MN

D0160489

THUNDER IN THE MOUNTAINS

THUNDER IN THE MOUNTAINS
A Portrait of American Gun Culture

CRAIG K. COLLINS

LYONS PRESS
Guilford, Connecticut
Helena, Montana
An imprint of Rowman & Littlefield

Lyons Press is an imprint of Rowman & Littlefield

Distributed by NATIONAL BOOK NETWORK

British Library Cataloguing-in-Publication Information available

Library of Congress Cataloging-in-Publication Data available

ISBN 918-1-4930-0385-3 (hardcover)

♾™ The paper used in this publication meets the minimum requirements of American National Standard for Information Sciences—Permanence of Paper for Printed Library Materials, ANSI/NISO Z39.48-1992.

To all the victims of American gun violence—more than 100,000 annually—their families, loved ones, and communities. I offer this work of prose, meager in the face of an epidemic so vast, with the greatest of humility and respect.

Contents

CHAPTER ONE

The shot cracked sharp through the crisp October sky. It echoed once, boomed twice, and tore off into the distance like the fading hiss of a car speeding toward the horizon.

Its first concussive wave had slammed into boulders across the ravine. One thunderous clap raced up an aspen-filled draw toward the top of a 10,000-foot Northern Nevada peak. The other plunged down a creek-carved canyon before spilling onto sage-covered flats a half-mile below, rumbling, nearly spent, through glades of yellow-leafed cottonwoods.

Somewhere, a deer flinched, then froze, waiting for the sound to roll by. A man in an orange vest cocked his head, trying to discern the origin of the shot, certain that one of his fellow hunters had encountered good fortune.

And then silence. Aspen quaked gold. The sage was riffled by an autumn breeze. The sun blazed cool amid some gathering clouds.

My ears rang as though someone were holding up a tuning fork. The high-pitched whine consumed me. I had been sitting on the ground, my back propped against a large boulder with my legs stretched out during a break in my trek through rugged deer country. My .30-30 Winchester lay on my lap. It was just like the one Chuck Connors had wielded so deftly in *The Rifleman*. My grandfather had reluctantly given it to me after some prodding by my dad. He'd had misgivings about arming a thirteen-year-old with a high-powered deer rifle. My dad? Not so much.

Trembling, I leaned forward to inspect my foot.

Moments before, I'd plopped down against an inviting rock nestled amid the sage and bitterbrush. Bored, I'd decided I should make sure I had a full complement of bullets loaded into my gun. And, just like the Rifleman, I had cocked the Winchester's lever-action handle. An unspent shell flipped out of the chamber, twirled through the air, and landed in the dirt. Concurrently, a lever had pushed back the gun's hammer while simultaneously sliding a new shell into the chamber. I was fascinated by the ingenious mechanics—a series of interconnected metal parts that functioned like a compact Rube Goldberg device. I'd cocked again. Another shell had flipped out of the chamber and onto the dirt. And again, the hammer was cocked back. It coiled above the firing pin, which was designed to be about as stable as a mousetrap. The slightest pressure, the smallest jiggle, would release the hammer, which would slam into the firing pin, which would pierce the brass primer, which would spark the gunpowder-filled brass casing, which would flame in a contained violent explosion, which would hurl a one-third-ounce lead slug out of the muzzle at roughly two and a half times the speed of sound.

I'd cocked the lever once more. Another shell flipped skyward. My index finger had carelessly slipped off the trigger guard. I'd snapped the lever back into position, and the trigger guard had clamped a small sliver of skin between it and the trigger. Time slowed. The brass shell gleamed gold as it hung in midair. My finger jerked. My mind said, "No." The trigger tensed. A spring clicked. The hammer slammed. The shell exploded. The barrel jumped. The trigger went limp. The shot echoed. My ears rang.

In the days and months and years since, I have often pleaded to have that moment back. I have startled awake from a nap or winced during a daydream—always reaching my hand into the cold, rushing stream. Always with my fingers outstretched. Always hoping to grab a fistful of water. Always hoping to stop time. But the brass shell never freezes in midair. My finger never avoids the trigger. The muzzle never moves away from my boot. Rather, the seconds hurtle onward. And I am always left sitting, stunned, with a high-pitched whine in my ears, wondering what happened to the bullet.

Ah, yes, the bullet.

My eyes widened. My chest tightened. My stomach knotted. I waited for a rush of pain. And waited. And waited.

It didn't come.

Maybe I'd missed. Maybe the slug had slammed harmlessly into the dirt.

Maybe.

I hoped it was so. And then I breathed. I squinted warily at my hunting boot, afraid of what I would surely see. I knew the damage a .30-30 could inflict. I expected to witness half a foot dangling from a shredded ankle. Instead, my intact boot was still propped leisurely on a rock, seemingly no worse for the wear. I leaned closer. Nothing was amiss, aside from an almost imperceptible tear in a seam on my dust-covered leather uppers.

But still, a calm terror gripped me. I was like a fugitive looking for an escape, for an explanation, for a slug in the dirt. My chest was still tight, my stomach nauseous. I wasn't fully convinced of any good fortune. I wasn't sure I'd literally dodged a bullet. And then the bottom of my right foot began to tingle. It felt like I'd stomped hard on a concrete sidewalk. Perhaps that was from the shock of the gun going off so close. Perhaps the bullet had hit a rock and ricocheted harmlessly into the sole of my boot.

Perhaps.

CHAPTER TWO

My dad, brother, stepbrother, and I had been up at dawn for what had proven to be an eventful opening day of deer season. By 7:30 a.m. we had downed a large doe with a clean shot behind the shoulder blade. This entailed field-dressing our quarry before hefting it a half-mile back to camp.

By mid-morning, we were back at it, hiking along a high ridge, when my stepbrother, who was sixteen, spotted a magnificent five-point buck a hundred yards off, lying stealthily amid a thicket of brush. My stepbrother slowly kneeled, pulled the butt of his .30-06 snug to his shoulder, fixed the scope's crosshairs on his prey, exhaled nervously, and gingerly squeezed the trigger. The explosion lifted the gun's barrel into the air and jerked my stepbrother's shoulder violently. The big buck jumped, instinctively clambering to its feet. It stood, quivering. Without a fight, it sank to its fore knees, dropped its heavy antlered head to the ground, and huffed its last breath into the dry Nevada dust.

The buck had been felled by a clean shot through the neck. A small red stain the diameter of a pencil eraser was barely visible at the center of its throat. The back of the animal's neck was a different story. A .30-06 (pronounced *thirty-aught-six* in hunter parlance) is a powerful weapon. Its ammunition was engineered during World War I. The US Army had entered the war late. The Germans had machine guns with range and accuracy up to 1,000 yards—over half a mile. The Americans needed to catch up; thus, the M1 round was developed. It's still in military use today, and is ideal for piercing light armor. Its civilian cousin became the .30-06, perhaps the most popular big-game ammo of all time. The shell is about 3.3 inches long. The actual bullet weighs ten grams—or about one-third of an ounce. Its core is composed of soft lead encased in a zinc-copper jacket.

When the trigger of a .30-06 is pulled, a firing pin strikes a small brass primer built into the base of the bullet cartridge. The primer sparks and ignites a chamber filled with gunpowder. A violent explosion ensues. The force of the explosion causes the soft lead core of the bullet to expand slightly, generating enough of a bulge in the copper-alloy jacket to make slight contact with the hard steel barrel of the gun. This happens almost at a molecular level between the steel and copper. But it's an important interaction. The inside of every rifle or handgun barrel contains small, spiral grooves called *rifling*. These grooves escort the bullet as it explodes down the barrel. The effect is much like a quarterback throwing a tight spiral. The rifling gives the bullet a true ride to its target. As a result of this split-second symphony of chemistry and physics, the .30-06 bullet exits the muzzle with supersonic fury.

The slug that brought down my stepbrother's trophy buck left the barrel, spinning at a rate of about 5,000 revolutions per second and traveling at a speed of over a half-mile per second, which is roughly 2,000 miles per hour—faster than an F-22 at full thrust. It covered the distance between my stepbrother and his quarry in about one-tenth of a second. The spinning, copper-jacketed projectile splashed into the buck's thick, muscular neck with the pressure of 60,000 pounds per square inch. Upon impact, the bullet then did exactly what it was engineered to do by the war merchants of the early twentieth century: It exacted maximum damage upon its target. The lead core began to flatten, splitting the protective alloy jacket. Released from its enclosure, the soft-lead interior flattened into the shape of a mushroom, expanding from less than half the diameter of a dime to the size of a half-dollar—all the while still traveling at supersonic speed. The bullet ripped through muscle. It exploded through bone. It tore out swaths of nerves, arteries, and veins. It created a vacuum as it exited, pulling and bruising the surrounding tissue, which stretched outward toward the bullet before snapping back in a gelatinous mess. The big buck was dead, but wouldn't yet know it for another twenty seconds or so.

It was a remarkable animal, easily the largest mule deer I'd ever seen up close. It weighed nearly 200 pounds—perhaps 185 after we'd field-dressed it. We were three miles from camp and a mile and a half from the nearest road. My dad and stepbrother Monte went back to get the truck. My brother Kirk, who was a year older, and I were assigned the task of dragging the animal to the dirt road snaking through the sage flat below.

There is no graceful way to haul 185 pounds of dead weight through the dirt and brush and rocks. We each grabbed an antler and foreleg and tugged. The first mile was manageable, but the final half-mile had devolved into an exhausting tug-of-war. We were like galley slaves pulling on oars to a drumbeat in those old black-and-white movies. We'd heave the buck ten feet in unison, stop, rest, and repeat. Ten feet at a time, we crept toward our rendezvous point. We were cloaked in sweat and dust and blood. The deer's tan, bristled hide had begun to scrape off, exposing the sinewy muscle of the buck's hindquarters. Finally, my brother and I collapsed along the four-wheel-drive trail and waited for our dad, who was rumbling toward us in a cloud of dust, bouncing up the rugged road in our old, red Dodge pickup.

By the time we made it back to camp, it was a little past noon. A trophy buck and a doe meant that we'd have a freezer full of venison. Our half-day of work had harvested more than some hunters reap in a full season. But we were on a roll, and our party of four had two more deer tags. So my dad led my brother and me on another foray over the rugged slopes and ridges. We'd hiked five more miles without seeing another deer. It was starting to get late; a cold breeze began drifting down the slopes, and clouds began bunching on the northern horizon. My dad informed my brother and me that we'd take a ten-minute break, rustle through our lunch bags for a snack, and then head back to camp before darkness descended.

I quickly plopped down on a level patch of dirt with a small boulder to lean back on and some rocks to prop up my tired feet. My dad and brother looked around and then opted to hike about fifty yards up a slope to a small shelf that offered a wider expanse of level ground.

Left alone with nothing but my curiosity, exhaustion, and boredom, I would soon be puzzling about a seemingly missing .30-30 bullet.

CHAPTER THREE

Leroy Knight's sister, Misty Knight, was a classmate of mine at Winnemucca Junior High. She was tall, cute, and had a really cool name.

Leroy was like a lot of boys in Winnemucca. He rode dirt bikes, hunted, fished, played basketball, and rode horses.

On a spring day in 1973, I was playing baseball with friends at the Little League diamond across the street from the town's hospital. As I stood in center field, the wail of a siren started small and grew big. Soon it drowned out the chatter of kids on a ball field. Quickly, I could see the pulsing lights of an ambulance rushing up the street.

Fielders abandoned their positions. Bats dropped in the dirt. The ball was tossed aside. There was a rush to the right-field fence, which afforded the closest view. Hands gripped the chain link. The chest-high rail strained against a cadre of teen boys stretching to get a glimpse of possible disaster.

The ambulance shut off its siren yards from the hospital. Its engine raced and its tires skidded to a stop in the wide crescent driveway. A team of nurses and doctors rushed forward. Doors opened, doors slammed. Orders were barked. Nurses replied in loud, assured voices. We watched in mesmerized fascination. The safety latch to the back of the ambulance was thrown. The double doors flung open, and out spilled the cries of a young boy.

"Mama! Mama! Mama! Mama!" wailed the boy on the gurney.

Two men hoisted the gurney out of the ambulance.

"Mama! Mama! Mama! Mama!" wailed the boy.

A nurse grabbed the boy's hand and stroked his forearm. "It's going to be okay. You're going to be okay," she commanded in her loud, reassuring voice. Nonetheless, there was a quiver of excitement in her words that offered the slightest hint that this was indeed serious, and that things wouldn't be okay.

"Mama! Mama! Mama! Mama!" wailed the boy.

More workers rushed from the hospital. More orders were barked. More nurses answered.

"Mama! Mama! Mama! Mama!" wailed the boy.

The gurney clanked; the wheels began to roll. The medical team trotted alongside.

"Mama! Mama! Mama! Mama!" wailed the boy.

Glass doors slid open.

"Mama! Mama! Mama! Mama!" wailed the boy.

Glass doors slid shut.

We leaned against the fence in silence. The afternoon was gray and getting cold. It was April, but the weather hadn't yet turned. I shivered.

One of the boys leaned forward, cocked his head, and said, "Wasn't that Leroy Knight? It sounded like Leroy Knight."

"Yeah, it did," agreed another boy.

Soon we all nodded our heads. It did sound like Leroy Knight.

A couple of Leroy's close friends threw down their mitts, pulled themselves over the fence, and ran across the street. The doors to the emergency room slid open and then slid closed. We stood and stared. Minutes passed. A few kids spoke in hushed tones. I held my mitt to my face and smelled the leather.

The doors slid back open. Two boys walked out, shoulders slumped. They looked each way for traffic, then jogged toward us. They grabbed the chain link. We huddled around as though we were listening up for our coach.

"It *was* Leroy Knight," the first kid said.

"Gunshot to the head," said the second.

"Twenty-two," said the first. "We heard them talking. Went into his eye and through the top of his skull. He was out shooting rabbits with Ed Smith. That's all we know. It's bad. Real bad."

The game broke up. We wandered back, picked up bats, balls, and gloves, and started walking home in clumps, speculating whether Leroy would live or if he would be a vegetable. I felt sorry for Misty. I could imagine her crying as she learned the news.

And, of course, it wasn't okay. Not for Leroy. Not for Misty. Not for their parents. Not for anyone.

The following school year, Misty and I became good friends. We began eating lunch together. She asked me to walk her home. Then she asked if I wanted to come in, say hi to Leroy, and hang out for a while—though she made it clear I had to leave well before her mom came home.

"Sure. Why not?"

Few people had seen Leroy since the accident. But I'd heard stories.

Misty bounced up the steps of her front porch. She was lithe and cheerful and pretty. She wore jeans and a T-shirt. I wasn't sure if I really wanted to see Leroy. I was mostly looking forward to hanging out in Misty's room and listening to records. The thought of seeing how much Leroy had changed was disturbing. I never told Misty about the day at the ballpark—about how I was there when her brother was brought in. In fact, I'd never talked to Misty about Leroy at all. It was too upsetting.

She put her hand on the doorknob, leaned close to my face, and spoke in a tone as though we were about to visit something exotic at the zoo.

"Leroy's not the same," she instructed. "He's missing most of his left frontal lobe. He lost an eye and wears a black patch like a pirate. And he has to wear a football helmet until some of the operations on his skull fully heal. He won't remember you and can't really talk. But just be happy and nice around him. He likes that."

"Okay." I nodded.

Misty turned the knob and swung the door open. Leroy was sitting on the couch watching TV with his home-care nurse.

Leroy sprang up, smiled excitedly, clapped his palms together, made some small jumps, and swayed his helmeted head back and forth.

"Hi, Leroy," Misty chirped. "I'm home."

She bounded toward him and wrapped him in a hug.

Leroy continued to hop up and down in her arms—continued to clap his palms together.

"Gaaaaa! Gaaaaa!" Leroy said excitedly. "Gaaaaa! Gaaaaa!"

"Leroy, I brought a friend to see you. This is Craig. He knew you from before. Say hi."

Leroy broke from Misty's embrace and bounced toward me.

"Gaa haa waa! Gaa haa waa!" Leroy said.

"He wants you to hug him," interpreted Misty.

I gave Leroy an awkward hug. His helmet banged into me. His movement was erratic and ungainly. Leroy laughed and clapped. Misty took him from me, put her arm around him, led him back to the couch, and sat him down.

"I'm going to go to my room now, Leroy, to listen to records with Craig. You sit here and watch TV, okay?"

Leroy grinned. His helmet swayed.

Misty held my hand and led me to her room.

"Leave the door open," the nurse hollered behind us.

I never did tell Misty about the day I saw her brother arrive at the hospital. I never walked her home again. And that was the last time I ever saw Leroy.

But I certainly thought about him now, as I sat atop a high mountain ridge in the remote Nevada wilderness, my foot tingling and a bullet gone who-knows-where.

CHAPTER FOUR

My dad came bounding down the hill in huge strides, crashing through the sage.

He was tall, strong, and fit. He was also calm in a crisis. He had saved a man from drowning at Lake Tahoe when I was five. My dad had purchased a yellow canvas inflatable raft just for fun the day before. My brother, sister, and I had spent most of the morning paddling around the cold, crystalline water in it. About a hundred yards offshore, a trio of scuba divers had been practicing and testing their equipment. Few people paid them much notice. And then there was a faint yell. One of the divers was waving and flailing in the water. A crowd gathered on the shore. No one knew what the diver was saying. It was a herd of people, staring and blinking and not knowing what was going on or what to do.

My mom ran and got my dad, who had been back near a picnic table, barbecuing hot dogs. My dad, who'd been trained extensively in lifesaving through both his time in the National Guard and his federal job with the Bureau of Land Management, immediately recognized that someone was drowning, and seconds counted. He ran back to the picnic site, grabbed the small, inflatable raft, splashed into the lake, and furiously churned his paddle as he made his way to the stricken diver. He bobbed nearby for about a minute while loading a limp, wet-suit-clad body onto the small, two-man raft. I could see my dad beginning mouth-to-mouth resuscitation. He then paddled strong for about twenty yards, before stopping and bending over the diver again. He repeated this several times before he made it to shore.

A crowd of about fifty people stood there, mesmerized. When he got about ten yards from shore, he was met by three men, who grabbed the boat, and, pulling it, hurriedly splashed their way out of the lake. The crowd parted to make room for my dad and the still-limp diver, who was dragged from the boat and onto the hot, coarse sand.

My dad instructed the crowd to give him some room. They did. Someone said an ambulance had already been called. I stood on the outside of the wall of adults, unable to see what was happening, and only able to get an occasional glimpse of my dad breathing into the diver's mouth and pumping his hands on the diver's chest. Soon an excited murmur began to rise. Men gasped with relief. A woman exclaimed, "Thank the Lord! Thank the Lord!" Sirens wailed. An ambulance bounced along a rutted car path through the pines and down to the beach. Two medics pushed through the crowd with a stretcher and some oxygen. They put a mask on the diver, lifted him onto the stretcher, hoisted him into the back of the ambulance, slammed the doors, and bounced away.

My dad stood with his hands on his hips, clearly exhausted. Two men in wet suits stood by him, patting him on the back. The crowd broke into a respectful applause as though someone had just sunk an impressive putt at a golf tournament. On the way home, my dad simply said he did what he was trained to do.

But apparently the diver wasn't the only person my dad had saved. My mom frequently made him tell the story to friends about the time he was earning his way through college by working the night shift at the Union Pacific rail yard in Pocatello, Idaho. A freight train had just been given clearance to leave on its journey. The lead engine roared, and the train creaked to life. The cranky wheels rolled into motion with short metallic screeches. The couplings on each boxcar snapped tight one by one, all the way down the line, leaving the cars shaking and shuddering as the engine huffed forward. A man shrieked. The train chugged on. The man shrieked again. And yet again.

My dad ran into the rail yard from the icehouse where he was using metal tongs to sling 300-pound blocks of ice down a chute into boxcars in the waning days before every car was built with refrigeration. Two foremen stood in overalls and work gloves over a homeless man who'd been trying to cross the rail yard when the train began to roll. The homeless man had figured he could easily scramble beneath the slow-moving train before it picked up any speed. He'd done it dozens of times before. As he crawled on his stomach over the rail bed, the train was beginning to roll above him, metal clanking, steel rails flexing, and wheels grinding. The man had crawled over the second rail but couldn't seem to find anything to kick his foot against in order to get enough traction to make the final roll away from the tracks. Then he felt something grab his left leg. He instinctively kicked at the rail with his right leg in a futile effort to break free. The man looked back in horror as a big metal wheel rolled slowly over his knee and lower thigh. Bones crunched. Ligaments popped. Muscles tore. A second wheel rolled slowly behind the first. This time there was little crunching or popping. The man kept kicking at the rail, finally sliding free after the wheel rotated by.

My dad ran to the man, who was still howling, his frantic screams filled with the stench of booze. The foremen were holding him down and trying to keep him calm until the ambulance arrived. My dad had already whipped off his ROTC belt—one of those army-green jobs with double prongs and dual metal eyelets running its full length. It was ideal for holding up a soldier's pants or for use as a tourniquet. My dad wrapped the belt around the man's stump, trying not to pay attention to the severed femur, shredded muscle, and torrent of blood. He yanked the belt once. The man howled. He yanked twice. He finally pulled as hard and tight as he could, slid the double tines into the eyelets, and relaxed. He'd done all he could do.

The man was no longer shrieking, but rather lying wide-eyed—shivering and shaking. He was clearly in shock, but ended up living. In the years after, my dad often saw the still-disheveled man hobbling with one leg and a crutch around the streets and alleys of downtown Pocatello. My dad never introduced himself or spoke to the man. As a nineteen-year-old, he'd done what needed doing, calmly and coolly. That was enough. There was nothing more to be said.

And that's what was so distressing now. My dad was neither calm nor cool. There was unmistakable panic and fear in his voice. It was something I'd never heard before. Maybe things were worse than I thought. Maybe I was in a situation more dangerous than I could imagine.

"Craig! Craig!" he yelled as he crashed down the hillside through waist-high sage.

"I'm down here," I yelled back in a weak voice.

He was still a couple strides away.

"Oh, dear God! My son! What have you done? What have you done?" His voice was high and filled with anguish.

"I think I'm okay, I think I'm okay," I answered, trying to reassure him.

He finally slid on his knees to my side and put his hand gently on my upper back.

"Oh, God, where are you hit—where are you hit?"

"I dunno. I dunno. I think I missed."

"You missed? You think you missed?" he repeated in a high-pitched panic.

"Yeah, I think so."

"Are you sure?" he asked, his voice quavering. He put his hand on my chest, pushed me slowly upright, and inspected my stomach.

He later told me that when he'd first seen me doubled over—I'd been leaning forward, inspecting my boot—he was sure I'd shot myself in the stomach or chest, which, of course, would've been a certain death sentence, so far from the nearest hospital.

"No, my foot, Dad—my foot."

I leaned forward and pointed at my right boot.

"Did you shoot your foot?" my dad asked, his voice lowering and his demeanor of calm-under-crisis returning.

"I'm not sure. I might've missed."

"Can you feel anything?" asked my dad, not convinced that I'd been so lucky. Plus, he later said that he could tell by the sound of the shot that I'd hit something. He said the gunfire's pitch was lower than what would've been made by an unobstructed trajectory.

"Not really. My foot feels fine, except that it's tingling a little."

"Okay, now, don't move. I'm going to take a look. Just be calm."

I wasn't sure if my dad was talking to me or to himself. Either way, he'd regained command of the situation. My dad shuffled his knees and began inspecting my boot. He looked at the top, and then carefully examined the bottom of the sole. He ran his finger over the small tear in the leather seam. He shook his head, completely puzzled.

He looked up at me and pointed to the tear in the seam.

"Was this here before?" he asked.

"I'm not sure. I don't know. It might've been. Probably?"

"Well, there's no exit hole, and that looks too small to be an entrance hole."

He shook his head again as he reexamined the boot.

"Okay," he said. "This is what we're going to do. I can't tell whether the bullet went in or not. I'm baffled, really. And I'm not supposed to do this. If you have been hit, you're supposed to leave your boot on. I could do a lot of damage taking it off, but I don't think we have a choice here. So I want you to sit really, really still. Okay? I'm going to unlace your boot as much as I can and try to remove it with as little strain as possible. Tell me if you feel anything or if it hurts. Okay? Are you ready?"

CHAPTER FIVE

BATTLE BORN.

This is Nevada's official motto. It's on the state flag.

That's because Nevada was born prematurely in 1864, the whole of its 110,000-square-mile, sage-covered, sparsely populated territory birthed into the Union during the depths of the Civil War—all for the bounty of a forty-square-mile strip of fabulously rich earth known as the Comstock Lode. The Union wanted silver to finance war; Nevada wanted statehood. It was a marriage of convenience.

BATTLE BORN.

And while it's a fitting motto for Nevada, it could very well be a national motto for America in general, and the American West in particular.

As Americans, we are all battle born. Whether we know it or not, it's a legacy we live with every day. As a people, we have butchered and slaughtered and hacked and hewed and hoed and chopped and knifed and shot our way from wilderness to civilization.

From our beachhead at Plymouth Rock, we pushed forward relentlessly on horses, mules, oxen, wagons, and plows. We axed forests, we tilled plains, we exterminated species, we snuffed out peoples. We built great cities, roads, and rails. And through this entire fantastical foray into the future, we had one constant companion: the gun.

For there were always guns in America.

One such gun on this journey was a Sharps .50 caliber rifle. It hung for eighty years on two pegs above a fireplace on the F. V. H. Collins ranch on the Rosebud River near Forsyth, Montana, not far from the Little Bighorn. My grandfather—the same person who gave me his .30-30 to hunt with—often lifted the Sharps .50 from its resting place and played with it as a boy. Before it was eventually purchased in 2000 by a collector in Great Falls, for $25,000, the gun had originally belonged to Peter Jackson, one of the territory's early pioneers and, by all accounts, the most prolific of buffalo hunters. Jackson was married to my grandfather's aunt and was an Indian scout for General Nelson Miles. He'd come to Montana in the 1870s, with my great-great-grandfather, Corporal Solomon Byron Finch.

Solomon Finch was raised on a farm in Wisconsin. He was a descendant of the Fighting Finches of Koshkonong, Wisconsin—twelve Finch brothers who had come in 1832 to fight in the Black Hawk War. Following that clash—a genocide, really, that killed and pushed the Fox, Sauk, and Winnebago Indians from their native lands in the Upper Midwest—the Fighting Finches were given to horse stealing, farm raiding, drinking, brawling, and, of course, shooting.

When the Civil War broke out, young Solomon was already well versed in riding and shooting. At the age of nineteen, he mounted his best horse, rode to Minnesota's Fort Snelling, near present-day Minneapolis, and enlisted as a private in Company G of the Iowa 5th Cavalry. Over the next six years, he got his fill of riding and shooting. That's because the Iowa 5th Cavalry covered more ground and fought longer than all but three units in that long and desperate conflict.

Finch's cavalry division fought for three years along the Western front and saw bloody action at Corinth, Shiloh, and Vicksburg. Shortly after the fall of Vicksburg, the Sioux had taken up arms against encroaching farmers in the plains of Minnesota and the Dakotas. Settlers had been shot. Indians had been hung.

The Iowa 5th was re-formed into Brackett's Battalion and sent north to quell the Sioux Uprising. For the next three years, Finch's cavalry unit rode in pursuit of the elusive Sioux throughout the Dakotas and eastern Montana. In 1866, they cornered Sitting Bull at Killdeer Mountain in present-day South Dakota. The Sioux were overrun and scattered. The campaign was declared a success.

During the Civil War, millions of young American men like Solomon Finch were trained to be superb marksmen and fearless fighters. The Sharps .50 was a popular weapon, particularly among sniper units. It was favored for its range of up to a thousand yards, as well as the blunt killing power of its 450-grain (one-ounce) slug, which could drop a man or buffalo at a distance of over half a mile, and maybe even farther, if need be. The term *sharpshooter* is a Civil War–era word derived from the Sharps rifle.

Following the war, veterans like Finch and Jackson spilled into the West. And, of course, they made sure to bring their guns, which they wielded with deadly accuracy and destruction.

Jackson brought his Sharps .50. Of his weapon, the *Billings Gazette* wrote in a 2004 article: "With the big gun braced against his powerful shoulders, the Norwegian immigrant felled somewhere between 4,000 and 5,000 bison, killed thousands of deer and antelope, and downed hundreds of elk."

In his old age, he dictated the following story to his daughter—my great-aunt—Edith Jackson Finch: "It is estimated that within the triangle formed by the Missouri, Musselshell, and Yellowstone Rivers, approximately 300,000 buffalo roamed in 1880. My interest in hunting as a livelihood and my greatest achievement came during the year 1873. I spent my time hunting on the Musselshell River near Harlowton and the spring on the American Fork. I killed a bear weighing about 1,000 pounds."

Jackson told his daughter about stacking buffalo hides high upon barges that made stops on the Missouri River in order to transport them to markets in the East.

Within a decade, men like Peter Jackson had converted the American Plains from an ecosystem as rich in fauna as the African savannah to something tame, sterile, and better suited for ranching and farming.

Jackson concluded the telling of his story to his daughter: "I did little hunting after 1883. I laid my old Sharps .50 to rest over the fireplace made of sandrock and clay."

The buffalo were dead. Sitting Bull had been subdued. The gun remained.

CHAPTER SIX

"Now, don't look," my dad said. "You're probably not going to want to see this."

"I think I missed," I muttered—tense and desperately hopeful.

My boot had been completely unlaced and my calf was propped on my dad's knee.

Kirk kneeled beside me, silent.

In spite of my dad's warnings, I was unable to turn away. I was now breathing fast, grimacing in anticipation.

My dad gripped my calf tight with his left hand and gently, steadily pulled on the heel of my boot with his right until the boot began slowly sliding off, its back collar pointing downward. It was as though I'd walked through a deeper-than-expected creek and had sat down to pour the water out of my boot. Except instead of water, this time, I was pouring blood. A bright, red stream gushed and then trickled from my boot, dripping, splattering, and pooling in the dirt.

"Oh, God! Oh, God!" I cried. "Oh, God! Oh, God!"

I'd been shot. I'd been really, really shot. I tensed. Panic streaked through my body.

I moaned through clenched teeth, trying to stifle my screams.

I imagined my shattered foot hanging by a tendon. I thought about amputation and what it would be like to walk on a prosthesis. Would I have to get special shoes? Would I be able to run? What about the basketball team and the season that was starting next week? Oh, dear God in heaven, I'd been shot. I'd been really, really shot.

"Come on, now," my dad said in his strong, controlled voice. "I need you to be tough. We're going to get through this, but I need you to be calm and tough. Can you do that?"

"Nnnnn!" I moaned through gritted teeth.

"Okay. I'm going to take the rest of the boot off. Look away."

My dad removed the boot and inspected my foot. It was difficult to assess the damage through my blood-soaked sock. "Well, you're definitely shot," he said. "I can't really tell how bad it is, and I definitely don't want to remove your sock to find out. But it's plenty bad."

My dad rotated my boot, trying to figure out why there was no bullet exit. He pulled at the sole, the entirety of which flapped free from the leather uppers. By chance, the bullet had entered through a leather seam on the uppers. The entry hole had been disguised and was hardly discernible. It could've been just a small tear in the stitching. The bullet then tore through my foot, shattering bone and shredding muscle. By the time it hit my boot's hard rubber sole, the bullet had flattened to the size of a half-dollar. Instead of blowing a hole through the bottom of my boot, it simply tore the tongue of the sole from its stitching. In less than a millisecond, the rubber bulged. It flexed violently outward. The bottom of my boot flapped open, the bullet passed, and the sole flapped back into place. It was certainly a peculiar display of physics.

Regardless, I'd been shot. My mind had turned far away from the mystery of the boot and bullet, focusing instead on, "What's next?"

CHAPTER SEVEN

Tracy Logan sometimes rode her horse to school.

While she was in class, she would keep the animal in a small corral out behind the football field and across from the maintenance sheds. That's where all the 4-H and FFA kids met after school. In addition to the occasional horse, they also had sheep, rabbits, and chickens.

On the days Tracy rode her horse, I would hear *clip-clop, clip-clop, clip-clop* on the trail behind me as I walked alongside the Union Pacific tracks on my way to Winnemucca Junior High. As the sound grew louder and closer, I would then hear the pace quicken to *clip-clop-clop, clip-clop-clop, clip-clop-clop*, followed by, "Hey, Craig, you want a ride?"

I looked up and squinted into the cold morning sun and shivered. It was late March and still frosty. My stepmother had hollered at me to wear a jacket before leaving the house, but I had ditched it in the closet on the way out the door. I wanted it to be May and warm. And though the temperature was around 35 degrees at 7:30 in the morning, it was sunny, and I was an optimist. It would surely break 60 today, and I wouldn't want to be playing basketball at lunchtime in a jacket. It was my way of willing the winter away and the summer into being.

Tracy swayed high above me atop her horse, fading in and out of the silhouette made by the bright spring sun. I shaded my eyes. She reached her hand down and clasped mine. I put my left foot into the stirrup, gave a hop, swung my right leg over the big animal's light-brown hindquarters, and settled in behind the saddle, riding bareback atop the horse's loins. I put my arms around Tracy and locked my hands together around her stomach. She was wearing a knit cap and a big down jacket. She was clearly not as optimistic about the weather as I was—probably because she didn't have to prove to a bunch of boys that she was tough and that the cold hardly fazed her.

I held tight. *Tt-tt*, Tracy told the horse.

We bounced lightly along the path. I clenched my knees into the animal's sides and tried to find the horse's rhythm. Occasionally, I would get out of sync and my rear would collide with its rump as we trotted.

Bam-bam-bam. Whatever I was in the middle of saying would come out sounding rat-a-tat-tat. My back would jar, and my kidneys would ache. I would then clench harder with my knees, lift up, and recalibrate to the horse's rhythm.

Tracy's straight, blonde hair smelled nice. She'd just washed it. I put my chin on her shoulder and pressed against her back. She was warm, and so was the horse.

"Whoa," Tracy said as we approached Bridge Street, one of Winnemucca's main thoroughfares. Morning traffic passed by. No one gave us a glance. A horse trotting near downtown Winnemucca was hardly unusual.

Tt-tt, Tracy told the horse.

Clip-clip-clip-clip-clip went the horse, trotting fast across the asphalt during a break in traffic.

"The past is never dead," wrote William Faulkner. "It's not even past."

That is true about the South, as Faulkner had intended. But it's also true about the American West. It was certainly true about Winnemucca in 1973.

The horses, the ranches, the railroads, the mines, the brothels, the gambling, and, oh, yes, the guns. They were all around.

Only two blocks from where Tracy and I had crossed Bridge Street stood the First National Bank. It was a stout, secure building made of gray granite blocks—a style popular among late-nineteenth-century buildings in Nevada. And though it would seem counterintuitive for a bank to give any indication of vulnerability, First National has always been outright proud of one of its robberies.

A time-darkened brass plaque had been set into the granite near the bank's entrance. It read: ON SEPTEMBER 19, 1900, BUTCH CASSIDY AND HIS WILD BUNCH GANG ROBBED THE FIRST NATIONAL BANK OF $32,500 OF GOLD. (That's nearly $1 million in today's dollars, adjusted for inflation.)

The Pinkerton Detective Agency provided this account of the robbery: "Three men . . . entered the bank and held up the cashier and four other persons. Two of the robbers carried revolvers and a third, a Winchester rifle. They forced the five persons to go into the inner office of the bank while the robbery was committed. Two of the men who committed this robbery were: George Parker, alias 'Butch Cassidy.' Now in Argentina or Chile. Harry Longabaugh, alias 'The Sundance Kid.' Now in Argentina or Chile.'"

The bank president was one George Nixon. He knew his way around even the roughest of Nevada mining towns and had amassed a small fortune through investments in claims around Goldfield, a fabulously rich boomtown about 300 miles south of Winnemucca. During the robbery, a Bowie knife was held to Nixon's throat while a robber coaxed him into opening the safe. Nixon kept his cool and dutifully obliged.

As soon as the Wild Bunch had departed, though, Nixon grabbed a six-shooter from his office and directed W. S. Johnson—a customer and local horse buyer who'd just happened to stop in prior to the robbery—to pull the pump shotgun off a rack on the wall behind the teller's counter.

Johnson jumped a fence behind the bank and found two of the robbers securing bags of gold coins to their saddles. He lifted the shotgun to his shoulder and drew a bead on an outlaw who was likely to have been Kid Curry, the wildest of the Wild Bunch—a cold-blooded killer who was renowned as one of the fastest quick-draws in the West.

Curry stared into the barrel of Johnson's 12-gauge with widened eyes. Johnson calmly put his index finger to the trigger and squeezed without hesitation. He'd expected an explosive thud from the barrel, followed by a strong kick from the butt of the gun into his shoulder. Instead, there was a lonely click. The chamber wasn't loaded. He lowered the shotgun slowly and found Kid Curry glaring back over the barrel. Curry finished cinching a sack of gold to his saddle, looked back at Johnson, and started to laugh. For whatever reason, the man who'd shot and killed nine lawmen was feeling magnanimous. Either that or he was just in a hurry. Instead of reaching for his pistol, he hoisted himself into the saddle, tipped his hat, and galloped away with his fellow outlaw.

George Nixon, meanwhile, had charged out the front door and into the middle of Bridge Street, his six-shooter blazing. Never mind that the notorious Butch Cassidy was already galloping well out of range. Nixon at least wanted to make a good show and be able to later tell of how he'd attempted, without fear, to gun down the Hole-in-the-Wall Gang. A posse was quickly formed, and Nixon saddled his best horse, joining over a dozen lawmen in the chase.

Cassidy and his gang thundered north into a vast, empty land that stretched a hundred miles to the Idaho border and then another hundred miles beyond that before the next hint of a town could be seen in the farmlands of the Snake River Valley. For eight days the posse doggedly pursued the robbers. But they were no match for a small band of cunning outlaws and a big stretch of seemingly endless wilderness.

For Nixon, all was not lost. In fact, much was gained. He'd achieved statewide and even national notoriety from the incident, using it as a springboard into politics to win election as one of Nevada's US senators.

Five months after a Bowie knife had been held to his throat, Nixon was chagrined to receive from the Pinkerton Agency a portrait, taken in New York City, of the very men who had robbed him. The outlaws, it seems, had put their gold to work, purchasing fine suits and bowler hats before posing for a portrait that would later become iconic in Western lore. It would also be the last photo taken of the gang before they departed on a steamship from New York to South America. Nixon studied the photo, pursed his lips, and then sent it out to be framed. It hangs on the wall of the bank today.

In 1973, there were still a handful of people living in Winnemucca who remembered that day when the First National Bank was robbed, and how the Wild Bunch had dashed down Bridge Street beneath a hail of gunfire with bags of gold cinched to their saddles.

The past is indeed never dead.

Tracy trotted her horse along the dirt road that led from the railroad tracks to the school.

"Yah, Trixie!" she yelled.

The horse lunged. I squeezed Tracy tight, and we leaned into the gallop. Gone were the short, staccato jolts of a slow trot and the accompanying *clip-clop* of hooves. Trixie stretched her neck forward, her forelegs reaching ahead and her powerful hind legs pushing from behind.

"Yah! Yah!" Tracy yelled, coaxing the horse ever faster.

A cold wind blew strong in our faces. Tracy's shoulder-length, straw-colored hair slapped the side of my face. I pressed my cheek against her warm neck and savored the faint whiff of shampoo. Trixie's long neck was the color of coffee with cream. Her mane was a deep chestnut and rippled in dark contrast. The horse's head bobbed in perfect rhythm with its muscular haunches. I rode easy atop the hindquarters, undulating in smooth cadence to the horse's long strides. My eyes watered in the cold wind, and the sagebrush that lined the sides of the road whisked by in a peripheral blur. The horse reached top speed. Its hooves dug strong into the dirt, flinging soil and leaving clouds of dust in our wake. Tracy and I rose and sank in tandem. We could both feel in our bodies the reverberation of Trixie's hooves striking the ground, each time generating a sonorous rumble that went *Th–th–rmph, th–th–rmph, th–th–rumph.*

We raced past the school's tennis courts and then the football field before Tracy pulled back on the reins.

"Whoa," she called to the horse. "Whoa, Trixie, whoa."

Trixie lifted her head and slowed. The fluid gallop ended abruptly, and we were back to a jarring trot.

We stopped on the dirt road behind the school. I swung my right leg over Trixie's hindquarters and stood with my left foot in the stirrup. Tracy looked me in the eyes, smiled, and gave me a quick, playful kiss on the cheek. I laughed and noticed her straight, white teeth and freckles. I ran my fingers through her hair and gave her a quick kiss back. I jumped to the ground and gently patted Trixie's rump. The horse snorted lightly and shook its mane.

"Thanks," I said, turning to walk to class.

"Yah!" yelled Tracy, her horse breaking into a fast trot on the way to the corral.

Later that year, after several horse rides, Tracy and I became boyfriend-girlfriend, of sorts. It was an arrangement that mostly consisted of sneaking out of the gym during halftime of the high school basketball games in order to kiss in the cold and the dark.

The following spring, her father, who was a local businessman and school board president, lost his seat as a county supervisor in a narrow election. Three days later, he shot himself in the head in the kitchen of his home.

My parents read the news of his death in the paper. They discussed it vigorously. Why would a man do such a thing? A man with a family? Just because of a few votes? My parents didn't know about my horseback rides with Tracy or our halftime rendezvous. I kept my head down during dinner, poked at my mashed potatoes, and offered nothing to the conversation.

Tracy didn't come to school for a week after that. And when she did return, she didn't talk much, and her eyes were swollen and red. I never asked about her father. And she never offered to talk about him. She never rode her horse to school again. The past might not die, but sometimes it fades quickly.

CHAPTER EIGHT

My dad reached into his hunting vest and pulled out a green-and-tan topographic map. It was government-issue from the US Geological Survey. He spread it on the ground, studied it, and carefully oriented it to the terrain around him. He stood, scanned the ridges, the canyons, the streams, and the peaks. He kneeled, adjusted the map again, and calmly, firmly, told my brother and me the plan.

"We're right here," he said, pointing his index finger near the center of the map. He pointed upward.

"That's God's Pocket Peak." It was a 10,000-foot mountain. We were about 1,500 feet below the summit.

"The camp is about five miles that way," he said, pointing across a steep ravine to a mountain ridge. On the map, he ran his finger down the spine of the eastern flank of the big, imposing peak.

"There's a jeep trail coming from the canyon along this ridge up until about nine thousand feet. If we hike up through those aspen," he said, pointing at the slope that rose behind us, "we should run into it. I'm going to carry you up there. Then you and your brother are going to sit tight while I go back to camp, get the truck, and see if I can make it up the jeep trail, or at least get close enough that we can carry you out.

"All right," he continued assuredly. "I'm going to kneel down, you're going to put your hands around my neck, and I'm going to carry you piggyback up to the top of the ridge."

I gingerly sat up, still dazed from the surreal nature of my predicament. I'd been shot. That didn't seem possible. It was something that happened to other people, but not me. I'd taken several gun safety courses. I'd been around guns and had accompanied my father on hunting trips from as early as I could remember. This couldn't be happening.

But it was. I stood on my left leg, gently lifted my right foot off the ground, leaned into my dad's back, and wrapped my arms around his neck—just like we'd done when I was a child. He grasped my right leg below the knee, pulled my left leg above his hip, and hoisted us both up.

"How's your foot?" my father asked.

"It doesn't hurt—it just tingles," I replied.

"Okay, hang on. Tell me if it starts to hurt. We're going to be going through some trees, so be careful not to bump it on anything."

My dad took two tentative steps, readjusted me on his back, and then began striding up the embankment, digging the toes of his boots into the flinty soil with each step in order to ensure that he didn't slip or fall.

My brother had gathered up all our gear—hats, guns, daypacks, lunch bags, jackets. He clambered upward, arms full, clattering several yards behind.

We entered an aspen grove that covered the north-facing slope. Above us, the small, round leaves fluttered gold and yellow in the slightest breeze. My dad labored up the hill with a methodic *crunch-crunch-crunch*, while a cool whisper floated above as the leaves shimmied and the sun flickered.

This was a mature stand of aspen. The slender white trunks were four to five feet in diameter and widely spaced. The grove's blazing gold canopy rose to twenty-five feet overhead.

This was lonely, remote country. The nearest paved road was 30 miles to the east. The nearest hospital was either in Elko, Nevada, about 110 miles to the south, or Twin Falls, Idaho, about 100 miles to the northeast. The Basque sheepherders, who summered in these high elevations in the late-nineteenth and early-twentieth centuries, knew about the dangers of these rugged mountains—about the expanse of isolation, and how an accident, large or small, could cascade and then swallow your life.

That's why the trees were carved with exotic glyphs and words. The carvings were unmistakable—the raised black lettering contrasting starkly against the aspen's smooth, papery-white trunks.

Through the trees, the Basques were able to speak across the years and the decades.

They would say simple things like:

etcheberrin campua 10 aug 1904.
(Etcheberri's camp, August 10, 1904.)

Or sometimes they were poetic and introspective:

baso honetan pasatu zuten
negu luze ta gogorrik
nahiz ta etxetik urrun egon
bada oroimen xamurrik
hutsik ez dago erran beharrik
gure historia ez dela egin
euskal herrian bakarrik.

(In this forest they endured
long and harsh winters;
even though they were far from home
one finds nostalgic memories here.
Needless to say,
our history has not been made
only in the Basque Country.)

On the ridge above this aspen stand, a person can look a hundred miles to the east and the west and the south and not see another human being, or even a trace of a human being. If you look intently, you might be able to see the faint line of a dirt road cutting through the sagebrush some twenty miles distant. But that is all.

Far from their native villages near Oñati, Urretxu, or Pamplona, the sheepherders would mostly write their names and dates on the aspen as a way to rail against the solitude, and declare for as long as the tree might stand, "I am here; I matter." It was also a recognition that if they were hurt, help would not come. And if they were to vanish in the wilderness, someone would be able to get word back to their family—maybe in a year or two hence—that, say, Miguel Marcuerquiaga last left his mark in the Jarbidge Range of Nevada, and that his soul is now resting somewhere in the vicinity of God's Pocket Peak.

CHAPTER NINE

Spring came riotously to Winnemucca. And the warm weather was hard-earned.

Winters were long and cold. The town was flanked by 10,000-foot peaks. On clear nights in January, the stars would glimmer in the dark winter sky and the cold would sink from the snow-covered slopes, settling into the Humboldt River Valley. One night it got down to 35 below. Some ranchers said their thermometers read minus-42 near the river west of town. The following day, a sort of frozen fog hung over the valley. It was so cold that ice crystals glittered and danced in the air beneath a weak sun that hung low on the horizon. The hard cold lasted through February. Snow still fell in March, and sometimes in April. There were numerous false alarms. A morning would dawn with warmth and sun and promise, but by noon it would be washed out by dark clouds carried above by a chill wind.

But when spring really did arrive, there was no mistaking it.

And today was such a day. It was the second week of May, and the lilacs hung in fragrant, lavender bunches in nearly every yard in town. The season's first scent of fresh-mowed lawn made a person smile and breathe deep. It was like savoring an almost-forgotten memory. The sun was warm without a hint of cool. There would be no stiff breezes flaring in the afternoon or clouds arriving suddenly to spritz the town in a cold spring rain. No, winter was gone for good.

Kids arrived at school early, gathering outside in large cliques, an excited chatter rising into the warmth of the air. There were no hats, no gloves, no jackets bulging over bulky sweaters. Basketballs bounced on the asphalt courts. Several boys brought their mitts and were tossing baseballs on the football field, atop tall, green grass that had just been watered.

At lunchtime, it was more of the same. Everyone—students, teachers, and staff—was outside. It was as though the whole world had been freed—released from the straitjacket that comes with the cold, the snow, the wind, the short days, and oppressive clouds.

I stood at lunch talking with Ray Upton, a tall, burly friend who was unafraid of a fight and nearly always in search of trouble.

The day was getting hot. It was over 80 degrees, maybe pushing 85. A layer of heat was shimmering above the asphalt playground.

My brother Kirk approached me from behind and tugged on my arm. He wanted to talk. It looked urgent. He pulled me aside and in an important, hushed tone said, "You need to come with us. We have something really, really cool to show you."

I looked up at my brother's friend, Tony Timerez, who was standing impatiently, arms folded, a few feet away. Tony and Ray hated each other. Tony was taller and stronger. When they were both over at our house at the same time, my brother and I would always worry that a boxing match would break out.

"Where? What is it?" I asked.

"I can't tell you until we get there. It's not far, but it's off campus."

There were strict rules about leaving school during lunch. Once you were off school grounds, it was as though you'd entered a no-man's-land. Anyone—a teacher, parent, cop, store clerk—could simply call the school and report you. It was a sentence that carried at least three days of detention. And because the town had a population of about 3,500, absolutely everyone knew who you were, knew who your parents were, and knew the phone number to the school. Leaving campus was nothing to be undertaken lightly.

"I need to know where we're going," I insisted.

"Trust me—you'll thank me when we get there. Just follow."

I was intrigued. My brother wasn't given to wanton exaggeration. I looked back at Ray and told my brother, "He's coming, too." I couldn't just abandon a friend, especially if this turned out to be as amazing as my brother's tone suggested it might be.

My brother looked back at Tony. He shook his head.

"Then I'm not coming," I bluffed, even though my interest was now so strong, I'd have ditched my friend without much hesitation. I added, "He's probably just going to follow us anyway."

My brother glanced again at Tony, who had grown impatient. Tony finally nodded, giving in to my demand.

"Okay," my brother snapped, waving the four of us into a tight huddle. "Here's the deal: What we're going to show you—you have to promise, promise, promise never to tell anyone. Got it?"

"Got it," I said.

Tony and Kirk looked up at Ray.

"Got it," he said in a bored tone, clearly dubious about the merits of this mission.

"No, really," my brother demanded. "This is serious. You. Can't. Tell. Anyone. Ever. Or Tony and I will make you sorry you did. Got it?"

"Okay. Got it," Ray and I muttered in unison.

"All right, let's go," Kirk said, breaking huddle. "And make sure no one sees us."

We trotted to the north side of the playground, bounding down a gentle grassy slope before sprinting across the road. Tony looked back to make sure we hadn't been seen or followed.

We disappeared through a trail that led toward a thicket of river willows and cottonwoods.

CHAPTER TEN

My dad picked his way up the slope and through the trees. As we neared the ridge, the rise became gentle, the trees smaller, and the gaps between them narrower.

Sweat soaked through the back of my dad's shirt where I clung. His chest heaved, and I could hear him breathing hard. He reached out to steady himself against an aspen trunk to our left. Then he staggered right and the heel of my bloodied stockinged foot banged against a small aspen no more than eight feet high.

A sharp pain electrified my right leg.

I let out a shriek, surprised by the sudden intensity.

"Sorry," my dad huffed, beginning to stagger under my weight.

The pain quickly subsided but was replaced with a dull throbbing in my foot.

My dad marched out of the aspen grove and onto a flat, narrow ridge, where mountain mahogany grew in dark-green clusters. And just as the map had depicted, twin dirt tracks made their way up the crest of the steep slope, over rocks, and through thick brush. My brother laid his jacket on the ground in an open space between some sage and a big mahogany that had sprung from between two large boulders, sending its reddish, gnarled branches into the sky. It was a good location to hunker down, with the mahogany there to protect us from the worst of any wind that might start to blow.

My dad carefully lifted me off his back, sat me near the jacket, and instructed me to lie down. He and my brother gathered some large, flat rocks, stacked them to make a footrest, and then carefully placed my leg on the rocks to keep my foot elevated. My dad had tied part of a torn T-shirt below my calf to help minimize the bleeding. Nevertheless, my white sock was soaked completely red. Concerned by the amount of blood, my dad took out the remaining shreds of the T-shirt and wrapped it gently, but firmly, around the whole of my foot. I still had no idea exactly where

I'd been shot, and my mind flickered between images of a few amputated toes or a fully amputated foot. Both were possibilities.

My dad stood and squinted at the jeep trail. We had a garden-variety Dodge pickup, not a four-wheel-drive. He was surely thinking there was no way a two-wheel-drive, low-clearance truck could make it up such a rugged trail. And he was right. He pulled out the map again, looked at the big peak to the north, back at the map, and then at the ridge to the west.

He knelt down next to me. My brother knelt, too.

In a low, calm voice he said, "I'm going to leave now. You both have everything you need—matches, flashlights, coats, water, food, a compass, and a map. I don't know how long it's going to take, but I'll definitely be back. Do not leave this spot, no matter what. I'll be back. Remember: If you leave this spot, no matter what the reason, I might never find you. Also, it might get dark before I can return. So, Kirk, go gather some firewood now while it's still light, so you don't have to do it in the dark. Keep Craig warm, and make sure he drinks plenty of water—that'll help ward off the possibility of shock. The pain's going to get worse before it gets better. Just be tough. I'll be back."

My dad stood, turned toward the aspen grove, started jogging, and disappeared into the trees and down the slope. A breeze blew, the trees whispered, and the pain came.

CHAPTER ELEVEN

The Humboldt River is one of the loneliest in America. It flows east–west across Northern Nevada, through the sage desolation that is the Great Basin. Along the way, it dissects perpendicularly the gaps in a number of north–south mountain ranges that comprise one of the Great Basin's unique features. Snowmelt from the Ruby, Jarbidge, Mahoganies, and Santa Rosa ranges feed high-altitude streams that rush down canyons choked with aspen, elderberry, and wild rose before widening and slowing upon reaching the flat plateau that the Humboldt meanders through. Like all rivers, it seeks the ocean. But the Humboldt never finds it, and thus spills unsatisfied into the Carson Sink, a desert marshland in the eastern rain shadow of the Sierra Nevada.

The river was first discovered by Hudson's Bay Company fur trappers as early as the 1820s. The mountain men scoured the river and its tributaries, relieving the watershed of most of its beaver and muskrat populations. In the mid-nineteenth century, the river escorted thousands of pioneers in covered wagons on their way to California riches. After the Civil War, the Central Pacific Railroad stitched its way along the Humboldt River in its race to join the eastern line of the Union Pacific in Promontory, Utah. Then came the ranchers, the miners, the gamblers, the rail workers, the sheepherders, the outlaws, and, oh, yes, the brothels and prostitutes.

Like the Humboldt River, the state of Nevada in the nineteenth century began nowhere and ended nowhere. It was beyond the reach or the interest of most of those in the East who made the laws. So Nevadans simply made laws of their own, adapting them to fit the people, the terrain, the hardship, and the work, not vice versa.

Gambling? Sure. What else is a miner to do for entertainment in the middle of nowhere?

Guns? Absolutely. The range is filled with mountain lions, deer, hostile natives, and all manner of bad men.

Brothels? Naturally. It gets lonely amid all this sagebrush and all these men.

"This way," my brother hissed, waving at us to follow and ducking beneath a low-hanging willow branch. We were getting close to the river, and I could smell the water, the reeds, and the mud banks. A mourning cloak butterfly flitted in the spring air before alighting on a wild rose, its gold-trimmed wings flexing slowly, flashing an iridescent purple-black in the warm sun.

My brother huddled us together again.

"Okay," he told Ray and me in a hushed whisper filled with urgency. "We're going to go over to that fence and take turns boosting each other up. Craig, you go first. Ray, you're second. I'm third, and Tony's last. You need to be absolutely quiet. Don't say anything. Don't make a sound."

We all nodded and followed, hunching down in single file as we crept through the open meadow before arriving at a seven-foot-high wooden fence that looked as though it might be part of someone's suburban backyard.

Tony clasped his hands together. I put one foot in, balancing myself on his shoulder as well as the pine fence. I could smell the wood, which was honey-colored and warm to the touch. The broad slats looked fresh from the lumberyard.

Tony hoisted. I wrapped my fingers around the top ledge of the rough-cut pine and pulled my nose level with the top of the fence. The sun glared hot off the light-colored wood. Sweat trickled down my temples. My knees wobbled.

I looked down at what appeared to be the backyard of a garish purple house. There were a dozen women in plastic lounge chairs you'd typically find by the deck of a pool. Only there was no pool. But there were tables with pitchers of lemonade, towels, and tanning lotion. The women were facing the sun, pointing toward us at about a 45-degree angle. And they were topless—employees of Mona's Place, Kitty Corner, and Irene's, enjoying a spring respite.

Brothels had been part of Winnemucca since before the arrival of the railroad in 1868. The Winnemucca Hotel was built less than a year after Lincoln signed orders in 1862 to begin construction of the transcontinental railroad. The hotel became a way station. Today it still serves Basque dinners favored by the sheepherders who had come to Nevada from the Pyrenees. Not coincidentally, the hotel is located only a few yards from the town's brothel district on Riverside Drive. Though the world was modernizing around it, many pockets of Nevada saw no need to change. In fact, frontier libertarian views on gambling, prostitution, and guns persist to this day.

Sweat trickled from my forehead and into my eyes. I didn't dare lift my hand to wipe it away. I tried to stay as still as possible. I breathed quickly and quietly into the pine fence. It was the first time I'd seen the live breasts of a real woman. I was astounded. There were large breasts. There were small breasts. There were perky breasts. There were sagging breasts. There were pink nipples. There were dark nipples. This spring day had delivered a cornucopia of good fortune. My brother tugged at my pant leg. I kicked at him, signaling that I needed more time. Fifteen seconds later, he tugged hard. My time was up. Tony lowered my foot to the ground.

Ray took his turn, and then my brother, and then Tony. I pointed up again, suggesting that we each take another look, but my brother pointed at his watch, intimating that we were out of time. The tardy bell would ring soon. If we were seen sneaking across a deserted playground, we would be easily spotted, and it would be obvious that we'd been off campus.

We crept away from the fence. Once we'd gone about ten yards, we broke into a full gallop, racing each other back to school. My brother reached the road first. He stopped behind a willow and called us together for one last huddle. The first bell had just rung, and kids were streaming back into the classrooms.

"Okay," he said. "Here's the deal—we meet here again tomorrow right after the first lunch bell. Don't be late, or we'll leave you. And here's the important part: You can't tell anyone, and I mean *anyone*. Got it?"

"Got it," we confirmed in unison.

"Now, everyone needs to swear they won't tell anyone. Swear?" he asked, pointing at me.

"Swear," I proclaimed.

"Swear?" He pointed to Ray.

"Swear," declared Ray.

"Swear?" He pointed to Tony.

"Swear," Tony said.

"I swear, too," said my brother.

We ducked from behind the willow, dashed across the street—covered in sweat and bits of brush—and headed back to class.

CHAPTER TWELVE

Most people think a bullet goes through a person in the same manner as a drill goes through wood—in effect, by boring a neat hole as it passes through the body.

This is a misconception.

Rather, the bullet crushes and shreds the tissue in its path. At the same time, it flings surrounding tissue in a radial motion, producing a temporary cavity that can be up to twelve times larger than the diameter of the bullet in a high-powered hunting rifle. This temporary cavity balloons and then collapses in the span of about five milliseconds.

Velocity is the most important factor in determining how much damage a bullet is likely to inflict. That's because a bullet in motion delivers kinetic energy to its target. The laws of physics state that a doubling of the bullet's mass doubles its kinetic energy, while a doubling of the velocity quadruples the kinetic energy.

That's why a .30-30 rifle firing a ten-gram bullet will pack over twelve times the kinetic energy of a .38 handgun firing a similar-sized bullet. Speed kills.

As a result, high-velocity hunting bullets deliver different and more devastating wounds. As the rifle bullet enters the body, there is a "tail splash," or backward hurling of injured tissue—much in the same manner as a meteor creates a ridge around its crater. Soft-lead hunting bullets are designed to expand, or mushroom, as they travel through tissue. This causes pieces of lead to fly off the main bullet and act as secondary missiles, further expanding the size of the wound cavity and the radius of damage. The bullet also injects bacteria in and around the wound track, making the risk of infection high. When these high-velocity bullets hit bone, they cause catastrophic destruction, sending shards exploding outward through the surrounding tissue.

—Adapted from *Gunshot Wounds: Practical Aspects of Firearms, Ballistics, and Forensic Techniques,* by Vincent J. M. Di Maio, MD (1999)

The dark clouds that only half an hour ago crouched in the distance on the northern horizon began to drift in on cold gusts. A shadow passed over the stand of aspen. The gold, luminous leaves flicked off, then on. Another cloud passed, and another. A great gust rustled through the stand. Leaves whooshed from their moorings and fluttered down the canyon in a yellow swirl. Clouds gathered around God's Pocket Peak, casting a shadow of gray gloom upon the mountain. The golden glow from the aspen leaves flicked off for the day.

My foot began to throb with each beat of my heart. I started to moan. I wondered how much of my foot was left. I wondered if I had any toes. I kept thinking about seeing if I could wiggle my toes just to find out. I knew it was a bad idea. I knew I might not like what I discovered. But the thought wouldn't leave. My foot throbbed harder and deeper.

I flexed my toes. A sharp pain shot up my leg. It seemed like my big toe couldn't move, but my other toes could. I wiggled again. My small toes definitely moved, but I could feel them sticking on what felt like large slivers. I learned later that a bone in my foot had been nearly vaporized. Shards and slivers had exploded outward—driven through the surrounding tissue, far away from the original wound.

An electrifying jolt shot up my right tibia and femur. And then another. The level of pain was stunning. It was like nothing I'd ever felt before. Like a dentist drilling deep into a tooth without anesthetic. Only worse. Again. And again. And again.

My brother returned with the firewood he'd gathered.

Another jolt of pain electrified me, this one lasting several seconds. I grabbed the spindly trunk of a nearby sagebrush. My hand clamped shut in a spasm. My back arched. The air was squeezed from my lungs. A full-throated scream left my mouth. My brother dropped the firewood on the open ground to my left. Startled, he knelt at my side and grabbed my left arm. I involuntarily screamed again, every muscle and every bit of air in my lungs devoted to the noise. That same scream in the morning would have rung through the wilderness, carrying far through the crisp, clear air, and echoing off canyon walls. But now, my screams were merely swallowed by the clouds and the cold and the wind.

The pain—hard, sharp, deep, and relentless—consumed me, overwhelming my muscles, my bones, my breathing, my vision, my hearing.

It was mind-bending. It was hallucination-inducing.

I screamed into the wilderness. And screamed. And screamed. And screamed. The wilderness did not care.

My brother tried to help, tried to get me to stay calm. I could hear his words but couldn't understand them. I tried to meditate, tried to take my mind elsewhere. But there was no escape. The pain always found me.

My back arched. My fingers dug into the dirt. Another scream shrieked into the wind.

I began to think about all the animals I'd ever shot. Now I knew how they felt.

There was the big, plump sage grouse that jumped up in front of me, wings beating furiously with a feathered buzz. I'd quickly and calmly raised my shotgun to my shoulder, steadied the barrel, put the bead about a foot in front of the bird, and slowly squeezed the trigger. With a booming thud and a poof of feathers, the grouse had folded its wings and crashed into the brush. I trotted thirty yards and found that it was instinctively and desperately trying to hide beneath the sage. Its left wing flapped, but its right wing was damp and red and remained tucked. The bird kicked its feet and beat its one good wing. I reached under the brush, grabbed it by its neck, and pulled it up. It scratched at my forearms with its feet, while its one good wing slapped into my wrist. I swung the bird hard clockwise by the neck. Once. And then twice. There was a *crunch, crunch*, and then the flapping and the kicking had stopped. Feathers and blood stuck to my hand. I'd tucked the bird into a pouch on the back of my hunting vest, wiped my sticky, feathered hand on my jeans, picked up my gun, and marched on.

Maybe that's why I'd been shot. Maybe I had it coming. Maybe.

I felt sorry for the buck my stepbrother had shot earlier in the day. And for the doe. And for all the deer that all the hunters in Nevada had ever shot.

I felt sorry for all the soldiers in all the wars, and for all the men lying shot in the jungles or the rice paddies in Vietnam.

In between screams, I started confessing my hunting sins to my brother. I told him of my new kinship with wounded and dead soldiers. My brother just looked back at me, worried.

CHAPTER THIRTEEN

The big white clock with the long black hands ticked slowly above the teacher. The day dozed onward. The windows were tilted open to let in the fresh, warm air. Butterflies flitted along the hedge in front of the school. A big, metal sprinkler went *chk-chk, chk-chk, chk-chk*. The first teacher droned on about how to diagram a sentence. The clock ticked slowly. The second teacher spoke about how the two Roosevelt presidents pronounced their names differently, and we should, too, if we wanted to be learned and correct. It was Teddy RUSE-a-velt, and Franklin ROSE-a-velt. The clock ticked slowly. Warm spring air wafted through the windows. The third and final teacher described the pH scale, informing us that solutions with a measurement of less than 7 were acidic, while those above 7 were alkaline. The clock ticked slowly, and the day dozed onward.

I couldn't think about verbs, nouns, prepositions, RUSE-a-velts, ROSE-a-velts, or pH scales. I could only think of big, beautiful breasts basking in warm, open sunshine.

Benjamin Franklin once wrote, "The only way to keep a secret between two people is if one of them's dead."

As usual, Ben was right.

The minute I'd sat down after returning from yesterday's lunch break, I knew with certainty that I was, for the first time, absolutely the coolest kid in school. I watched in agony as the clock ticked in math class. But I'd made a vow and couldn't break it. I did jumping jacks in PE, thinking philosophically, "What's the point of being the coolest kid in school if no one knows you're the coolest kid in school?" And the clock ticked.

By geography class, I'd thought about all the secrets my brother had spilled at my expense—about all the times he'd ratted me out to my parents. I looked at Joey Buchan sitting across the aisle from me. The clock ticked. It was 3:10. Only ten more minutes until the end-of-day bell rang. Joey looked pretty dependable. He was sort of a friend. We'd been on the same flag-football team. I could trust him. Besides, who would he tell?

I leaned toward him. The teacher droned on.

"You'll never guess what we did at lunch," the conversation began . . .

Joey didn't believe me—so much so that he threatened to punch me in the shoulder. I told him he didn't have to believe me; he just had to meet me tomorrow across the street after the first lunch bell. Don't tell anyone, and don't bring anyone—just yourself, I said. And don't be late, or we'll leave without you.

CHAPTER FOURTEEN

"Pleeeeease, God!" I screamed into a swirling, cold wind.

"Pleeeeeeeeease! Make it stop! Make it stop! Make it stop!" I cried.

But the pain didn't stop. It only grew—and in ways that didn't seem possible. My entire body was pain. I no longer knew where I'd been shot. My knee hurt. Maybe I'd really been shot in the knee? My arm hurt. Maybe it was the arm? My teeth hurt. Maybe it was the jaw?

My dad had been gone less than an hour, but time had slowed. I felt searing pain with every beat of my heart and every pulse that went up and down my leg. I measured time in heartbeats. I knew it would take my dad at least two, maybe three, hours to return, and then God knows how many hours to get to a hospital.

I wouldn't make it. I couldn't make it. It wasn't humanly possible.

"Oh, dear God, puh-leeeeeease! I'll do anything! Anything! Puh-leeeeeease! Please make the pain go away. Dear Lord, please hear me. Please answer my prayer. Puh-leeeeeease!"

The wind buffeted and shook the tops of the sage.

My brother spoke often, but I could no longer hear or see him. I was only vaguely aware of his presence.

"Please, God!" I screamed. "I'll go to church every Sunday for the rest of my life! Please! I'll never again doubt you. Please! I'll never again lie to my parents. Please! I'll always help others. I'll live a life that is good and holy. Please! Anything! Please make it stop!"

And then I waited. Surely God had heard me. How could he not? He was kind and forgiving. How could he let pain like this exist? How could he visit it upon a young boy? How? Why?

Perhaps he was testing me. Perhaps he was testing my faith in him. Perhaps he didn't think my belief in him was pure and true.

I screamed the Apostles' Creed in its entirety into the gathering storm. I'd been made to memorize it in the third grade at St. Teresa of Avila Catholic School in Carson City, Nevada. Sister Victoria had told me that God heard us always, and that if we were sincere and our motives pure, our prayers would all be answered in good time.

I believed her.

"I believe in God, the Father Almighty, creator of heaven and earth . . ." I began, doing my best to ignore the pain so I could concentrate enough to make it through the prayer I'd been reciting laboriously every Sunday in church. I struggled through each line before concluding, "I believe in the Holy Spirit, the Holy Catholic Church, the communion of saints, the forgiveness of sins, the resurrection of the body, and life everlasting. Amen."

I then tried mightily to push the pain out of my mind long enough so I could just be silent and listen. To not yell. To not moan. But to wait for an answer, which was sure to be forthcoming. Because Sister Victoria had assured me it would.

The wind buffeted and shook the tops of the sage. The aspen bent and the leaves rattled.

I waited. I listened.

I looked up the slope at God's Pocket Peak. The clouds had all gathered and had begun to sink. In the West, you look for storms by watching the big peaks, because when one comes, it first swallows the tallest mountain and then the next. And then it sinks down the slopes before filling the valleys. To this day, the only two things in nature that fill me with a sense of eternity and dread are clouds swallowing a mountaintop in advance of an impending winter storm, and an ocean churning gray and green and infinite beneath the wind and rain.

So it was that the clouds sank down upon God's Pocket Peak, and the mountaintop disappeared into an ominous gray.

And then the snow began to fall.

CHAPTER FIFTEEN

The next day was a carbon copy of the previous one. Lilacs bloomed. Butterflies flitted. Kids played catch. The scent of mowed lawn wafted sweet on the spring breeze.

In class, teachers droned and windows tilted open to let in the enticing warmth.

And the clock ticked. It was almost noon—almost time for the Big Rendezvous. My knee bounced nervously beneath my desk. One by one, several boys in my class asked for permission to go to the restroom. When the fourth boy asked, the teacher told him she'd already given enough hall passes, and that he'd simply have to wait until the noon bell.

The clock ticked. The bell rang. I dashed down the hall through a crowd of students. As I ran across the playground, I noticed several other boys running, too. By the time I reached the field, there were at least a dozen kids jogging ahead of me.

How could this be? I'd only told Joey Buchan. He could be trusted. Who would he tell?

By the time I reached the big fence, I could see at least three pairs of boys giving each other boosts. Then there was yelling. I could hear a lady on the other side telling us to leave—saying that she'd called our principal.

Some kids retreated. Some didn't. There were kids running down the trail toward the fence and kids running back the other way toward school.

"Shit, she's called the school," one retreating kid yelled as he ran back against a tide of boys.

I looked up and could see three or four of the male teachers running across the street toward the field. They were grabbing boys by their arms and hauling them back toward campus. Kids fled in every direction.

I saw my brother in the melee. He turned to me and said, "Shit— don't get caught."

Indeed. My stepmother was a very popular elementary school teacher. She knew everyone. If the teacher posse spotted me, she might get a call.

My brother crashed through a thicket of willows and brush on a path that led down to the river. I followed. We ran for about a quarter-mile before making our way to the rural highway that looped behind the school. We jumped a fence by the maintenance sheds and made our way nonchalantly across the football field and back to the main school building. There we saw Ray and Tony. We once again huddled, this time by the outdoor basketball courts, away from members of the teacher posse returning from the fields with some of their quarry.

"What the hell happened?" shouted my brother.

"I have no idea," said Tony.

"Who talked?" asked Kirk.

There was silence. We all looked down.

"I mentioned something to my brother," said Ray. "But he's in high school, so what does it matter?"

"I only told one guy," I protested. "And I know him. He didn't tell anyone."

"I told a guy," confessed Kirk.

"Me, too," said Tony.

"Well, from here on out, just keep your mouths shut," warned Kirk. "Let's hope none of this comes back to us."

The teacher posse was able to nab only a few of the three dozen boys who'd attempted to witness the spring glory that was Mona's Place. The phone never rang at our house regarding the incident. And the brothel staff stopped sunbathing topless—during lunchtime, at least.

The goose had been cooked. The golden eggs were no more. They proved as fleeting as the first warm days of spring.

—◆—

And, indeed, spring was nothing more than a transient in Winnemucca. Here one week, gone the next. The season was squeezed between the hard, cold elbow of winter and the broad, torrid shoulder of summer. Soon the sun would rise high and hot above the dung-colored land. The surrounding expanse of sage-covered hills would be unable to provide even the slightest solace of shade, thus submitting fully to the pounding heat—a heat that, once here, would march relentlessly, day after day, in an unbroken string of triple-digit or near-triple-digit numbers, all the way until the final days of August or the first days of September, when the heat, which by then, no one ever expected to end, would be broken by the quick, sharp stab of the coming autumn's first freeze, killing overnight all the tomato plants in all the backyards of the town, and catching all the gardeners by complete surprise, even though it happened this way year after year.

And as soon as the hot days had come, spring would be nothing more than a memory. Lilac bushes would be left with shriveled flower stems—dark and burnt and tucked between the plant's broad, deep-green leaves of summer. And though perhaps it wasn't even ten days prior to last Tuesday when the heat had first arrived, you would find yourself straining to even remember the dusty purple flowers that hung in heavy bunches and produced a florid fragrance that traveled thick on a soft afternoon breeze and made you stop in place to take a deep extra breath before continuing on your way. And when the heat enveloped you fully in July, and you reminisced about the glory of grown women sunbathing topless in the backyard at Mona's Place, it all seemed like a distant dream, and you questioned whether it had really happened, even though you were almost certain it had.

But there was one place in Winnemucca where memories were absent and time was frozen in slabs of granite and marble. That place, of course, was the cemetery. And on an evening in late June—a little over a month after the fiasco at Mona's Place—a mother, distraught, knelt in the grass and placed a bouquet of blue and yellow irises gently atop a small tombstone. Into the granite was carved the following: OUR BELOVED SON. SCOTT M. HAINES. MAR. 27, 1958. JUNE 29, 1971. She ran her fingers like feathers across the letters before sobbing softly into the twilight and repeating, "Our beloved son, our beloved son, our beloved son."

Of course, we all knew the story of Scott Haines. One of our classmates was there when it happened and had told us the story in gory detail. Plus, Scott was an accomplished golfer. His father was the manager and golf pro at the nine-hole municipal course. During the summer, we would brave the heat because we were young and impervious. For $28, you could buy a season pass that would enable you to play as much golf as you could stand during the summer. Which we did. We'd play hole after hole after hole. Our record was 108 holes in one day—all walking, from sunrise until we could no longer see the ball, well after sunset.

We were not big on the finer points of golf etiquette in Winnemucca. When stuck behind some doddering duffers, we would simply leapfrog them by skipping a hole and playing on. On the next trip around the course, we would play the skipped hole twice. As a result, Mr. Haines was eternally infuriated at us. He would come racing toward us in his red golf cart, bouncing over the rough and gliding down the fairway before skidding to a stop on the grass next to us after a loud, angry stomp on his brakes. He would get out of his cart, gather us around like a Little League baseball coach, pull out his USGA Rules of Golf handbook, wave it in the air—open to a pertinent page—and explain to us in detail the three or four rules he'd seen us violate just that day. He'd tell us that he knew we could do better, and that if we didn't show more respect for the proud and ancient traditions of golf, then he'd have a talk with each of our fathers, all of whom he knew on a first-name basis, and demonstrated it to be true by reciting, "Ben, Dave, Herb, and Joe." He then handed us each a USGA Rules of Golf handbook of our own and advised us with an air of certitude that we'd all grow up to be more civil and well-rounded men if we'd just take the time to read through the list of rules and memorize a few.

We nodded politely, and vowed to do better, just as he'd asked. As we watched him glide back down the fairway and then bounce back over the rough on his way to the clubhouse, we'd lower our heads and flip through the handbook disinterestedly, before stuffing it into one of the pockets of our golf bags with the four or five other handbooks Mr. Haines had given to us previously.

We were always puzzled by Mr. Haines's earnest attempts to turn us into better golfers and better men. It was 105 degrees. The only people on the course were a slow threesome of retirees and a foursome of teenage boys with nothing better to do. This wasn't St. Andrews; it was Winnemucca. It hardly seemed fair or reasonable that the proud and ancient rules of golf should apply right here and right now. But we never argued or talked back to Mr. Haines. We were always polite. And I did once make an attempt to read the Rules of Golf from cover to cover, although I lost interest somewhere around Rule 19-5a, the one where it's a two-stroke penalty for hitting another player's ball on the green with your ball while putting.

Mr. Haines never did discuss our on-course oafishness with our fathers that we knew of. And in spite of the fact that we were teenage boys—the most narcissistic, least self-aware, and most self-centered of all types of humans—we always felt a certain sorrow and maybe even compassion for Mr. Haines whenever he came around.

That's probably because we all knew the story of his son Scott. For Scott was once one of us. And his story was this:

Winnemucca was infamous for its gnats. Mosquitoes, everyone expected. And, yes, there were plenty of those. But gnats? Their swarms were biblical, and there was something unfamiliar and unholy about them. They were as small as the period at the end of a sentence. But they were voracious, relentless, and multitudinous—like speck-size vampires in search of their nightly fill of fresh blood. They were nowhere to be seen during the shimmering heat of the day, but as soon as the sun set, they would billow up in great clouds from the oxbows, sloughs, and stagnant ponds of the Humboldt River just north of town. They would rise ominously from the evening cool of the river willows, and if the breeze were just right, they would blow into town, blanketing people, pets, and livestock.

You might be outside at a neighbor's, barbecuing hamburgers, or perhaps just taking a walk and enjoying a summer evening, when you would look down and notice that your forearms were carpeted with black spots. The amoebic cloud would then descend upon you, and the faintly buzzing specks would stick to your eyelashes, become tangled in your hair, and get sucked inside your nostrils. You would flail your arms uselessly at the swarm while running in terror for the nearest door, which you would slam behind you and lean against for good measure, all the while still slapping at your arms, head, ears, back, legs, and face.

Maybe a day or two later, you would see a biplane, traveling back and forth along the river, dipping just below the trees and releasing roiling clouds of white dust and smoke, which would fall softly atop the willows and the waterways. This would stifle the gnats for a week, or sometimes more, but they would always be back, often more plentiful than ever. Who knows what was in that concoction dropped by the biplane? For the residents of Winnemucca, it didn't really matter. It could've been DDT or napalm—anything to relieve them of the nightly plague of ravenous gnats.

Scott and his best friend had spent most of that particular day playing golf. Each time they played the gopher-infested sixth hole—with its fairway that bordered an open field; hence, the gophers—Scott's friend would boast about how he'd just received a .22 rifle from his dad for his thirteenth birthday, and how they should both come back just after sunset to make quick work of the pesky rodents.

Later that afternoon, just as twilight arrived, Scott had stopped by his friend's house, eager to begin the great gopher hunt. However, their plans were slowed by clouds of gnats. They poked their heads out the front door, looked up into the sky, and saw that the gnats were impossibly thick.

Undaunted, Scott and his friend went to the garage to douse each other with bug repellent. One boy would stand like Jesus on the cross, his arms stretched straight out, his eyes closed, and his lips pursed tight. The Jesus boy would exhale fully, take a deep breath, and then hold it while his friend sprayed everything except the soles of his feet, causing the Jesus boy to fade behind a thick aerosol of fog. Both boys would then run to the opposite corner of the garage, each coughing from the oily, medicinal smell of the bug spray. The other boy would then assume the Jesus position so he, too, could be inoculated against the winged bloodsuckers that lurked in the night.

The door leading from the house to the garage flung open, and the friend's father took two full strides toward the boys before stopping, waving his hand in front of his face, and breaking out into a fit of coughing.

He stepped back, composed himself, squinted suspiciously through the cloud of bug spray, and bellowed, "What in the Sam Hill are you two doing?"

Jesus boy—the man's son—coughed and stepped away from the fog. Scott stood, red-handed, holding the can, his finger on the aerosol button.

"Just spraying each other for mosquitoes and gnats," said Jesus boy, offering nothing more than the obvious—name, rank, serial number.

No shit, the father thought. And having once been a teenage boy himself, he knew to be suspicious of such goings-on. He pressed his case.

"Why?" he asked loud and slow, as though he were speaking to someone who was both daft and hard of hearing. "Planning on going somewhere?"

Both boys were silent, giving each other furtive glances while they worked out an unspoken agreement as to who would field this simple question that begged only for a simple answer.

The friend stood tall and declared to his father: "Out."

He'd hoped, of course, that his tone and conviction would bring the interrogation to a close. But the father was as experienced in such parrying as one of those lawyers you'd see in the black-and-white TV shows.

He rolled his eyes, took a deep breath, and said—still loud and slow so there would be no mistaking his meaning—"Out where?"

Silence hung in the garage as thick as the bug spray.

The boys looked to each other, hoping one of them could come up with an answer that was suitably evasive. But after some seconds, they both slumped their shoulders.

Scott cracked first.

"We saw a bunch of gophers on the sixth hole this afternoon," he explained, all the while thinking that the plan already didn't sound as brilliant and airtight when said out loud to an adult as when he and his friend had first cooked it up. But he forged ahead anyway. "We thought we could take the new twenty-two and kill a slew of them." For good measure, he added, "They're doing terrible damage to the fairway."

There was silence. The father looked first to Scott and then to his son.

He bellowed, "Like hell you are."

He strode to his son, pulled the can of bug spray from his grip, and gave him a gentle shove in the back toward the door to the house. The two boys, their evening's adventure dashed, shuffled away in dejection.

The father put the bug spray on the shelf, shook his head, and hollered after his son, "You can't go off shooting gophers now anyway. Christ, it's almost dark."

"We have flashlights," the son said indignantly, just to show that the plan wasn't as half-baked as his father thought.

The father shook his head again, gathered a scathing response, but then thought better of it. He simply let it go before quietly shutting the door to the garage behind him.

Scott plopped on his friend's couch, content to stay at home and watch a summer rerun of *The Mod Squad*.

"Well, let me go get my gun, anyway," said the friend, still eager to show off his new present.

"Sure," said Scott, as he slouched into the cushions, clunked his large, tennis-shoe-shod feet onto the coffee table, and let his head loll to the side. The TV blared with '70s cop-show music.

"Check it out," said the friend, holding the rifle in his right hand, just above his hip, and inattentively waving the barrel around the room. Scott didn't notice. He was tired and hot and transfixed by the TV.

"This is the safety," said the friend, pointing to a place near the trigger, while still ignoring the gun's muzzle. "You press this tiny pin here to the left like so, and no matter if you pull the trigger, the safety won't let the gun go off."

The friend gave a demonstration. There was a startling bang and a flash, and smoke from the muzzle swirled toward the ceiling, rising eerie and blue through the flickering light of the television.

Scott arched his back, and stayed that way, stuck. His fists clenched and jaw tightened, a guttural scream tried to escape through his teeth, without much success. Blood began to stream down the middle of his forehead, across the bridge of his nose, and down the side of his left cheek.

His friend, terrified, didn't say a word. He laid the gun gently on the coffee table, careful now to point it away from Scott. He then ran down the hall to get his father.

The ambulance wailed down Mizpah Street on the way to the hospital. It skidded to a stop beneath the brightly lit EMERGENCY sign above a crescent driveway. A team of nurses and doctors rushed forward. Doors opened, doors slammed. Orders were barked. The safety latch to the back of the ambulance was thrown, the double doors flung open—but all was quiet. Two men hoisted the gurney out of the ambulance. One looked over to the nurse and slowly shook his head. The team rolled the gurney through the sliding glass doors, but they trotted forward without a sense of either urgency or hope. The doors slid shut behind them with a mechanical *snick*. Outside, the air was still thick with gnats, and the only sound was the insects' faint buzzing.

And that's how Scott's mother came to find herself in the Winnemucca cemetery, running her fingers across the chiseled granite before her, on the second anniversary of her son's death—kneeling, sobbing, and muttering, "Our beloved son, our beloved son, our beloved son." The pain was the same as when she'd first realized all was lost, when she had stood helplessly in her driveway, watching the ambulance pulse red as it roared away into the night, its siren wailing big at first before fading to small.

The mother grieved over many things in between her sobs. But she mostly grieved about the end of memories. Of how her son would never celebrate another birthday, never play another round of golf, never again feel the warm spring sun on his face, never graduate, never have a career, never know the love of a caring woman, never marry, never have children, never grow old.

Never, never, never, she thought.

He would be forever young, forever frozen in time and place, just like the words and dates carved in the granite slab that stood just beyond the position of his head.

Thomas Wolfe, whose father had made a business of carving angels and cherubs and names and dates into North Carolinian granite and marble, once wrote: "[W]e can't turn back the days that have gone. We can't turn life back to the hours when our lungs were sound, our blood hot, our bodies young. We are a flash of fire—a brain, a heart, a spirit. And we are three-cents-worth of lime and iron—which we cannot get back."

Perhaps.

But at least we, the living, have memories. They, the dead, do not.

And as the mother knelt and sobbed, knelt and sobbed, the darkness grew. Mr. Haines was there, too. He stood to her side, transfixed, still staring off to the place where he'd watched the sun set some thirty minutes earlier. He did not cry. Instead, he wrestled wearily with the lump in his throat, the knot in his stomach, and a grief so deep that it seemed to emanate from his bones. He noticed that the trees along the Humboldt were no longer green, but rather black silhouettes against the twilight. A cool, damp breeze blew in from the river bottom, beckoning a pestilent cloud of gnats, which now billowed darkly into the evening sky of silver-blue.

CHAPTER SIXTEEN

"Wow, that's a beaut," said the doctor, inspecting my foot during a trip to the emergency room sometime in my late-twenties after spraining my ankle in a game of pickup basketball. "I'm guessing a thirty-aught-six or a thirty-thirty, right?"

"Pretty good," I replied, impressed. "Thirty-thirty."

"Thought so. How'd it happen?"

"I was deer-hunting in Nevada in the middle of nowhere when I was thirteen."

"Bet it hurt like hell."

"You have no idea."

"Actually, I do. But whoever patched you up did a decent-enough job, considering what they had to work with. You're just a little bit lucky you didn't die."

"Die? C'mon. You can't die from a gunshot wound to the foot."

"Well, actually you can. Especially when it's from a high-velocity rifle shot into the bone. Those are the most dangerous and painful kinds. And if you don't get medical attention right away, the risk of slipping into shock is quite real. I was a medic in Vietnam. I saw plenty of guys shot in the extremities who'd had to spend several hours or longer in the bush before getting evacuated to an army field hospital. Some of them were in so much pain and had lost enough blood that they went into shock and didn't make it.

"Others ended up with severe infections and died later from septic shock. It was rare, but it happened. If you have an open-fracture gunshot to your lower leg, and it takes you longer than six hours to get treatment, you have about a fifty-fifty chance of developing either shock or sepsis. Before World War I, such an injury was a death sentence that could only be solved through amputation. A nineteenth-century surgeon would've probably just taken a bone saw to you right about here," he said, pointing to just above my ankle. "Like I said—coulda been worse."

Confusion, panic, and disorientation are killers in the wilderness. They are to be avoided at all costs. They cause people to do stupid things and often either contribute to or hasten one's demise. They are also precursors to shock, a dangerous affliction that, once started, is difficult to stop. Shock is like a falling line of dominoes. Once the first domino tips over, it's only a matter of time before the chain reaction claims them all. Initially, the central nervous system becomes overwhelmed. Then the circulatory system. Then the kidneys. The liver. The brain. The lungs. The heart.

"Craig! Craig!" my brother yelled.

He was kneeling over me, almost nose to nose, holding my face with both of his hands.

He was staring straight into my eyes. I tried to focus. I tried to stare back. I used all my mental energy to push the pain away and to stop screaming and to listen. His eyes became clear in my vision.

"Craig! Listen to me," Kirk said loudly and slowly, as though he were talking to someone several feet away with a hearing problem. "I know it hurts, but you need to calm down. Screaming's not going to help. It won't make anything go faster. Dad'll be back soon. You need to do everything you can to try to stay calm. Can you do that?"

I didn't think I could, but I nodded weakly, nonetheless.

"Okay," said Kirk. "Let's see how long you can go without screaming. Show me what you've got."

Between the intermittent flurries of snow, I could see the sun flicker faintly through clouds on the horizon far to the west. I tried to do some calculations to help ward off the pain. My dad had been gone about an hour. The sun would begin to set in about an hour and a half. We would then have about thirty minutes to an hour of dusk before total darkness. We had to get out by then. My dad had to get back to us before it got dark. Lots of things can go wrong in the wilderness at night. He could get lost, he could get disoriented. He might have to wait until morning.

Pain and panic returned. I screamed into the wind.

"That was good," Kirk said, staring into my face. "You went almost thirty seconds without a scream. See if you can do a minute."

I closed my eyes and, for whatever reason, thought of fish.

I was with my grandfather—the one who'd given me the gun. We'd been fishing along a stream high in the Sawtooth Mountains of central Idaho. We were busy catching cutthroat trout. The stream ran beneath a canopy of trees. Everywhere it was green and shady. My grandfather stopped and pointed. In the middle of the shallow current was a fish bigger than any trout I'd ever seen. It looked completely lost and out-of-place. It was blood-red, and its humped back stuck out of the water. It was facing upstream, its tail waving slowly, rhythmically, from side to side.

"That's a sockeye," my grandfather said in a low voice. "He came all the way up here from the ocean. There used to be lots of these here this time of year. But this is the first one I've seen in nearly a decade."

We walked to the stream's edge. The fish was almost three feet long and weighed at least twelve pounds. I stepped out on a rock not more than a foot from the fish to get a closer look. The salmon blithely accepted my presence, its tail swishing slowly in the current. I reached out to touch its back. The bright-red color almost glowed in the forest. My hand hovered above the water, mere inches from the fish. The salmon splashed with its tail and torpedoed upstream about thirty feet.

And then the pain returned.

I screamed again. And again. And again.

"That was good," my brother replied. "That was over a minute. See if you can go longer."

I focused hard. I was fishing again with my grandfather. One of his favorite places was atop the American Falls Dam on the Snake River in southeastern Idaho. He first took my brother and me there when I was about five. But in order to get to the large concrete platform where you could fish into the deep waters of the reservoir, you had to cross a narrow catwalk that hung precariously across the dam's spillway. The catwalk was suspended by a pair of steel cables and had wood slats for a base. You had to walk single file, each hand grabbing a cable on either side. To the left, the greenish-brown reservoir water drifted slowly by. To the right, the water plunged white, roaring over a hundred feet and relentlessly pounding the black lava rocks below. The air reverberated with the thrumming of the crashing water, and a mist wafted up from the canyon below.

The first time my brother and I had crossed, we were terrified. There were no safety rails or netting. Many adults, who had arrived to fish with friends, saw the catwalk, shook their heads, and turned back. But my grandfather nudged us across, and by the afternoon, he had to scold us for running back and forth and playing tag on the catwalk. Our mother would've been horrified.

Again I screamed. I was tired of playing mental games. I just wanted to give up—to give in to the confusion, panic, and disorientation.

"You're doing great," Kirk said. "That was two minutes—two minutes! Good job. Hang in there. You're going to make it. Keep doing what you're doing."

I went back to American Falls with my grandfather. This time we were at the base of the dam—below the spillway. There was a kokanee salmon run under way. These were small salmon that stayed in freshwater and never went to the ocean. They had made a run up the Snake from another reservoir downriver, but there was no way they could get past the dam. Idaho Fish and Game allowed people to net the fish since they would die there anyway. We opened the creaky metallic door of my grandfather's old Chrysler. My brother and I—eight and seven (respectively) at the time—spilled out and looked up at the towering dam, with water tumbling over the top, turning into a curtain of falling white, and then thundering into the river and the rocks below. The air shook, and you had to yell to be heard.

My grandfather opened the trunk of his car and pulled out a large, white bucket and a green nylon scoop net with an eight-foot-long aluminum handle. He then told us to stay put while he walked out on the lava rock and scouted along the river's edge. He came back, placed his hands on his hips, leaned down to us, and yelled into the roar, "Who wants to go first?"

My hand shot up, and I dashed to the river. My grandfather caught me from behind, holding the back of my shirt collar with one hand, the bucket and net in the other. But when we stepped out onto the basalt shelf that was black and wet from the mist, I became terrified.

My grandfather yelled, "Don't be afraid. I've got you, and I won't let go."

He was strong and stocky, and grabbed a handful of my jeans along my belt line with his thick right hand.

He yelled into my ear, "I'm going to lean you over the water, and you're going to dip that net into the river as deep as you can, and then pull up some fish."

I wasn't at all sure about his plan. And I would've handed the project over to Kirk, but this was one of the rare times where I'd gotten to take a first crack at something. Sibling rivalry wouldn't allow me to turn back.

My grandfather set his feet. He lowered me almost parallel to the water. Just beneath me, the river boiled and pounded into an angry white froth. Blobs of water and foam danced in the air. Occasionally, a small, dark fish would jump, wriggle, and fall back into the foam.

I wondered what it would be like to just let go and plunge into a pillow of raging white. But my grandfather held tight.

I stabbed the net into the water, holding the handle tight with both hands. The net was tugged and jerked by the current. I swished it forward, turned, and swished it back.

My grandfather then lifted me off the rock and carried me two steps back from the edge. A bounty of kokanee wriggled silver and black. I smiled as my grandfather set me back on the ground.

Again I screamed. The veins along my neck and temples bulged. I was exhausted from the pain. I wanted to escape it, but there was nowhere to hide. No matter where I went, it always found me.

"All right, you're doing good," Kirk said. "You're doing good."

"No, I'm not!" I yelled. "No, I'm not. I can't take it anymore, I can't take it. How come God hasn't answered my prayer? How come?"

"I don't know. Say another one. Say another prayer."

"Hail, Mary, full of grace," I yelled. "The Lord is with thee. Blessed art thou among women, and blessed is the fruit of thy womb, Jesus. Holy Mary, mother of God, pray for us sinners, now and at the hour of our death. Amen."

The snow swirled in the wind. Fortunately, it wasn't a wet, heavy snow, but rather a light, dry dusting with small, round flakes that gently pelted your jacket.

Maybe this was the hour of my death; maybe it would just be easier to let go. Anything to escape the pain.

I began to shiver. With each shake, my body was jolted with even more pain.

"I'm cold," I said to my brother. "I'm cold."

He had already started to build a fire. The sun was getting low on the horizon, the clouds were sinking farther down God's Pocket Peak, and the light was growing dim.

With just one match, the kindling flared. My brother had stacked larger branches of wood at 90-degree angles on the outside of the kindling, creating something of a chimney to bring the flames to life.

The fire whooshed upward. The wood crackled and sparked. My brother stood and scanned the horizon for any sign of a truck. There was none.

The fire leaped into the darkening sky, and tiny pellets of snow swirled in and out of the light.

CHAPTER SEVENTEEN

My stepbrother had shot and wounded an owl.

We all felt bad about it.

"I didn't think I'd actually hit it," he complained.

But he did hit it, and the damage had been done. Nevertheless, we were all now in this together. We quickly formed a confederacy of conspirators—my brother Kirk, my stepbrother Monte, and me. My dad must never find out what really happened. He worked for the Bureau of Land Management (BLM) and was well versed in environmental issues, wildlife management, and endangered species. He was also a stickler about gun safety, hunting protocol, and shooting only what you planned to eat. Not to mention that it was against federal law and punishable with a felony to shoot a raptor like a great horned owl. No, telling my father the truth about the owl just wouldn't do. As coconspirators, our story would be this: We were out hiking and came across an injured owl. Someone must've shot him. Bastards. We rescued him, brought him home, and planned on nursing him back to health. How noble were we?

My brothers and I had begun the day hiking from our house to the dirt road that led up to Water Canyon, where my family had an A-frame cabin and a corral with horses. We'd brought a .22 rifle and a .410 shotgun with us for target shooting, and in case we came across any rabbits. It was a hot day in late August. The temperature was already above 90 degrees at ten a.m. when we'd set out.

Water Canyon was carved into the flank of Sonoma Peak, a nearly 10,000-foot, sage-covered mountain that rose just south of Winnemucca. White Creek began just below the highest ridge that led to Sonoma Peak and was fed by melting snow and mountain springs. Between the steep, brown canyon walls, the small creek rushed and burbled and snaked its way down to the Humboldt River, escorted on its journey by an oasis of cool, green cottonwoods, willows, and alder.

My brothers and I tromped through the hot dust toward the canyon some three miles away. The sun beat down and the ceaseless buzz of cicadas rose with heat that made the distant ridges shimmer. My back sweated against a pack that carried our lunches and a canteen of water.

We arrived at the canyon and found a trail that ran beside the creek and beneath a canopy of trees. We'd stopped to drink some water and eat a sandwich when Monte saw something move high in the big cottonwood about fifty yards away. We all looked where he'd pointed. A head swiveled. Big eyes blinked. The bird was perched on a branch and tucked against the dark-brown tree trunk, his color and form indiscernible from the bark.

Monte slowly raised the .22 to his shoulder and aimed into the tree.

The small rifle popped, sounding more like a firecracker and lacking the thunder that the big rifles and shotguns produced. There was no hard kick to the shoulder or ringing in the ears.

The owl hadn't flinched. It sat motionless, looking down with big, yellow eyes.

Monte aimed again.

Pop went the gun.

Nothing.

The owl lost interest, swiveled his head forward, and closed his eyes.

"I don't think you're supposed to shoot an owl," I offered in a less than halfhearted protest.

"Don't worry," said Monte. "I'll never hit him from this far away. I just want to get him to fly."

Monte raised the gun again.

Pop.

Startled, the big bird stood on the branch, stretched its wings, flapped twice in irritation, and hopped into the air, expecting to make a silent, graceful glide away from the menacing trio of boys.

Instead the bird spiraled left. Panicked, it began flapping wildly. But that did not stop the plunge to the ground thirty feet below.

We all stood looking at each other.

"Shit. You hit him," said Kirk.

"Crap," said Monte. "I didn't mean to."

We ran over to where the bird had fallen.

The great horned owl stood in a clearing beneath the tree, looking naturally nonchalant. He was one of the largest birds in North America, and clearly wasn't used to getting shot at. He stood two feet tall with a sharp, pewter-colored beak, strong, menacing talons, and two trademark tufts that stuck straight up from either side of his head.

We stopped about twenty feet away, not sure what to do.

The owl was intensely focused on us, standing his ground and bobbing his head from side to side.

"Should we kill him and put him out of his misery?" I asked.

"I don't know," said Kirk. "I don't think he's that badly hurt. Might've just winged him."

"Well, we can't just leave him here on the ground for the coyotes."

"No, you're right. We should take him home. I think we can nurse him back to health."

I'm not sure if the owl's well-being was the foremost priority for my brother. His altruism probably stemmed mostly from the irresistible notion of having an owl as a pet.

"Yeah, but you're never going to get him home," said Monte. "Those talons will tear you apart."

"I'm not sure, but I think I can get him to calm down, then get him to ride home on my wrist after I've wrapped it with a shirt or something," Kirk muttered, thinking aloud.

When it came to animals, Kirk had something of a gift. He was calm, graceful, and fearless in their presence. And for whatever reason, the animal—be it a bug, lizard, bird, horse, or dog—responded in kind.

We all had lots of practice with exotic pets. Our home housed a menagerie of animals. We had an English pointer, a champion bird dog who wasn't happy unless he was out in the field sniffing for quail, chukar, or pheasant. We had two cats and the occasional batch of kittens. We sometimes had ducks and chickens, as well as a coop full of fantail pigeons.

And those were just the regulars. Because of his job, my dad spent some time out on the range, counting wild horses, documenting the health of the ecosystem, and checking cattle-grazing permits. He was responsible for overseeing a swath of federally owned rangeland stretching throughout most of northwestern Nevada. His coworkers called him Black Rock Benny because he spent a lot of time in the Black Rock Desert, now famous for the counter-culture Burning Man Festival. And he was always coming home with critters that disgusted my mom but delighted my brother and me.

There were lots of king snakes and garter snakes, as well as the occasional blue racer. He brought home horned toads, leopard lizards, and collared lizards. And every now and then, he would bring us an especially creepy tarantula or Jerusalem cricket. We would care for our new pets usually for about a month or two, until we either lost interest or a new boarder arrived. My dad would then make us have a ceremony in which he would remind us that these were wild animals; they weren't really pets. They were simply on loan and eventually needed to be returned to nature. My dad would walk us out to a nearby field, boxed critter in hand, where we would say our good-byes and release the animal from its captivity.

Sometimes there would be tears.

When I was about five, my father had returned from one of his trips to the range with a baby magpie that had fallen from its nest. The magpie became a family project. We built a cage in the house and took turns feeding it sugar water from an eyedropper. The bird grew from a small ball of gray fluff to a noisy jay with long, stiff feathers of black and white. One morning, we walked into the room where we'd kept it and were startled and delighted to see that it had gotten out of its cage and was recklessly flapping and careening through the air and into curtains and walls.

"He can fly! He can fly!" my younger sister Camille shouted, clapping with glee.

My dad surveyed the situation and then informed us that we would now have to release our pet. My sister wailed. My brother and I protested. But my dad held firm.

The following day, we took the magpie into the backyard. Our dad reminded us that this was a wild animal. We were only temporary stewards. The magpie would be much healthier and happier living in its natural environment. My sister cried. My brother and I fought back tears.

Scraw-scraw! shrieked the magpie. *Scraw-scraw!*

My dad held the bird with both hands, clasping its wings to its body.

Scraw-scraw! Scraw-scraw!

My dad held the bird out so that each of us could say good-bye and pet its head one last time.

Scraw-scraw! Scraw-scraw!

My dad threw the magpie into the summer sky. It flapped wildly and flew awkwardly upward. It then stabilized and began flying toward the neighbor's trees.

Atop a nearby poplar, a red-tailed hawk perched. It watched the ceremony with interest, drawn irresistibly to the squawking of a young bird.

The magpie flew toward its first taste of freedom. The hawk unfurled its wings, hopped from its high perch, flapped twice, and tucked its wings. It fell like a bomb that'd been dropped from a plane.

The hawk collided with the magpie only yards from where we'd released it. The air exploded with black-and-white feathers. My sister screamed. Even my dad was caught off guard.

Scraw! Scraw! Scraw! Scraw! Scraw! Scraw! shrieked the magpie.

The hawk flew with the smaller bird in its talons to the neighbor's roof.

Scraw! Scraw! Scraw! Scraw! Scraw! Scraw! shrieked the magpie.

The hawk landed with its prey and began tearing at the magpie with its talons and its beak. More feathers flew. And then the shrieking stopped.

My dad herded us back into the house. Fumbling for something to say, he could only come up with, "Well, that's nature. There's a lot of death and dying. It's not like a Disney movie."

We'd learned at an early age that nature abhors the weak or the wounded. Nevertheless, in trying to decide what to do about the owl, my brother still thought the creature could be mended and safely returned to the wild.

Kirk took off his shirt and wrapped it around his wrist.

Monte and I had little faith in his plan, but we shrugged and followed my brother toward the owl. The big bird bobbed its head warily. My brother came within a couple steps. The bird stretched its wings out to their full four-foot span, hissing and clicking and lifting its outstretched talons one by one at my brother. The owl's left wing drooped. The bone on the wing's leading edge had been broken.

My brother retreated, thinking better of the plan.

"Okay, how 'bout this?" he mused. "I'll toss my shirt on him, then grab him from behind, holding his wings together."

While Kirk was plotting his strategy, the owl turned away, hopping and flapping through the sage. It tumbled down a ravine and into a dry creek bed. Kirk followed. The owl turned to make a stand, hissing and clicking furiously. Kirk approached, dangling his shirt in front of the owl like a bullfighter. The owl flipped onto its back, both sets of talons outstretched. Kirk tossed his shirt onto the owl. The bird hissed and flapped and thrashed, its talons kicking and slicing the cloth. Kirk grabbed the tail of the shirt and pulled it back. It was in shreds.

We huddled again, looking at my brother with *What now?* expressions.

He wandered beneath the cottonwoods for a few minutes and came back with a long, weathered branch. He approached the owl again. The bird hissed and clicked, still on its back, waving its talons in the air. Kirk put the end of the branch against the owl's fearsome feet. The owl instinctively clamped onto the branch with full force. Kirk lifted the owl into the air, leveling the branch on his shoulders. The owl flapped upside down, refusing to release its grip. My brother rotated the branch until the owl was upright.

My brother looked at the owl. The owl swiveled its head and stared back. It hissed once more, tucked its ruffled wings, swiveled its head forward, and then adjusted to its perch.

We walked three miles back home carrying a large owl cantilevered on a branch. When we arrived at the house, we gathered some leather straps, made a tether, and tied the owl to a branch in our backyard apple tree.

We kept the owl for nearly three months. After about a week in the apple tree, the owl let us approach him without hissing. After about ten days, he let us feed him chopped pieces of raw steak from our leather-gloved hands. After about a month, we heard a loud *Hoo-hoo, hoo, hoo, hoo* in the night.

Most of the neighbor kids would come over to see the owl. Tom Schwartz would walk by my house on the way to school and see me feeding it. Tom was chubby and shy. I waved him over one morning and let him feed the big bird. Tom was thrilled. He stopped by every morning afterward, and we started walking to school together. Tom wasn't one of my usual friends. Guys like Ramon Sanchez were.

Ramon was the quarterback on my flag-football team. He was tall and athletic with dark curly hair. When he threw you the ball, it came at you in a tight spiral, arriving with a smack and making your hands sting.

At lunchtime, Tom found me in the cafeteria, set his tray across from mine, and asked me about my owl. We sat talking as the cacophony of plates and trays and silverware and teenagers clattered around us.

Ramon Sanchez slid next to me.

"Hey, Craig," Ramon said with a smirk. "Why are you talking to this guy?"

I leaned back in my chair. Tom got quiet, looked down, and bit into his sloppy joe.

"Hey, Tom. Why don't you tell Craig about your brother?"

Tom's shoulders slouched. He stopped chewing.

"Well, if you won't, I will," said Ramon with a measure of sarcastic glee.

Ramon nudged me and pointed at Tom. I didn't like where this conversation seemed headed, but I also didn't feel like standing up to Ramon.

"Tom and I used to live on the same street. Two years ago, Tom and his brother had gotten their dad's guns out and were running around the house playing cops and robbers. And this dumbshit here pointed a thirty-aught-six at his brother's chest and pulled the trigger. He was too stupid to check and see if the gun was loaded. He shot and killed his own fucking brother. Didn't you, Tom?"

Tom sat silent, his cheeks bulging with a mouthful of sloppy joe and his eyes welling with tears.

"C'mon, Craig, you don't want to sit here."

Ramon picked up his tray. I tried to swallow a mouthful of my lunch, but couldn't. So I picked up my tray, too, and followed in stunned silence.

I've regretted this incident often in life, wishing I'd stood up to Ramon that day, wishing I'd told him what a cruel SOB he was, and wishing I'd stayed and said something kind to Tom.

But I didn't.

A few days later, I went out in the morning to feed the owl. The tether dangled from the apple tree branch nearly to the ground. The owl had finally gnawed through it. I looked for the bird, but it was nowhere to be found.

My brother came out to help look. We heard a *click-click* in one of the high branches. The owl swiveled its head side to side and stretched out its wings. We'd done our best to mend its injury, but it had healed at an awkward angle. One of the wildlife biologists who worked with my dad had even stopped by. He said the bird would never fly, and we should just put it down. The owl stood on the branch and flapped, not yet letting go with its talons. It did this several times before finally hopping from its perch and flying unevenly to the field across the street, where it landed amid the sage. We ran after it, but before we arrived, it jumped from the brush and flew another twenty yards. And then another, and another, before disappearing from view.

The bird could fly, but barely.

My brother and I stood silently gazing into the horizon, hoping for the best.

"Well, maybe he'll be okay," said my brother.

I shrugged.

"I mean, once he gets used to that wing, he might start flying better."

I nodded as we turned to walk toward the house.

But my brother and I both knew that nature was cruel to the weak and the wounded.

CHAPTER EIGHTEEN

"Oh, God, please," I begged once more. "Make it go away. Make it go away. I'll do anything. Anything."

"Craig! Craig!" Kirk yelled into my face. "Settle down. Settle down."

"I can't," I cried. "I can't. I can't take it anymore. I can't take it. When's Dad coming back? He's been gone for five hours. When's he coming back?"

I was growing hoarse from the screaming. I'd lost my sense of time. I didn't know if it was day or night. I didn't know if it was today or tomorrow.

"Listen," Kirk said. "Dad'll be here soon. It's only been two hours. He'll be here soon."

"Oh, God, I'm not going to make it," I cried. "Why hasn't God answered any of my prayers? Why? Not a single one. I'm not going to make it."

"Okay," said Kirk. "Think of something else. Think of something to take your mind off it."

I couldn't. My mind was done thinking.

"God! Oh, God! Oh, God!" I cried, half sobbing, half screaming. The fire crackled to my left. I could feel the heat through the denim of my jeans. "How can you do this? How can you do this? I've prayed to you. I've begged you. Please, please. I think you're a mean God. How could you do this to me? What did I do to deserve this? Why me?"

I was becoming angry with God. Nothing else was working, so why not?

"Stop it. Stop it," said Kirk. "Calm down."

The sun sank behind a far mountain ridge, and the clouds crept heavier and farther down the flanks of God's Pocket Peak. And then the gray and the gloom were upon us. Soon, we would be consumed by snow and darkness.

"I hate you, God, I hate you," I ranted into the storm. "I'm never going to believe in you again. You're a fraud, a fraud. You don't exist. I know you don't exist, because no God would ever do this to a kid. I hate you. I hate you."

The wind shook the tops of the sage, the snow swirled, and the darkness descended.

I thought of the worst thing I could say to God—any God.

"You don't exist," I croaked hoarsely into the wind. "Fuck you, God. You're a bastard. Fuck you. Fuck you."

The wind shook the tops of the sage, and the snow swirled.

My brother slapped me in the face. Hard. And then he slapped me again.

My eyes focused.

"You can't say things like that about God," he warned, hand raised, ready to slap again.

He then stood, scanned the horizon, and prayed.

I muttered, defeated, into the wind, "But it's true, it's true."

— ◆ —

My dad was exhausted—as exhausted as he'd ever been. He'd been running for nearly an hour and wasn't exactly sure where the truck was. He had to keep dropping into ravines in order to try to maintain a straight, short route. There were also disorienting stands of aspen and hillsides of tall, thick bitterbrush. He was pretty sure the head of the canyon where we'd set up camp was just over the next ridge. He hoped it was, anyway. He prayed it was. Because if it weren't, he'd have to get out his compass and topographical map and spend precious time reorienting himself, not to mention perhaps having to backtrack an extra mile or two if it turned out he was indeed off course.

My dad scrambled uphill and pulled at the sage to help him reach the top of the ridge. Sweat drenched his denim shirt, which was dark, wet, and blue around his armpits, back, and chest. He scanned the terrain. The sun was low, the clouds were darkening, the temperature was dropping, and an occasional flake of snow swirled in the wind. His chest heaved, and he worried that if the snow began to fall in earnest, he would likely not be able to get me off the mountain until the morning. He spotted a landmark that he recognized, and for the first time was certain he'd drawn

70

near to our camp. He trotted up the ridge and came to the headwater of a small creek that splashed and tumbled into a narrow valley filled with tall, yellow cottonwoods. He trotted downhill along the creek and could smell the campfires of other hunters. A four-wheel-drive trail appeared and he pushed himself hard until he saw his red Dodge truck, white canvas tent, and two dressed deer hanging by their hind legs from a wooden pole resting on branches between two trees.

Monte was sitting by the campfire when he saw my dad running toward him.

My dad, exhausted, only said, "Craig shot himself . . . in the foot . . . throw everything in the back."

Within five minutes, they had broken camp and had tossed everything, deer included, in a jumble in the truck bed. My dad studied his topographical map, searching for the quickest way to get back to the base of God's Pocket Peak. It would certainly be tricky. Again, he couldn't afford to make a mistake. There might be an error on the map. A dirt road that was supposed to run up and over a canyon might have washed out two years ago and never been repaired. Or a supposedly easy road might now be rugged. If the truck got stuck in the sand or high-centered on a large rock, I would likely be stranded on the mountainside until morning.

The road that led out of the canyon where we'd camped ran for ten miles in the opposite direction of my location. It connected to another dirt road that ran in a wide crescent for fifteen miles across a sagebrush flat before winding up a steep, narrow canyon for five miles, eventually leading to the base of the ridge where I lay wounded. My dad hoped he could find another hunter somewhere along the way who had a four-wheel-drive. Otherwise, he, Monte, and Kirk would have to carry me off the mountain—an arduous, painful prospect that my dad wanted to avoid at all costs.

The red Dodge bounced and rattled down the canyon. My dad could only drive twenty to thirty miles per hour. Any faster, and he'd risk getting stuck or breaking an axle on a big rock. When he reached level ground, he was able to drive up to forty in places. It was a long, slow trip. Dark clouds gathered, and the snow began steadily swirling for five or ten minutes at a time but wasn't yet sticking.

By the time my dad reached the narrow canyon below God's Pocket Peak, the road had become steep and rugged before finally turning into a barely noticeable four-wheel-drive trail that was impassable for his truck. He'd come to the end of the line, and still he hadn't seen another hunter. He parked the Dodge, got out, and looked up the ridge. In a clearing beneath the cottonwoods to his right, he saw a campfire. There sat a dad, his teenage son, and teenage daughter. Beside them was a four-wheel-drive International Harvester.

A modicum of hope and relief visited my dad for the first time since the ordeal had begun. He knew then that he'd be able to get me off the mountain before sunset. He only hoped that I wasn't in too much pain, and that it wasn't too late to save my foot. With that in mind, he jogged up to the four-wheel-drive owner and asked the man for help.

CHAPTER NINETEEN

Sonoma Sun Stone was a champion pointer.

He was the best hunting dog my dad had ever raised, and those who had the good fortune to hunt with him agreed that he was the best they'd ever been around.

My dad had been in the market for a new dog after his big Weimaraner had died, so he visited a field trial near Winnemucca. These were events where hunting enthusiasts and their bird dogs would gather to compete in displays of pointing, retrieving, and obedience. There were also breeders at these events with pedigree pups for sale. One could often watch the dams and sires in action to get a sense of which litter might be best.

The most decorated dog at the trial was an English pointer named Sunrise. My dad observed it in competition and was impressed. He met with the dog's owner and asked to take a look at the pups. The breeder led my dad down to his truck, lifted a large metal cage from the back, set it on the ground, and pulled a latch. Out tumbled seven white-and-brown puppies no more than twelve weeks old.

English pointers are medium-size, short-haired dogs with long, straight tails and a white coat marked by large, irregular spots of tan or dark brown. The dogs have a tremendous sense of smell, which they use to track upland game birds such as quail or pheasant. They're extremely fast and have remarkable endurance. A good pointer will sweep back and forth about fifteen to thirty yards in front of a hunter. When they come upon a fresh scent, they will crouch, nose close to the ground, and begin stalking. When they get within five to ten yards of the bird, they will freeze, nose aimed forward, tail stiff, eyes unblinking, and right paw lifted off the ground and tucked under their chest. And then they'll remain in that pose for as long as it takes for the bird to flush. After the bird is shot, the pointer will break its freeze, dash after the quarry, pick it up gently in its mouth, and return it to the hunter.

While the breeder pointed out to my dad some of the prized characteristics of each round-bellied pup, one adventurous littermate trundled away to inspect a nearby sage. The breeder called it back, but the pup ignored him, instead staring intently into the brush. The breeder called again, but the pup didn't move. My dad walked over to retrieve the dog, but it started yelping when my dad tried to pick him up. My dad gave the brush a kick with his boot, and a quail burst vertically into the air, wings beating and throat chortling as it flapped into the distance.

My dad turned to the breeder and said, "I'll take him."

During bird season, we mostly hunted chukar. They were about twice the size of a quail and half the size of a chicken. They'd been introduced to the Great Basin in the early 1900s from their native range in the Himalayan foothills, and quickly flourished. Northern Nevada's rugged terrain, high plateau, vegetation, and climate were similar to that found in the mountain regions of Pakistan, India, Afghanistan, and Iran.

These partridges are nearly impossible to hunt without a talented dog. They look something like oversize quail, with gray backs and rust-colored legs and beaks. They have white-and-black bands on their flanks and a black bandit mask across their eyes. The birds blend in perfectly with the terrain and are nearly impossible to see as they scamper on the ground. Chukar are quick runners and typically fly as a last option. They use the rugged landscape to their advantage, scurrying uphill when pursued by a predator and then launching into flight when they reach the top of a ridge.

The game of polo had been created by Persians in the first century BC in part because of the chukar. Polo was practice for the horsemen of Central Asia, who typically hunted the birds on horseback, chasing them down as they ran and smacking them from atop horses with mallets, or snagging them with snares.

My dad, brother, and I had spent the day hunting chukar in the Granite Peak area north of Gerlach, which was a wide spot in the road that featured a gas station, market, and a bar facetiously called Bruno's Country Club. In spite of the town's small size, Bruno's was a busy place. As one of the few drinking establishments in the Black Rock Desert, Bruno's was filled with hunters, ranchers, miners, hikers, drifters, and adventurers. They would inevitably pass through Bruno's to shoot a game of pool, down a cold beer, eat a hamburger, or play a hand of 21. The town of about two hundred souls was over eighty miles from the nearest city of any consequence, and sat amid a great salt flat that stretched east and west for dozens of miles.

It was getting late in the day, and we were headed back to the truck. We'd bagged half a dozen chukar—a good result, requiring a full day of hard work. About four hundred yards from the truck, our dog bolted from our side. He dashed full speed—barking—about a quarter-mile up a steep hill. He stopped in front of a rock wall just below the ridge and froze, his tail erect and his right paw tucked.

"Stoney!" my dad yelled.

The dog was oblivious.

Thhhhhhhwiiiit, my dad whistled sharp and loud.

Nothing.

Thhhhhhhwiiiit. "Stoney!" *Thhhhhhhwiiiit*.

Nothing.

"Goddammit, Stoney, get your cur ass down here!" my dad yelled in frustration.

He then turned to me and said, "I've never seen him act like this. Wonder what he has up there? It's certainly not a bird."

We waited for several minutes. The dog still pointed. After more whistles and curses, my dad handed my brother his gun and instructed him to head to the truck, get things packed, and start cleaning the birds.

He then turned to me and said, "C'mon, let's go get the dog. He'll stay there all night in a point if we let him."

"Oh, man," I whined. "Can't I go back to the truck?" The last thing I wanted to do was slog up a steep hillside after a full day of slogging up steep hillsides.

"No. Your brother cleans the birds quicker and better than you do."

I huffed and then handed my brother my 20-gauge. At least I could travel up the hill a little lighter.

"Keep the gun," my dad said. "Just in case."

I pulled the gun back and began trudging side by side with my dad.

We got within about fifty yards of the dog, and he was still frozen. We stopped. My dad yelled, whistled, and even threw some rocks in his direction. Stoney remained on point, just as his instinct and training had instructed him to do.

We got within thirty yards and could see that he was stationed about two feet from the rock wall, pointing into a small cave.

We yelled and whistled some more, but Stoney wouldn't budge.

We took a few steps closer. The ground leveled, and in the sand I could see what looked like dozens of paw prints that a housecat might make, only they were about four times larger. I signaled to my dad and pointed at the ground.

"Shit," my dad whispered. "It's a mountain lion."

He slowly dropped to one knee for a closer look, adding, "It's got cubs," and then pointed to a crisscross of smaller tracks.

My dad stayed on his knee, thinking out loud.

"What the hell are we going to do? I can't just leave my dog here. Shit—he'd probably stay pointing like that for three days, or until he dropped. Damn."

Dogs and mountain lions are natural mortal enemies. Dogs hate lions, and lions hate dogs. That's because when a mountain lion sees a dog, it really sees a wolf. Dogs were culled from their gray wolf lineage only 10,000 to 30,000 years ago by humans. A typical dog still has more than 99 percent wolf DNA. Both lions and wolves evolved over millions of years, competing for prey at the top of the food chain. Any chance a wolf pack has to kill a lion, it will take it. And any chance a lion has to kill a wolf, it will return the favor. Hence, the standoff between Stoney and the lion.

"Okay," my dad whispered, finally formulating a plan. "Here's what we're going to do. You're going to walk slowly about ten yards behind and to the left of Stoney. You're not going to have a clear shot into the cave, but try to get as far left as you can. I'm going to slide over to that rock wall a few yards to the right of the dog. I'll creep along the rocks until I get to him. Then I'll grab his collar, and we'll beat it."

My heart began racing, and my palms got sweaty.

"Now," my dad whispered loudly for emphasis, "a few key points. If that lion bolts out of there, just pull the trigger. Don't think. Just do it. If you have to kill the dog, too, I hate to say it, but that's just too bad. The last thing I need is a mountain lion in my lap. And if you have to shoot, aim low. Be sure not to shoot me. Given the choice, I'd rather take my chances with the cat. Ready?"

I put the shotgun to my shoulder, clicked off the safety, and crept slowly to my position. The rocks crunched under my boots. I got into position and stood, ready to fire, about ten yards from the cave's entrance. I tried to calm my breathing. My stomach was queasy, and I could hear my pulse pounding in my temples. My index finger rested lightly on the side of the trigger.

I'd been nervous before when sighting a deer, but nothing like this. The thought of a big, snarling cat lunging at you from out of a dark cave stirred the most primal of fears. I'd never hunted anything that could hunt me back.

My dad had reached the rock wall. He slowly walked toward Stoney. The dog stood like a statue.

I kept breathing, purposely inhaling deep and exhaling fully in order to try to keep calm. My left arm, which was extended to hold the grip below the barrel, began to wobble. I flexed my arm muscles to keep them from tightening. My left shoulder began to burn. My dad reached over, grabbed the dog's collar, and yanked him away. Stoney finally broke point and began jumping up and down. My dad motioned for me to stay in position. He attached a leash onto Stoney's collar and tied the dog to a nearby sage. My dad then picked up some rocks and crept back toward the cave.

Crap, I thought. *Now he's just being curious. Let's get the hell out of here.*

From the side of the rock wall, he slowly peeked his head into the cave. Then he threw in a rock. Then another. Finally he stood up, relaxed, and told me to lower my gun.

"Well, there was definitely a lioness and a couple cubs here, but she must've seen us and bugged out before the dog charged up the hill. Hell, she's probably watching us right now."

The sun dropped behind a ridge and the temperature began to fall sharply as my dad and I returned to the truck. I hopped into the cab, exhausted and eager to leave. My dad was clunking hunting gear in the back of the truck bed while my brother and I tuned the radio, searching for one of the big 50,000-watt superstations. That was usually the only reception you could get in the middle of the desert. After the sun went down, it was fairly easy to pick up KGO out of San Francisco, or KSL from Salt Lake, or even KOA from Denver. The San Francisco station crackled through the static. The play-by-play of a 49ers game faded in and out. My brother fiddled with the knob.

"Leave it there," I commanded.

My dad slid into the truck, jammed it into gear, and we started slowly rumbling down the dirt road toward Gerlach.

My dad looked over at me and saw that I hadn't put my shotgun away. I was too tired and lazy. The butt of the gun was planted firmly on the floorboard with the barrel pointed away from me toward the top of the cab.

My dad shook his head and said, "I hope that thing's not loaded." Normally he would've stopped and made me put it in its case and place it in the back, but he, too, was tired, and didn't want to bother.

"Don't worry, it's not," I confirmed.

The truck bounced and rattled down the hill. The sky blazed orange in the west and deep purple in the east. The white alkali of the dry lake bed reflected the sky and glowed violet in the gathering dark. Gerlach, with its small cluster of lights, glimmered in the distance. The announcers shouted excitedly above the static, describing the long, arcing touchdown pass thrown by John Brodie.

We pulled into the Gerlach gas station and my dad hopped out to fill the truck's tank. My stomach grumbled as I thought about sinking my teeth into one of Bruno's hamburgers.

"You didn't unload your gun," Kirk said, matter-of-factly.

"Sure I did."

"No, I watched you—you didn't."

I became indignant.

"I absolutely did. Why wouldn't I?"

"You didn't," my brother chided.

"Fine, I'll prove it," I said. I flicked the safety off and put my finger near the trigger. I looked up to make sure the barrel was pointing away.

"Don't, you idiot," my brother hissed. "I'm telling you, it's loaded."

My dad went into the gas station to pay.

"No, it's not," I insisted. "When I pull this trigger, all you're going to hear is a click."

"Don't, don't," my brother pleaded, not wanting to wrestle the gun away from me lest it go off.

I was enjoying torturing my brother. I inched my finger toward the trigger. Doubt crept into my mind. I was sure I'd unloaded the gun before I hopped into the cab of the truck. I always did.

"Okay," I compromised. "Five dollars says it's not loaded."

"You're on."

I squeaked the heavy truck door aside, hopped to the cement, pushed a lever, and breached the gun. The shiny brass base of a shotgun shell sat snug in the barrel.

My eyes widened. I imagined pulling the trigger in the cab and blowing a hole in the roof of my dad's truck. I wondered if the shotgun pellets would've all gone clean through, or if some might've ricocheted inside.

A bell on the gas station door clanged and rattled against the glass as my dad swung it open.

"Shit," I muttered.

I pulled the shell from the barrel, stuffed it into my pocket, and snapped the gun shut. I hopped up into the cab and slammed the big metal door.

"Don't tell Dad," I whispered to my brother.

"Just make sure you pay me that five dollars," he replied.

—✦—

Ray Baker was a big man. I always had to look way up at him whenever he came over to our house. He and my dad worked together at the BLM.

Baker had thirteen kids. Everyone in town referred to them as the Baker's Dozen. The boys were all strong and athletic. Don and Dan, twins, were teammates of my brother Kirk on the Albert M. Lowry High School Buckaroos championship wrestling team.

Baker and his sons were avid hunters. He and my dad frequently talked after church about how someone they both knew had been near Orvada and had seen huge coveys of quail. Or about how one of the wildlife biologists from the Forest Service said the deer count was particularly high this year around the North Fork of the Humboldt.

It was early November, and Big Ray had taken Don and Dan to see if they could bag a trophy buck in the Santa Rosas north of Winnemucca. The area was renowned for the number of five-point-and-better mule deer. But the old males liked to stay high, and the terrain was particularly rugged. The Bakers had hunted almost to the top of Paradise Peak. It had been a long day. They'd seen a few does and a couple of forkies— young bucks with only two points on their antlers. But the trophy deer had eluded them.

Big Ray had called it a day. The trio clambered into the cab of the GMC four-wheel-drive and squeezed shoulder to shoulder on the bench seat. Big Ray drove, and Don sat in the middle, next to his dad, which required him to pull up his left knee every time his father had to use the stick shift.

The rack mounted on the back window held only two guns. Don had to hang on to his rifle in the cab, pressing the butt against the floorboard and holding the barrel with both hands, making sure to keep it pointed upward.

The truck bounced and rattled its way out of the mountains. The dirt road leveled and Big Ray accelerated. His truck could likely have been seen from at least twenty to thirty miles distant. To a hunter standing on a faraway ridge, the truck would've looked like a schooner sailing across a vast sagebrush sea. The truck itself wouldn't necessarily be visible, except for the occasional flash of sunlight reflected by a chrome bumper, side mirror, or windshield. Other than that, there would only be a billow of dust inching across a desert expanse.

The truck rattled rhythmically and Don's eyes drooped. His head slumped forward and sleep came.

Big Ray began to slow for a cattle guard. He reached for the stick so he could downshift. Don's knee bumped to the right. The crumpled denim seam on the side of his jeans—where his knee bent—jammed into the gun's trigger.

An explosion roared through the cab.

Don's eyes shot open and his mouth gaped.

Big Ray stomped hard on the brakes. The wheels dug into the gravel and the truck fishtailed to a stop.

Dan flung the passenger door open and jumped. He could only hop up and down in the gravel, saying, "Oh, God. Oh, God. Oh, God." Blood gushed in squirts from Don's chest.

Big Ray, working in the close confines of the truck's cab, frantically tore off his own shirt and pressed it against the wound in his son's chest. Don's face turned blue. His eyes stared wide and vacant. Blood began to trickle from the sides of his still-gaping mouth. Don shook uncontrollably. And then he didn't.

A cloud of dust drifted forward and enveloped the truck, leaving the Bakers adrift in a sagebrush sea.

CHAPTER TWENTY

"Someone's coming! Someone's coming!" my brother shouted. "There's a truck crawling up the hill. It's going really slow."

I propped myself up on my elbows and craned my neck to see between the sage and down the hill. A pair of headlights was bouncing along the ridge in the fading twilight.

"Thank you. Thank you," I whispered to the sky.

My brother ran over to the jeep trail and began relaying reports.

"It's halfway up the ridge. Definitely not our truck. Maybe Dad found someone with a four-wheel-drive. Maybe they just saw our fire and are coming to see if we need help. It's going to take another ten minutes for them to get here, so hang tight."

The truck rumbled and crept over small boulders. It mowed through the sage that stood as high as its hood. My dad jumped out and ran to us, while the driver worked to back the truck closer to my brother and me.

"How're you doing?" he asked.

I grimaced. I didn't want my dad to see me crying and screaming.

"Not so good," my brother proclaimed. "The pain's been pretty bad. He's been delirious for the past hour."

Dad put his hand on my shoulder and leaned toward me.

"Any nausea? Did you pass out at all from the pain?"

"No," I labored, still trying not to scream. "But it really hurts. Oh, God, it hurts. Do you have anything for the pain?"

"No," my dad said. "I don't even have any whiskey."

"How long until we get to the hospital?" I asked.

"I don't know—maybe a couple hours. Maybe three. Depends on how quickly we can get off this hill and to a highway."

My dad and brother loaded me into the back of the four-wheel-drive.

On the one hand, knowing that I would soon return to civilization, paved roads, and anesthesia made the pain slightly more bearable. On the other, my foot jiggled in agony with every bump, rock, and rut we went over. I could feel my toe flex with each jolt, shards of bone grinding together as my foot vibrated. I could feel slivers of bone piercing into adjacent toes.

By the time we got to the bottom of the hill and had transferred to my dad's Dodge, it was dark, and about thirty miles of dirt road separated us from Highway 93—a two-lane ribbon of asphalt that stretched from Mexico to Canada, traversing the eastern edge of Nevada through some of the most remote country in the continental United States.

We came out of the mountains onto a straight, well-graded dirt road that eventually intersected with the paved highway. My dad stopped before pulling onto the asphalt. It was a relief to leave the dust and the rattling and the bouncing behind. The truck turned south and accelerated smoothly. Traveling at night in Nevada is always the same. The headlights wash the sage in white on both sides of the road. Everywhere else, darkness is total. Every few minutes—sometimes much longer, depending on where you are—a pair of headlights appears over a rise about a mile or two away. The lights grow larger and brighter until you can hear the oncoming vehicle—usually another truck—rushing toward you on the pavement. That's followed by a sudden *whoosh*. Then a deep-throated hiss fades quick and low. After that, you're back to the strain of your own engine, the sibilance of your own tires, and the flood of white light on the sage.

The Winecup Gamble Ranch is one of the largest cattle-and-sheep operations in the United States. It sprawls across the O'Neil Basin west of Highway 93 and to the foot of the Jarbidge Range, as well as east of the 93, all the way to the Utah border. Created in the 1870s and 1880s, the Winecup was part of a 75,000-head empire reigned over by cattle barons and, later, Nevada governor John Sparks. At its peak, the ranch and related holdings covered over five million acres and was larger than six current states: Massachusetts, New Jersey, Hawaii, Connecticut, Delaware, and Rhode Island.

Governor Sparks insisted that his friends and the general populace call him Honest John, though honesty was something of a malleable concept in the Old West. And it certainly wasn't compatible with the art of amassing huge swaths of cattle land. Sparks, a former Texas Ranger, had arrived in northeastern Nevada sometime around 1880. He first purchased water rights to every spring, creek, pond, and waterway in the region. He and his henchmen would then shoot at anyone or anything that came near. Area ranches, deprived of water for their cattle, became worthless. Sparks bought them for nickels on the dollar. He then hired friends, acquaintances, and passers-through to file homestead claims on adjacent public lands, later deeding the property back to Sparks. Honest John rose to power and prominence.

And then disaster struck in 1891 when heavy snows on the Winecup were followed by temperatures that plunged to 42-below. Honest John's massive herds of Herefords were decimated. When the spring thaws arrived, the Humboldt became choked with cow carcasses, which were so thick in the river that they piled up behind the bridges in Elko and caused flooding in the streets. Honest John moved just south of Reno, cobbled together another ranch, won the governorship, and died in office during his second term, heavily in debt.

A partnership that included the crooner Bing Crosby owned the ranch in the 1950s. He and his family used to spend considerable time here in an effort to get as far away from Hollywood as possible. Crosby and Co. later sold to another partnership that included Hollywood icon Jimmy Stewart. He, too, had a fondness for the West and a frequent need to get away. Today, the ranch is still in operation, and still huge, at just under one million acres.

In the midst of the Winecup Gamble Ranch, where its western tongue crosses Highway 93, for many years stood the Thousand Springs Trading Post. It was owned by the ranch and was never more than a wide spot along a very lonely stretch of road. It featured a Phillips 66 station (the only gas for twenty-five miles, either direction), a post office, a general store, and a roadside saloon.

My dad knew much about the Winecup. The ranch had numerous dealings with the BLM over land use and grazing permits. My dad also knew that the ranch maintained its own airstrip only a few miles from the trading post. He thought maybe he could find a ranch pilot who could fly me to Twin Falls.

Our tires crunched in the gravel as we pulled off the highway, eased across the dirt parking area, and stopped next to the old, wooden building with the neon beer signs in the window and a rustic sign overhead that read THOUSAND SPRINGS TRADING POST. My dad ran inside to use the phone.

A few seconds later, a plump waitress flung the bar door open and marched toward our truck with two tall ranchers following in single file. One of the ranchers yanked the truck door open.

"C'mon, son," the waitress commanded. "You're not going to wait out here. The pilot at the ranch can't fly you because it's dark and he's not instrument-rated. But the sheriff's on his way; so's the ambulance from Twin Falls. Larry and Charlie here are going to bring you inside, nice and gentle, and we're going to make you as comfortable as we can. I heard you were in a lot of pain. I can imagine so. I told your dad we should give you some whiskey, but he disagrees. C'mon, boys."

Larry, Charlie, and my brother carried me inside. It was a Friday night, and the bar-in-the-middle-of-nowhere was packed. Half a dozen men sat at a dark, worn mahogany bar that had likely been imported from the East Coast in the late 1800s. A middle-aged woman dealt 21 at a table to three ranchers smoking cigarettes and drinking beer. Two women played slot machines against the back wall, oblivious to everything except their cigarettes, quarters, and spinning displays. A couple of families sat at tables eating dinner. Larry, Charlie, and two attractive women in jeans and checkered shirts were playing pool at the table near the front door.

"Grab that chair over there," barked the waitress to Larry. "Pull it up to the pool table. Set him down on the chair and prop his foot up on the table. You need to get his foot elevated."

"But he's going to bleed on the felt," Larry complained.

"Oh, that's of no concern," said the waitress. "We'll just get some new felt. Probably need some anyway. Here, honey, have a Coke," she said, handing me a glass of soda that the bartender had just delivered to her. "Believe it or not, you're not the first gunshot victim we've had in here. We've had at least a couple of hunters come through since I've been here. Hey, Larry, remember that bird hunter that stopped in a couple years back? We were picking shotgun pellets out of him with tweezers. But don't you worry about any of that, honey; you're going to be fine. Just sit back, relax, and Sheriff Bill will be here any minute."

She then bustled off to take a dinner order from a couple who'd just walked in.

I sipped my Coke and moaned in agony. The pain had not subsided. But I was exhausted—all screamed out. I now sensed that help would soon arrive. Thus, I was able to keep my screams muffled and not make even more of a spectacle of myself. The men at the bar had glanced back when I first came in but quickly went back to their conversation. The ranchers playing 21 hardly even looked up from their cards.

The blood dripped from my heel and, drop by drop, soaked the green felt with a deep red stain. Larry went behind the bar and came back, plunking down a fifth of Jack Daniel's on the pool table next to my foot and then holding out a .30-06 cartridge.

"Hey, soldier," he said in a bad John Wayne impersonation. "How 'bout a shot of whiskey and a bullet to bite on?"

For some reason, that struck me as really funny. Maybe it was the absurdity of the situation—me bleeding all over the pool table, men drinking beer, families eating dinner. It was almost like this was a regular occurrence on a Friday night.

"No," I said with a weak laugh, appreciating Larry's attempt to cheer me up.

Larry examined the bullet, holding it up in front of his nose and turning it back and forth.

"I never understood why biting one of these would help anyone who'd been shot," he mused. "Go figure."

"They were different bullets," I said through gritted teeth. "In the Civil War, they shot soft, lead balls. They'd give you one to clamp your teeth on so you wouldn't bite your tongue while they sawed your leg off."

"Now that makes more sense," nodded Larry.

"Hey, kid, what's your name?" asked Charlie.

"Craig," I said.

"Okay, Craig," Charlie said, waving his pool cue like a wand over my foot before tapping it on the felt next to the bloodstain. "From this day forth, this pocket will be known as 'Craig's Corner.' Anyone who wants to sink a ball here will have to call it in Craig's Corner. How 'bout that?"

I was honored. Everyone laughed.

After about half an hour, Sheriff Bill, who'd driven up from Wells, walked in, consulted with my dad, and directed Larry and Charlie to lay me down in the back of his cruiser. The waitress, bartender, Larry, Charlie, and their dates all came out to wish me well. They told me to be sure to stop by on my way back home to let them know how I was doing (which we did). And then the sheriff sped north into the Nevada night toward a rendezvous with the ambulance that had already been dispatched from the hospital in Twin Falls.

CHAPTER TWENTY-ONE

My dad's grandfather, Benjamin Franklin Collins, was born on a Wisconsin farm in 1858, before the Civil War.

His grandfather, Colonel James Collins, was born in Pennsylvania, a decade after the Revolution. Only four generations separated my father from the founding of this country.

The past is never as far away as we sometimes think.

And, like America's, my family's quest for prosperity was a journey that began in the East and ended in the West. It was a trip marked by long periods of bucolic quietude, punctuated by spasms of horrific violence.

And always, there was the gun.

Just as a point of clarification: I'm not 100 percent certain that I'm directly related to Colonel James Collins. It's more like 80 percent. The documentation is a bit sketchy in parts. But I am related to a James Collins who lived, fought, and died in the frontier lands of southwestern Wisconsin. So close enough, either way.

Colonel Collins joined the army in 1812 as a way to get off the farm and have an adventure. After the war, he returned to farming, this time securing land of his own on the Ohio frontier.

Within a decade, much of the prime farmland in Ohio had already been claimed, and Americans began to hew the woodlands of Indiana and Illinois. Soon, settlers were clamoring to claim more farmland in northern Illinois and southern Wisconsin. Miners had already flooded the region near the Mississippi, digging for lead. The Sauk, Fox, and Winnebago Indians stood in the way, but that was a trivial matter.

In 1832, a small core of army regulars led several thousand American militiamen—farmers with guns—in pursuit of Black Hawk, the diminutive leader of the fugitive band of Indians. The Black Hawk War served, for better or worse, as a training ground for leaders in another, much bloodier conflict. Participants included future presidents Zachary Taylor and Abraham Lincoln, as well as Confederate president Jefferson Davis.

In the spring of 1832, Black Hawk and his troop of about 400 men and 600 women and children walked across southern Wisconsin from their winter home in present-day Iowa. They were attempting to return to their native lands in northern Illinois, where they could plant some summer corn. This was the third straight year that Black Hawk had attempted such a maneuver. In the two previous years, he had been met by American troops and talked into returning west of the Mississippi.

But this time, American forces seemed intent on ridding themselves of Black Hawk's nuisance and opening the lands of northern Illinois and Wisconsin for good. American officers traveled throughout Illinois and Michigan, raising a volunteer militia. About 2,600 enrolled for the campaign, augmenting a force of about 400 federal troops. They then spent much of the spring and summer of 1832 chasing and harassing Black Hawk and his followers.

The Americans entered the fray with an ample number of Indian interpreters. However, in military accounts of actions, it seems that the interpreters always seemed to have wandered off or were unavailable whenever Black Hawk asked to speak to the Americans.

In late July of 1832, the Indian chief stood on a ridge above the American military camp and gave an impassioned plea, asking General Atkinson for safe passage of his people back across the Mississippi to the Iowa Territory. Several aides counseled Atkinson to send emissaries to meet with Black Hawk. They told Atkinson that Black Hawk was pleading for peace. In Washington, President Andrew Jackson and his secretary of war, Lewis Cass, had already decided to rein in Atkinson. They sent orders to the frontier, relieving Atkinson of his duties. It took two months for the orders to reach him in the wilds of Wisconsin. Atkinson was as dismissive of his orders as he was of his aides. He prepared his troops for battle.

On July 31, 1832, Black Hawk and his band found themselves on the east bank of the Mississippi just below the confluence of Bad Axe River. Most of the Indians had begun to build rafts and canoes in an attempt to cross the river and escape the Americans. Black Hawk pleaded with his tribe that there wasn't enough time, and that the only hope for escape was to head north. Only a few heeded him.

On August 1, the steamship *Warrior* spotted the Indians busy at work along the riverbank. Black Hawk recognized the ship and knew its captain, Joseph Throckmorton.

According to military accounts and interviews with eyewitnesses, "Black Hawk called out to those on the boat: 'I am Black Hawk, and I wish to come and shake hands with you,' waving his hands to correspond, telling the women: 'Don't run. I will save you and the children by going on board and giving myself up.'"

At least two braves in Black Hawk's party waved white flags. Captain Throckmorton remained unmoved. He also claimed later that his interpreter was unavailable, rendering his crew unable to understand Black Hawk's request. Additionally, he thought Black Hawk was trying to trick him into asking for safe passage as a guise for launching an attack. Or so he said.

Captain Throckmorton opened fire.

"Finding their only object was to gain time," said Lieutenant Reuben Holmes in a post-battle briefing, "and at last assured they were the hostile Sauks by a woman on board who knew their language, fearing also that they could scatter so as to injure the efficacy of our fire, the order was given for a general discharge upon them commencing with the six-pounder cannon."

The *Warrior* fired at the Indians with cannon and musket for two hours before having to pull anchor because they were low on fuel. Over twenty-five Indians were killed.

In a post-battle interview, Black Hawk said, "The Winnebago [interpreter], on the steamboat, must either have misunderstood what was told, or did not tell it to Capt. [Throckmorton] correctly, because I am confident that he would not have fired upon us, if he had known my wishes. I have always considered him a good man, and too great a brave to fire upon an enemy when suing for quarters."

And though Captain Throckmorton said he had no interpreters available, Black Hawk said, "A Winnebago on the boat called to us to run and hide, that the whites were going to shoot!"

At sunrise the following day, the full force of the American divisions fell upon the Indians. Fighting ensued for about three hours. The Americans suffered six killed, nineteen wounded. The Indians? Reports said that the waters of the Mississippi ran red, and bodies floated downriver for days. General Atkinson and other American officers seemed vague about the number of Indian casualties but had all arrived at a general figure of 150 killed. Of course, that's not counting the 68 scalps that the Santee Sioux brought the Americans. They had been paid by the army to take up positions on the west side of the river in order to shoot and kill any of Black Hawk's band who had attempted to swim, or who might have made it across. Of the Indians in the battle, only 70 survivors were taken prisoner—all women and children, no men. After the incident with the *Warrior*, Black Hawk led a small band of Indians north, thus surviving the second day of the massacre.

So what happened to the other seven hundred or so Indians? Listen:

The Indians retreated toward the Mississippi, but kept up a retreating fire upon our front spies for some time until Gen. Dodge, who commanded, began to kill them very fast. The Indians then retreated more rapidly, and sought refuge in their main army, which was lying on the bank of the Mississippi, where they had joined in a body to defend themselves, and sell their lives as dear as possible, for now they found that they could not get away from us, and the only chance for them was to fight until they died.

—Surgeon's Mate John Allen Wakefield, Illinois Militia

Early in the morning, a party of whites, being in advance of the army, came upon our people, who were attempting to cross the Mississippi. They tried to give themselves up. The whites paid no attention to their entreaties, but commenced slaughtering them. In a little while, the whole army arrived. Our braves, but few in number, finding that the enemy paid no regard to age or sex, and seeing that they were murdering helpless women and little children, determined to fight until they were killed. As many women as could commenced swimming the Mississippi, with their children on their backs. A number of them were drowned, and some shot, before they could reach the opposite shore.

—Black Hawk

During the battle that ensued, my command killed fourteen Indians, and after a short time, say an hour's engagement, Gen. Dodge with his force, and Gen. Atkinson with his regular army, arrived at that place where I had engaged this party consisting of about forty Indians, and about the time of their arrival, we had killed and dispersed the whole party.

—Captain Joseph Dickson, Michigan Territory Militia

When we came upon the enemy, they were fixing their bark canoes to cross the river. Some of them had crossed, others had just launched their canoes, and some had not got them made. But I suppose all were busy in making the necessary arrangements to cross and get out of our way. But the Ruler of the Universe, He who takes vengeance on the guilty, did not design those guilty wretches to escape His vengeance for the horrid deeds they had done, which were of the most appalling nature. He here took just retribution for the many innocent lives those cruel savages had taken on our northern frontiers.

—Surgeon's Mate John Allen Wakefield, Illinois Militia

A little Indian boy concealed in the driftwood jumped from his hiding place and ran for his life. Dickson ordered Rittenhouse to shoot the child. The brave soldier raised his gun but [then] lowered it, saying, "Captain, I can't shoot a child!" Dickson thereupon cursed him and said, "Nits breed lice," and again ordered him to kill the boy. He again raised his gun but dropped it and said, "I tell you, Captain, I can't shoot that child." Just then a big Dutchman [John House] came up, and Dickson ordered him to shoot the poor boy. He did so, and sent a bullet through his heart. Presently, another jumped from the driftwood, and the Dutchman took aim and blew the top of his head off.

—Dr. C. V. Porter, *DeSoto Chronicle*

During the fight on the mainland, an Indian woman was killed. She had a young child at the breast, and the deadly bullet had passed through and shattered the arm of the infant and penetrated the left breast of the mother. When they were found after the battle, the

woman was lying dead, over the child, whose head protruded under the mother's arm. Dr. Addison Philleo, of Galena, surgeon of the volunteers, amputated the child's arm.
　　—Captain James B. Estes, Michigan Territory Volunteers

With Henry's men we killed in three-fourths of a mile, eighty-two Indians. We lost three men. Those not killed, got into the river. Henry's men were below on an island and killed those who floated down.
　　—Private H. S. Townsend, Michigan Territory Volunteers

When the Indians were driven to the Banks of the Mississippi, some hundreds of men, women, and children plunged into the river, and hoped by diving to escape the bullets of our guns. Very few, however, escaped our sharpshooters.
　　—Dr. Addison Philleo, Surgeon, Illinois Militia

During the fight, the river was full of Indian ponies with women and children clinging to them. [Captain] Lindsey saw six persons hanging on one pony. Many children were supposed to have been drowned. It was enough to make the heart of the most hardened being on earth to ache.
　　—Private H. S. Townsend, Michigan Territory Volunteers

In America today, guns are part of our country's creation myth. Seemingly everyone who owns one harkens back to a Founding Father—they're part Washington, part Jefferson, part Adams.

Perhaps Colonel James Collins is my ancestor. Perhaps not.

Regardless, we in America also harken to those who fought in the Black Hawk War—we're part Taylor, part Davis, part Lincoln. That much is inescapable. And as such, we all have the blood of Bad Axe on our hands.

CHAPTER TWENTY-TWO

William Collins was killed in the Civil War, leaving his son Benjamin Franklin Collins fatherless.

William's life was a restless one. He was a quintessential nineteenth-century American in perpetual quest of wealth and a better life. His father James brought young William and his older brother James Jr. to the frontier of southwestern Wisconsin perhaps as early as 1828. The prairie lands along the Mississippi were making rich the men who dug for lead—gray gold, they called it—that lay in great sheets just below the surface of the virgin flatland. Here the prairie was pocked by shallow mines and adjacent piles of dirt. The Indians thought it looked as though a plague of burrowing badgers had descended; hence, the official state nickname.

William toiled at lead mining and farming until 1848, when news of California gold swept through towns like Mineral Point, New Diggings, and Prairie du Chien. Any able-bodied man who owned a pick and shovel headed West. Within months, most towns in the area had lost up to 80 percent of their male population.

It's not certain where William went in California or precisely how he fared. It's only known that he didn't do well enough to stay there and build a mansion in San Francisco. But he apparently extracted a modest amount of wealth from the earth—at least enough to return to Wisconsin in 1854, purchase 160 acres of prime dairy land along the Wisconsin River south of Richland Center, marry, start a family, volunteer to fight the Rebels, and get shot. Today, the Collins Dairy and Stock Farm is listed on the Wisconsin historic registry, having operated in the family continuously for well over a century.

But Benjamin Franklin had little interest in dairy farming. Like his father, he was restless. And always looking west.

He crossed the Dakotas almost as soon as he could ride a horse. He settled on the Rosebud River in Montana next to the spread of Corporal Solomon B. Finch, who was likely a military acquaintance of his father

William. He claimed ranchland of his own, married Solomon's daughter Helen, raised a family, and ran some cattle.

But always there was the prospecting. He'd heard stories of his father's adventures in California. He dug for gold in Deadwood, South Dakota. He regularly packed his horse with a bedroll, supplies, pick, shovel, and rifle, and disappeared into the Montana wilderness for months at a time. He wasn't a great father, or a great rancher, or a great prospector. But he was relentless and driven. He was tough, hard, and spartan. He was at home in the vast emptiness that was the West.

The year 1908 found him in Boise, Idaho, staying with one of Solomon Finch's brothers. He'd met a pair of prospectors who claimed to have had luck panning for placer gold in the Jarbidge River near the Idaho-Nevada border.

Benjamin was getting old. He'd seen gold rushes come and gold rushes go. He'd missed on all of them and feared that perhaps his time had already passed, and that the West—like his youth—had already faded.

But still he dreamed.

His family dreamed, too. A prosperous brother in Wisconsin regularly funded his expeditions. Benjamin regaled his wife and daughters with tales of great riches hiding just beneath the earth, there for the taking.

His daughter Edna was unimpressed. She wrote to him in 1908, demanding, "Father, when are you going to send for us like you promised? If I have to spend another winter in Montana, I'll be as sad as a lost pup."

Benjamin settled into his saddle just outside Bruneau, Idaho, some seventy miles south of Boise. He gave the reins a shake, and his horse began trotting across the Snake River Plain, which stretched brown and dry and hot almost as far as Benjamin could see. It was June, and the heat reflected off the black basalt and rose above the sage. On the horizon, about another seventy miles south, a chain of mountains rose like an island, faint and blue and cool above the shimmer.

This was difficult country. Created two to ten million years ago by massive fissures that oozed oceans of lava, the Snake River Plain is a crescent that stretches across the whole of southern Idaho. It is bisected by the east-west flow of the Snake River, which is flanked on each side by an expansive plateau that tilts upward to the north toward the Sawtooth Range and upward to the south toward the mountainous rim of the Great Basin. As the plateau rises, the fertile farmlands near the river dissipate into arid sage and dry grass. Rugged, black basalt becomes the predominant feature. Sometimes the volcanic rock is smooth and hard. Sometimes it's cracked and jagged and brittle, evidence of the land's fiery, bubbling birth.

Benjamin and his horse picked their way through the lava fields for two days before coming to a great, black gash that twisted and wended through the high desert. It was the canyon of the Jarbidge, some 650 feet deep, with nearly vertical walls of basalt. The river originated from the island-mountains that still hovered faint and blue above the heat some thirty-five miles distant.

Benjamin and his horse dropped into the canyon and followed the river's edge. Every few miles he stopped, pulled out a large metal pan, and scooped up a mound of river sand. He deftly swirled it in the flowing waters and peered into the dark mud that had settled at the bottom. He looked intently for any small grains or flat flakes that glowed unmistakably in the sun. There were none. Undaunted, he and his horse trudged upstream, toward the river's source.

After two days, juniper and mountain mahogany dotted the canyon sides with green, and the river rushed colder and steeper and faster. Bighorn sheep clambered gracefully amid the boulders and rockfall, eying the man and his horse from above with a native wariness. Red-tailed hawks and golden eagles circled above, riding thermal uplifts and searching for meals of rabbits and gophers and snakes. All along the river's edge, Benjamin stopped, scooped, and swirled. Nothing.

Benjamin arrived at the base of the mountains, which rose sudden and stark out of the volcanic plateau. Though it was early summer, snowfields still covered the highest slopes. A quintet of imposing peaks rose in single file to over 10,000 feet, towering with patches of white over the hot desert plain. Straight south was Jarbidge Peak, then Matterhorn Peak, Cougar Peak, and Marys River Peak. About three miles east, on an adjacent ridge, was God's Pocket Peak. These were big, dangerous, isolated mountains that could swallow man and horse forever. Benjamin stopped, studied the landmarks, and pressed on.

The canyon narrowed. Water crashed and sprayed over huge boulders. The riverbanks began to fill with cottonwood and aspen. Benjamin hiked to a clearing that overlooked the east bank of the Jarbidge. The faint smell of sulfur wafted in the breeze. The ground was covered with a white alkali crust, and steam belched from holes in the earth. On the edge of the meadow, upwind from the hot springs, was a white canvas tent that stood strong and taut against the mountain backdrop. A team of three mules grazed in the grass. Supplies and mining tools were stacked neatly and covered with a canvas sheet.

A stocky, ebullient man jumped up from a camp chair, strode across the meadow toward my great-grandfather, stuck out his right hand, and declared in mid-stride, "Welcome to the Hot Hole! Dinner's almost ready. There's water by those trees for your horse. And after you eat, you can wash the dust off in those hot baths next to those big rocks."

David Alexander Bourne had a knack for following gold. And once he found it, he had an even better knack at telling the world, fanning a whiff of expectation into a crescendo of excitement that rose like a fever and broke in a cresting rush of investors, prospectors, merchants, hoteliers, builders, proprietors, and prostitutes.

David was born to Mormon pioneers in Utah but left the confines of his family and tight-knit religious community to seek his fortune in the desolate hills and rough-and-tumble mining towns of Nevada. He knew the land, the history, and the mines. He regularly sold stories about the quest for mineral riches to papers in Los Angeles, Chicago, and New York. That's because he knew that next to gold and silver, the most valuable commodity for a boomtown was people. A quick rush of speculators drove up prices and provided an avenue for cashing out to those who had gotten in early.

After years of dusty toil, he finally had a sizable strike of his own in Steptoe Canyon near Ely, Nevada—about two hundred miles south of Jarbidge. By the time Benjamin and David had met, David was flush with cash, having just sold his Alvin Mine for a considerable sum to a large conglomerate. He was eager to double down and repeat his success. Both men had spoken to those who had been to the mountains of northeast Nevada, and both were tempted by the geology and the stories they'd heard. They forged a partnership and set out to prospect one of the last untouched swaths of the West.

Tales of gold in the Jarbidge first surfaced in the 1860s, and then again in the 1880s. There were stories of a lost sheepherder's mine—never mind that nearly every mining district in the West had a variation of the same story. A sheepherder had wandered out of the mountains in a delirium, talking about a fabulously rich vein of ore and packing rock samples that glittered in support of his tale. But the sheepherder was bad at directions, his partner had died, and the heart of the lode was never again located. Instead, it sat waiting—a siren in the wilderness. There were also stories of a Bigfoot-like creature that lurked in the river-carved canyons. The name *Jarbidge* had been bastardized from a Shoshone Indian word for "devil" that sounded something like jah-HA-bits.

Neither David nor Benjamin paid heed to such silliness, though the tales made a good backstory for some of David's later self-promotion. Rather, the pair was most interested in the placer gold that had been panned the year before from the riverbed only three miles upstream from the hot springs and across the Idaho border in Nevada. The region was so remote that it had not been properly explored by men who knew where to look and how to spot the types of geology that were conducive to harboring pockets of gold.

Benjamin Collins was such a man. He was particularly intrigued by reports of large benches of exposed rhyolite, quartz, and andesite running along the canyon walls above the headwaters of the Jarbidge. It was an exquisite combination—a geologic signpost that screamed for attention. Benjamin surmised that the placer in the river bottom had washed down from somewhere, most likely from the rhyolite that streaked below the ridgelines.

The morning broke clear and cold. A mountain frost coated the tips of the meadow grass and the mules huffed small clouds into the chilled air. The mud pots bubbled, and geothermal steam billowed white into the blue dawn.

David and Benjamin cooked breakfast over an open fire before saddling their horses, loading supplies on the mules, and trekking up the canyon.

Three miles above the camp, Benjamin dipped his pan into the river bottom. The cold, clear water swirled across the black sand. He sluiced out the remnants and tilted the pan toward the sunlight. Five grains of color shone unmistakably against the dark backdrop. The gold was small, sharp, and angular. It wasn't the type of placer found in the streams along the Snake, which was typically flour gold that was more trouble to extract than it was worth. No; this had promise.

David and Benjamin didn't speak. A calm excitement overcame them. They moved methodically up the river, stopping every thousand feet or so to pan, pick out grains of placer, exchange glances, and then stand to study the rocks and ridges that rose on either side above them.

Eight miles above the camp, they came to a fork in the Jarbidge. Jack Creek flowed in from the east side of the canyon ridge, with the Jarbidge wrapping around the west side. Both looked promising, so the men split up—David following Jack Creek, and Benjamin staying with the main fork.

Three miles farther on, Benjamin dipped his pan into the river bottom, sluiced the water, and tilted the dark sand toward the sunlight. His excitement became electric. He wanted to yell, but there was no one in the canyon to hear. So the water burbled, the aspen leaves softly riffled, and the horse dropped his head to tug at the tall grass along the riverbank. More than twenty grains of color glowed with a bright luster. He knew immediately that he was in the midst of something extraordinary. He noted that the grains were large and irregular, and surmised that they'd spent less time in the water where their edges could be smoothed by tumbling sand. It might be that they'd been recently exposed because a spring flood had flowed over an inconsequential spur of quartz. Perhaps. But Benjamin didn't think so. Not this time. He stood and studied ridgelines and canyon walls. Somewhere nearby, he suspected, was a long, rich vein that had been sprinkling the waters with gold.

Benjamin soon came to a small spring-fed stream that trickled and splashed down the canyon's steep eastern slope. He hiked fifty yards up a gulch and then used his pan to scrape out another heap of dark sand. Benjamin deftly began swirling, swirling, swirling. Small clouds of mud trailed back into the stream. His mouth grew dry and his heart raced. He sluiced out the last of the sand and water, and held the pan close to his nose. Large flecks gleamed in the sun. He dabbed the biggest with his index finger and held it up for inspection. His hand trembled. Benjamin scrambled farther up the juniper-covered slope. Through the trees, he could see an outcropping of rhyolite that ran parallel to the top of the ridgeline in a large white-and-reddish band. He scrambled through the brush and the dust. Small rocks sloughed and clattered down the slope with each stride.

By the time he reached the ten-foot-high outcropping, his chest heaved and his denim shirt was soaked dark in places with sweat. He ran his hand along the putty-white rock. It looked like crystalized chalk and was mottled with red-brown streaks. Benjamin hammered off chunks of stone and then stabbed at the rock with a small pick. The mineral didn't flake or crumble, as it would if it were mica or pyrite. Instead, the brown streaks had dented, and the face of the stone was pocked with small holes from his hand pick. Benjamin stood and caressed the face of the ledge. He looked along either side and could see that the white rock ran exposed for over a quarter-mile before sinking back into the mountain.

Benjamin gripped his prospector's hammer, swung it back, and smashed parts of the ledge into fist-size chunks, which he gathered and tossed into his Stetson so he could run an assay back at camp. But that was almost a formality. This was easily the best gold country Benjamin had ever seen.

CHAPTER TWENTY-THREE

Whenever I see Canada geese flying high overhead in an elegant, purposeful, swept V, I think of cold. Not of a wet March cold or of a brisk October cold. But of a bitter, sunny, diamond-sparkling January cold.

That's when my dad first took my brother and me hunting.

I was four; my brother Kirk was five. My dad had asked us the day before if we wanted to go goose hunting with him. We answered with an enthusiastic "yes," even though neither of us had any idea what goose hunting entailed. But that didn't matter. We always wanted to do whatever our dad was doing. If he were hammering in the backyard, we would want to hammer, too. If he were sawing in the garage, we would want to saw, too. If he were mowing the lawn, we'd want to mow, too. It is the way with sons and their fathers. So, goose hunting? Sure.

My dad said it would be cold—very cold—and that we'd have to dress warm and promise not to complain. We promised. He said we'd have to get up really, really early, while it was still dark. We didn't care. It was an adventure.

My mother didn't like the idea. Not a bit. We heard her trying to talk my dad out of it. There would be ice. There would be cold. There would be a dog. There would be guns. There would be feathers. There would be blood. There would be death. And we were so young. We were her babies. Couldn't it wait until we were older? My dad said we'd be fine. My mother finally said okay. We were glad. She still wrung her hands with worry. It is the way with sons and their mothers.

My dad carried me from my bed to the small breakfast table in the kitchen. Winter's cold pressed black against the window. The kitchen lights were bright and made my eyes squint. My dad returned behind the stove, scrambling eggs with a spatula. He sipped coffee. Sausage sizzled. I closed my eyes, my head drooped forward, and my chin pressed against my chest. My brother sat across from me, still and quiet.

My dad shook my shoulder with his left hand and held an iron skillet filled with eggs in his right.

"Craig," he said in a low voice. "Craig."

He pushed eggs onto my plate and shook my shoulder again.

"Craig. Do you want to go back to bed?"

I fought sleep. I fought to open my eyes. I fought to hold my fork. I fought to keep from being left behind.

We ate in silence.

My dad told us to go get dressed and he'd be in shortly to help us with our jackets and snow pants. We went to our room and heard the clattering of dishes in the sink.

My dad joined us and began putting on extra layers of shirts and socks. He tugged wool caps down past our ears and pulled mittens snug on our hands. By the time he'd zipped our coats, my brother and I were hot and puffy with arms that stuck out stiff and wouldn't fall to our sides.

We waited by the front door while my dad made several trips to the truck, which idled in the driveway, the heater straining to warm the cab. My mother shuffled, arms folded, in slippers and a nightgown down the hall. She kneeled and hugged my brother, who gave her neck a squeeze and a kiss. She turned to me, tugged my cap to make extra sure my ears were covered, and said, "You be careful, little Craigy. Stay close to your brother. Don't go out on the ice. And be sure to do what your father says."

She pulled me close and kissed my cheek. I reared my head back and pushed her shoulders away with mittened hands. I was a goose hunter now; I didn't need kisses from my mother. She smiled, stared into my eyes, and gathered me so close that this time there would be no pushing back. I kissed her neck and she stood. She grabbed my dad's jacket tight with both hands, pulled him down to her, and kissed him quickly on the lips.

"Don't let anything happen," she warned.

"They'll be fine," he said.

My brother and I stepped onto the porch, and the cold was fierce. The truck's bench seat was made of a plastic material that crinkled as we slid onto it. The heater blew warm air, but the metal and glass that encompassed the cab shunted the heat, and our breath froze each time we exhaled. My dad turned on the headlights, pulled out of the driveway, and rumbled slowly down the street. The snow that had fallen two days earlier squeaked like Styrofoam beneath the wheels. There were stars in the western sky. There were none in the east. A faint glow was beginning to rise from behind the mountain range on the far side of Eagle Valley.

CHAPTER TWENTY-FOUR

The ambulance pulled into the emergency exit beneath a flood of lights. Latches clanked, doors slammed, sneakers scuffed on the cement. The two ambulance drivers hoisted my gurney and rolled me toward the twin glass doors that slid to each side as we approached.

A nurse—young, blonde, and athletic-looking—hovered over my face. Her ponytail bounced as she trotted alongside.

She held my hand and said, "So, here's the brave guy I've heard about. I'm going to ask you a few questions, okay?"

I nodded.

"How's the pain?"

"Bad, but they gave me something in the ambulance, so it's not as bad as it was before."

"On a scale of one to ten—ten being the highest—how would you rate your pain from earlier?"

"Eleven. No, twelve."

"Ha. Funny guy. What's it now?"

"Seven. Maybe eight."

"What day is it?"

"Friday."

"What time is it?"

"No idea. Eleven?"

"Close. Ten-thirty."

"And what time did this happen?"

"About two-thirty."

"Wow. That's a long time. We're going to have to give you a Purple Heart. And have you taken any medications today—other than in the ambulance?"

"A guy gave me a bullet to bite on."

"Did it help?"

"Not a bit."

"Did you get nauseous?"

"No."

"Did you pass out?"

"No."

"You're a tough guy. You'll be fine."

"Well, you didn't hear me screaming earlier like a little girl."

"Don't knock little girls; they're the toughest."

The rolling stopped. A young doctor walked in and examined my chart. He then asked me all the same questions the nurse had just asked, only he seemed more mechanical and preoccupied.

The nurse had a pair of scissors in her hand.

"Okay, Craig," she said, "I'm going to cut your sock off. And the doctor's going to examine your foot. Just put your head back, close your eyes, and don't look. This isn't something you're going to want to see."

"Oh, God," I moaned at the thought of losing my foot. "Is it really bad? Am I going to be able to walk?"

"You'll be just fine," said the nurse, gingerly cutting the crusted, blood-soaked cloth. She poured warm, soapy water over my foot, peeled the sock away, and then poured more water, dabbing at the dried blood with a sponge.

I propped myself up on my elbows. The nurse gently pushed me back down with her left hand and cupped her right hand above my eyes. The doctor leaned close and inspected the wound. The room was silent.

I craned my neck around the nurse's hand and caught my first glimpse of the bullet hole. And then I laughed—near ecstatic.

"Is that it?" I cried. "Is that it?"

The nurse and doctor both stopped and looked back at me, puzzled.

"I thought I'd blown it clean off," I explained. "And that's just a little hole. I'm going to be okay, aren't I, Doctor?"

"Well, let's not count our chickens here," he said. "This is going to be tricky, but I think I have a handle on what needs to be done."

The bullet had entered at the base of my big toe. The top of the wound looked like crater surrounded by a round ridge of pink hamburger. The bullet had passed through at such high velocity that the flesh had been pushed outward along the sides of the wound canal before getting snapped backward by the vacuum that trailed in the bullet's wake. Shards of bone and slivers of white protruded from the hamburger-like injury.

But the top of the foot was deceptive. What I couldn't see was the gaping exit wound on the bottom. That's where the real damage was. Skin, shattered bone, snapped ligaments, and shredded muscle dangled from the silver-dollar-size hole. The doctor squinted and shook his head.

The nurse removed my shirt, cut off my jeans, and swabbed my body with a warm, soapy sponge. She placed a cool, clean sheet over me and wheeled me down the hall to a large operating room. A man rolled in a cart and took out a needle. The nurse held my hand and said, "Okay, Craig, I want you to count to ten backward."

"Ten . . . nine . . . eight . . . seven . . ."

CHAPTER TWENTY-FIVE

Boomer was impervious to cold.

He lumbered toward us, head down, panting steam into the predawn gray. He rammed my brother slowly with a broad, massive head. Kirk wrapped an arm around Boomer's neck and began scratching an ear with a mitten.

Boomer leaned his hindquarters into me. I tried to grab hold, but my mittens just slid across his back, and I plopped on my rear in the snow. I stood to make another attempt, but Boomer's prodigious tail began thumping the side of my puffy coat with a *thwack-thwack-thwack*. I stood far to the side and instead watched my dad and his friend—Boomer's owner—hack their way through the near-shore ice with canoe paddles before gliding into open water, where they set out decoys with which they hoped to lure flocks of geese as near as possible to the blinds.

Two trucks were parked side by side on the shore of Washoe Lake, which sits a mile high between Carson City and Reno, Nevada, just east of the Sierra Escarpment. Headlights from the trucks washed over the dried reeds and cattails and turned the ice an eerie white.

My father and his friend returned, hauled the canoe ashore, and turned off the headlights. The sun was still a half-hour from rising, but at least the dark was gone and the sky was beginning to brighten. Far at the north end of the valley came the faint sound of what resembled a cart's squeaky wheel. The sound grew louder until it became a nasal clarion of *mip-mip, wa-haaa wa-haaa, mip-mip, wa-haaa wa-haaa*. We looked up, and about two thousand feet straight overhead flew a huge flock of Canada geese, driven ever southward by the cold, moving in three large Vs, which were in dark silhouette against the coming light.

My dad waved my brother and me over to the lake's edge and herded us into the duck blind. We walked atop snow-covered ice through a maze of dry, dead cattails before coming to two rectangular clumps of reeds. We stepped through an opening in the back and walked into what amounted to a reed-covered box. The blind had a plywood floor with three wooden milk crates to sit on. The roof was high enough for a man to stand up, and there was an opening in the upper half of the front wall, out of which a hunter could stand, aim, and shoot. When I sat on the crate, I could only see sky. When I stood, I could see the lake if I pushed down on the reeds and stood on my tiptoes.

My dad's friend and Boomer sat in the blind five yards to our left. Ice extended about ten yards from the blinds, after which was the open water where a dozen wooden geese lazily bobbed.

My dad took off his gloves, clapped his hands, and blew into his clasped fingers in hopes of generating some warmth. He pulled out of his coat pocket what looked like a long, wooden kazoo, cupping it in his hands and holding it to his mouth.

Mip-mip, wa-haaa wa-haaa, went my dad. *Mip-mip, wa-haaa wa-haaa.*

My brother and I laughed. We were well familiar with my dad's goose and duck calls. We often chased each other up and down the hall of our home, to my mother's eternal distraction, to see who could make the loudest quack or honk. But the best we could ever do was a shrill *Haaaa, haaaa.*

Mip-mip, wa-haaa wa-haaa, went my dad's friend. *Mip-mip, wa-haaa wa-haaa.*

Mip-mip, wa-haaa wa-haaa, went my dad. *Mip-mip, wa-haaa wa-haaa.*

The sun rose over the piñon pine–crested range to the east, and the cold sparkled. A frozen mist rose from the lake and glimmered. The dry, bitter-cold snow was sprinkled with small refractions of brilliant sunlight. Our frozen breath gleamed in the air before dissipating.

We sat and waited, staring expectantly into the bright January sky.

Mip-mip, wa-haaa wa-haaa, went my dad. *Mip-mip, wa-haaa wa-haaa.*

Mip-mip, wa-haaa wa-haaa, went my dad's friend. *Mip-mip, wa-haaa wa-haaa.*

We sat and waited some more.

Mip-mip, wa-haaa wa-haaa, went my dad. *Mip-mip, wa-haaa wa-haaa.*

Mip-mip, wa-haaa wa-haaa, went my dad's friend. *Mip-mip, wa-haaa wa-haaa.*

I was cold—as cold as I'd ever been. My lips stung and were beginning to crack. I could feel pinpricks in my cheeks. The inside of my nose frosted with every breath. My feet were numb and my fingers hurt.

I scooted my crate toward my dad and leaned my shoulder into his heavy coat. He put his arm around me, pulled me close, and rubbed my opposite arm with vigor.

"How are you doing?" he whispered. "Cold, isn't it?"

"Yeah."

But it didn't matter. I was a goose hunter, and goose hunters were tough.

"Do you want some hot cocoa?" he asked in a whisper.

"Yes."

My dad leaned his 12-gauge shotgun against the wall of the blind and reached down to open an army-green metal lunch pail. He pulled out a thermos with a stainless-steel top that doubled as a cup. I rubbed my mittens together to try to relieve the pain in my fingers.

Wa-haaa wa-haaa, wa-haaa wa-haaa, said the goose.

Mip-mip, wa-haaa wa-haaa, said all the other geese.

My dad dropped the thermos, grabbed his shotgun, and stood.

The lead goose flared its wings about five feet off the water and flapped furiously to change direction.

Pa-hoom went the shotgun in the dull, loud thud that shotguns make.

Pa-hoom, pa-hoom went the shotgun of my dad's friend.

The noise in the blind was sudden, shocking, and loud. I put my mittens to my ears and wanted to cry. But I was a goose hunter, so I didn't.

Pa-hoom, pa-hoom went my dad's gun.

Pa-hoom went his friend's a final time.

The friend whistled shrill and Boomer charged. He dug his paws into the snow and ice, and bounded powerfully toward the water, his head low and his ears flapped back. The big Labrador came to the ice's edge and flew upward, his front paws extending far forward and his back paws extending far back. He landed on his belly with a splash and churned his paws deep.

My eyes watered and my ears rang, but I could hear a goose honking in the lake and beating its wings frantically on the surface.

Boomer chomped his big mouth on the goose's breast and turned to swim back toward the blinds. The goose brayed wildly and hammered Boomer's face with its one good wing. But Boomer was impervious to goose wings. He closed his eyes and swam steady, stopping only once to readjust the reluctant goose between his jaws. Boomer clambered awkwardly onto the ice and trotted, his eyes still closed, to his owner. My dad's friend grabbed the goose by the neck and told Boomer to release it. With a quick twist, all was silent except for Boomer's huffing. My dad's friend whistled again, and Boomer charged back into the water to retrieve yet another goose.

CHAPTER TWENTY-SIX

"Hey, Hopalong!" hollered the mother of one of my neighborhood friends from the second-floor window of her house as I walked home from school with a cast that covered my foot and extended up to my knee. "How's the foot? I didn't know they were in season."

She meant well, and probably thought the situation called for levity, but I found it humiliating and not commensurate with the trauma I had suffered. From that day forward, she smiled whenever she saw me and called me Hopalong. I would be forever known in Winnemucca as The Kid Who'd Shot Himself. I was often the subject of ridicule—mostly from other kids—in a town that prided itself on its Western heritage and its cultural embrace of hunting. There would be awkward glances at my foot in the shower after gym class or basketball practice. And sometimes in the summer while standing with a group of teens by the side of the municipal pool, a girl would blurt out for all to hear, "Oh my God! What happened to your foot?" as though it were something that had occurred just that morning and that she'd felt obligated to call attention to because perhaps I hadn't yet noticed.

To an adult, such incidents would likely be a mere annoyance. To a teenage boy, they were a shameful burden.

For whatever reason—probably cultural—there are two places on the body you can get shot and people will find it funny.

One of those places is in the rear end—or "the buh-tox," as my son would say, impersonating Tom Hanks as Forrest Gump, who declared, "I got shaw-ought in the buh-tox."

The other is in the foot. People have an image of Yosemite Sam emptying his six-shooter into his boot, hopping around mad on one leg for about five seconds, and then scampering off in infuriated pursuit of Bugs Bunny.

I remain perversely jealous of a former classmate of mine from Winnemucca. To this day, friends call him The Bullet. It's much sexier and more mysterious than Hopalong or Yosemite Sam.

A couple years after I'd shot my foot, The Bullet, who was known to all simply as Mike Barry before he'd earned his stripes, was spending the night with his friend Alan Seals. It was almost noon on a Saturday, and Barry was still asleep, his tousled hair sticking out from beneath a messy pile of blankets atop a narrow twin bed jammed in the corner of Seals's bedroom.

"Get up," barked Seals. "We told the guys we'd meet them for lunch."

Something wriggled beneath the blankets.

Seals lifted his leg and poked at the lump with the heel of his Timberland boot, from which untied laces dangled. The room was dark and dank and filled with the flotsam and jetsam of teenage boys. A record player sat on a desk. A speaker stood in the corner, albums stacked precariously atop it. Posters of rock stars, swimsuit models, and football players were taped to the walls. The floor was littered with deep rumples of sweaty T-shirts, gym shorts, socks, jeans, and basketball shoes.

Seals kicked at the lump again.

"C'mon, Mike. Let's go."

The lump wriggled once more and then was still.

Seals stepped over to the curtains on the window above the bed and gave them a yank. A shaft of sunlight blazed onto the bed, filling the room with light and making even Seals blink.

The lump wriggled once more, and the tangle of hair atop the pillow slithered under the covers and out of sight.

"Go away!" came a muffled command.

"Mike," declared a frustrated Seals, "we gotta go. If you're not up in two minutes, I'm going to get a gun and shoot your ass."

"Go ahead" was the weary response.

Seals gave the lump one more push with the heel of his boot before wheeling around and stomping out. He went to the den, where, between the wall mounts of a stately mule deer and an elegant pronghorn antelope, was a gun rack. On the top rack was a .30-06 with a scope. In the middle was a 12-gauge shotgun. Seals grabbed for the gun on the bottom—a .22 rifle.

He returned to the bedroom and poked at the lump with the gun barrel. Barry, now truly annoyed, flung the blankets back and turned in bed to glare at his antagonist. He squinted, bleary in the sunlight, and focused quickly on the muzzle, which hovered steady about three inches away. The sun shone at just the right angle so he could see the fine spiral grooves inside the barrel.

"I warned you," said Seals. "You have ten seconds to get your lazy ass out of bed."

Barry lifted his head and propped himself up on his elbows. The gun barrel was almost touching his cheek. Barry squinted at Seals, and they locked eyes for several seconds without speaking.

Barry's eyelids drooped shut. He flopped his head back on the pillow, his eyes still closed. He pulled the blankets tight to his chin and with a tone of teenage ennui, told Seals, "Fine. Go ahead. Shoot. I don't give a shit."

Seals pulled the butt of the gun to his shoulder, leaned his cheek into the smooth, dark walnut stock, closed his left eye, and took aim at Barry's face.

There was silence. Motes of dust spiraled slowly through the shaft of sunlight.

The gun popped with the unexpected bang of a firecracker, its sharp report reverberating off all four walls. A blue cloud exploded from the muzzle. Its acrid smoke hung in the air, slicing into the dull smell of unwashed laundry.

Both Seals and Barry flinched at the abrupt sound.

Seals jumped back, dropped the gun, and blurted, "Oh, God. Oh, God. I'm sorry. I didn't think it was loaded. Oh, God. I'm sorry."

Barry, now alert and fully awake from a surge of adrenaline, sat up in bed and put his hand to his jaw—on the place where it felt numb and tingly. He could immediately tell that his jaw was wet. Puzzled, Barry pulled his hand away and lifted it into the sunlight a few inches from his face. His palm glistened red and the smoke swirled a hazy blue in the shaft of light. Barry coughed and gurgled and spit blood down his chin.

He looked up at Seals incredulously, holding his bloody palm out as proof. "You bathtuhd! You bathtuhd! Gahdammit! You thot me! You thot me!"

The slug had crashed through his jaw, through part of his tongue, and down his esophagus. It exited his shoulder and had come dangerously close to both his carotid artery and his spine. Another inch, and Barry would've been either dead or paralyzed. As it was, he came away with several scars after enduring a number of surgeries.

The summer following graduation from Lowry High, Seals was bombing down Second Street in Winnemucca when he lost control of his pickup and plowed into a telephone pole, turning himself into a quadriplegic. Those who embrace the notion of karma, and who like to believe that the forces of nature concern themselves with the doings of humans, take an odd comfort in the fate that befell Seals. Others simply see it as a stone-cold tragedy from start to finish.

Either way, no one fucks with The Bullet. Hopalong? Well, not so much.

Of course, there is no good place in the body to get shot. Bullets are deadly anywhere and do horrific damage, whether they travel through a foot, gluteus maximus, thigh, head, arm, stomach, or chest.

For when a bullet passes through flesh and bone in supersonic fury, those lucky enough to survive are forever damaged and disfigured. Getting shot is nothing like having an appendix surgically removed or having one's knee scoped or having a broken arm set and placed into a cast. Those are tidy procedures that leave small and sometimes imperceptible scars in nonobvious places. Bullets, however, are brutal, savage, and indiscriminate. They leave behind wound channels, bone fragments, jellified organs, and severed nerves. All this needs to be cleaned, disinfected, cut, removed, replaced, stitched, and sewn. And nothing is the same. Ever. A gunshot foot never works properly. Nether does a gunshot arm or leg or lung or, most certainly, brain.

Of course, that's compounded by the trauma that those who have been shot carry with them for the remainder of their days. There is no surgery for that. The memory of a bullet passing through your body, the deafening sound of the gun, the ringing in the ears, the horrific pain, the difficult recovery, the awkward discussions with friends and family who just don't know or understand, the futile hoping to be able to reach once into the stream of time and take back just a single second—these are the things that stay with you.

I have come to terms—as much as one can—with my injury. For many years it was something I simply never talked about. Once I moved from Winnemucca, I was no longer The Kid Who'd Shot Himself. I later discovered that the source of my pain and humiliation regarding the incident came from within, not without. I found that most people are too concerned with their own trials and tribulations to worry more than a few minutes about those of someone else. So you shot your foot. . . . When's the housing market coming back? So you shot your foot. . . . When are the Dodgers going to make it back to the Series? So you shot your foot. . . . When's Apple releasing the new iPhone?

And with that realization came a sense of acceptance.

My bullet entered at the base of my big toe. It cracked the first metatarsal—the main long bone that runs down the top of the foot toward the big toe. It completely disintegrated the first proximal phalange—the first joint of bone in the big toe. It sent shards of shattered bone into the second and third toes of the foot. It ripped open skin and muscle and bone just above the ball of the foot. It damaged growth plates and caused my right foot to cease growing.

Like many such things in life, I was both unlucky and lucky. Unlucky in the sense that an inch and a half to the left, and I would've missed. Lucky in the sense that an eighth of an inch to the right, and I would've severed the foot's main flexor tendon that attaches to the top of the ankle. The result would've been much messier, and likely would've rendered my foot nearly useless, perhaps even requiring a partial amputation.

As it was, the doctor removed the entire proximal phalange bone on my big toe and repaired my broken metatarsal. He then fused the distal phalange (the tip of my big toe) to the first metatarsal. Today, my foot looks a bit Frankensteinish—as though someone with a weird sense of humor chopped off my big toe and sewed the top half of someone's thumb in its place. My right foot is about two inches shorter than my left, which always makes for an interesting conversation in the shoe department. I have no nerves or sensation in the left side of the foot, but otherwise I've been able to run, walk, and play sports with abandon. For that, I'm eternally grateful. It didn't seem like it at the time, but in retrospect, and compared to most of the other gunshot victims in the United States, I got off cheap.

CHAPTER TWENTY-SEVEN

My mom heard the truck door slam and stepped onto the porch to greet us. My dad gathered caps, gloves, and lunch pails from the cab. My brother and I ran excitedly toward our mom, clutching a goose each by the neck. We held our bounty—which was almost as long as we were tall—straight out in front of us. The geese swung from side to side. My mom feigned delight as we told her about the heroics of the day—about the ice, the cold, the dog, the guns, the feathers, the blood, and the death.

We started to run into the house with the geese, but my mother stopped us, and with a hand on each back, marched us into the garage, where she'd already covered the floor with newspaper and had set out two buckets. She took off our jackets and snow pants, and my dad joined us in the garage with a goose of his own.

He took out a sharpening stone and spit on it, just as I'd seen my grandfather do whenever we'd gone fishing. He pulled a large hunting knife from its leather sheath and rubbed the blade in small circles on the stone. My brother and I watched his every move intently. When the knife was sufficiently sharp, my dad slit open the goose's stomach with quick sawing motions. He reached his arm inside the slit and pulled out a handful of brown and red and black. The garage filled instantly with a deep pungency. He continued pulling out handfuls and handfuls of entrails, and when he was done, he set the goose aside. Neither my brother nor I could resist doing whatever my dad was doing, so we asked if we could clean a goose, too.

"Are you sure?" my dad asked. "It's smelly and messy."

Of course, we were sure. We were goose hunters.

My dad took off our long-sleeved shirts, undressing us down to our Ts. He slit the bellies open of the remaining geese and my brother and I both reached deep. Blood stuck like goo up to our elbows, and the stench in the garage grew.

My mother stayed inside, preparing ingredients for side dishes and chopping carrots and onions. She never wanted to know what happened in the garage.

We sat at the table in the evening, and the goose—who had been born in the Arctic and who had flown as high as 16,000 feet and who had migrated 6,000 miles each of its ten years—sat elegant, brown, and glazed at the center of the table.

My dad cut slices from its breast and placed them on our plates. He reminded us to chew carefully and said that if we encountered any small, round pellets of shot, to be sure to spit them out onto the plate.

I cut a piece of goose, stabbed it with my fork, and chewed. It had a deep, lean taste that reminded me of a forest.

I cut another piece and smiled. It was good to be a goose hunter.

CHAPTER TWENTY-EIGHT

"There [is] $27,000,000 of gold ore in sight," Bourne told the *Los Angeles Times*.

This statement was picked up by media outlets in the United States and flashed around the world. Prospectors, farmers, ranchers, and city dwellers dreamed of another Sutter's Mill. The Old West was not dead yet, and the ground had not yet yielded all her secrets.

Forty men per day began arriving in Jarbidge, and seemingly over-night, a tent city of 1,500 sprang up in the narrow, high-altitude canyon that was accessible only by horse and mule. Jarbidge had become the last major gold rush in the United States.

Bourne and Collins filed seven mining claims that summer on what became known as Bourne Gulch. Within months, another seventy-one mining claims were filed. Bourne and Collins's claim became the North-star Mine. This was followed by the Bluster Mine, the Pick and Shovel, Flaxie, Pilgrim, Little John, Carrie Nation, and others.

Bourne's stories to the press later proved to be somewhat exaggerated. Prospectors weren't tripping over gold-filled rocks in the streets. How-ever, high-grade ore did abound, even though it was difficult to get at. The mining district produced precious metals for over twenty years, leading the country in gold production from 1917 to 1920. By that time, however, most of the early prospectors had sold out to large conglomerates. Bourne and Collins sold in 1912 for $250,000 to Elkoro Mining Company, a subsidiary of Solomon Guggenheim's Yukon Gold Company.

Over the course of two decades, the mines yielded nearly 500,000 ounces of gold and about 1.3 million ounces of silver. It wasn't the mother lode, but it certainly was respectable. The mines returned over $11 million in extracted riches to their owners. At today's precious metal prices, that much gold and silver would be worth about $750 million.

Benjamin did keep his word to little Edna, sending for his wife and three daughters shortly after the elation of his initial strike. My grandfather was born in nearby Bruneau about a month after Benjamin had found gold in Jarbidge. He was named David Alexander Collins, after my great-grandfather's business partner. The entire Collins family is listed in the summer of 1910 as living in the mining camp of Hot Springs, at the base of the Jarbidge Canyon.

Twenty-two-year-old Fred Searcy pulled himself up onto the buckboard of the mail wagon that served as the overland stage between the rail stop at Rogerson, Idaho, and Jarbidge. Fred was the driver for the last leg of the route—about thirty miles—that began in Three Creek, Idaho. He checked the Parker 12-gauge shotgun tucked into a holster on the right side of the wagon and peered at the sky. Four inches of snow had fallen in Three Creek overnight. Large, wet flakes were still floating sporadically at noon from a low, gray sky. To the south, the base of the Jarbidge Range could be seen through breaks in the clouds. The foothills were white and the snow was falling heavy at the higher elevations. Fred flipped up the collar of his tan duster, pulled down on the brim of his cowboy hat, and gave the reins a shake. The two horses in his team raised their heads, shook their manes, and began trotting down the wide dirt road that led through the snow-covered sage toward Jarbidge Canyon.

It was about a five-hour trip, and Fred would have to push his team hard if he wanted to make it by sundown. With the snow and the steep elevation, it was possible that he might have to stop for the night at Hot Springs before making a final push to Jarbidge in the morning. He'd hoped to get this run over with as quickly as possible. He'd taken the job only two weeks earlier at the request of a cousin whom he'd been ranching with near Mountain Home. He figured he'd work the route only until Christmas, at which time he planned to return home to his family's land near Pendleton, Oregon. Along with standard mail and supplies, he was carrying over $3,000 in payroll cash for the Jarbidge miners. Fred was one of the last overland stage drivers in the United States. The Elkoro Mining Company had tried running a supply truck up to Jarbidge two summers earlier, but it had proven unreliable. Between the harsh weather, rugged roads, and mechanical breakdowns, horses were still better suited to winter travel in this part of the country.

Ben Kuhl was a ne'er-do-well, even by the low standards of a mining camp like Jarbidge. Born to German immigrant farmers in Michigan, Ben was tall and wiry, with blond hair and blue eyes. From a young age, he'd read obsessively about the West, and at the age of sixteen, he'd hopped a train to San Francisco. From there, he'd made himself useful at some of the California mining camps near Nevada City and Grass Valley. He could do everything from running a sluice to shoeing a mule to cooking dinner for a mining crew. By the time he was twenty, he'd served a few months in a Marysville, California, jail for theft. Two years later, he headed north, where he got caught up in a horse-rustling ring and spent an even longer sentence in the Oregon State Penitentiary. Around 1912, looking for a fresh start at the age of thirty, he made his way to the remote gold and silver camps along the Reese River in central Nevada. When the mining there began to slow down, he showed up in Jarbidge in the summer of 1916 as a cook for the OK Mine. It was a convenient life for a mule skinner like Ben. There was always work, which meant he could haul ore for a couple weeks, take a break, build a fence line for a couple weeks, take a break, be camp cook for a couple weeks, take a break. In between, he could play cards, drink, or head out to someplace new.

But the fall of 1916 came in with a roar. The first dusting of snow arrived in mid-October. A series of blizzards buried the town in November, and by Thanksgiving, the drifts were fifteen feet deep in places, slowing mining operations and town activities to a crawl. Workers like Ben fell idle. He found himself spending most of his time at the Commerce Club, the Red Dog Saloon, the Success Bar, and the Jack Griffin Saloon. And then Ben's money ran low.

Bluster was a big dog. Part Vizsla, part wire fox terrier, and part something else, he stood almost to a man's waist. He had a frizzy, golden coat with grizzled whiskers that made it look like he was sporting a goatee. He was gentle, loyal, and friendly. He came to the camp as a puppy in 1910. His owner left, but Bluster stayed. And so it came to be that Bluster belonged to no one in Jarbidge, and to everyone. He had the run of the town, but of late, Bluster had adopted Ben the cook, following him around town and sitting dutifully nearby whenever Ben held forth at one of his favorite haunts.

On December 5, 1916, dark came early to Jarbidge Canyon. Snow had been falling all day, and by late afternoon, gaslights flickered along the street beneath halos of swirling snow. The hush of the storm muted men's voices, and horses walked quietly through the drifts.

Ben tied his horse to a hitch outside the Jack Griffin and opened the door to the warmth of a roaring potbellied stove. He stomped the snow off his boots, removed his black duster, and slapped his Stetson against his jeans. He took a seat at his usual table near the back and ordered a dinner of steak and potatoes with a beer. Bluster sat at eager attention, his nose level with the table. Every few minutes, Ben would flick a chunk of fat or gristle off his plate toward the floor. Bluster would snap the meat in mid-air, swallow it with a single gulp, and promptly return to attention, where he would intently observe every move of Ben's knife and fork.

After dinner, Ben ordered another beer and drank it quickly. He left two silver dollars on the table and clomped over to the door, where he buttoned his jacket to the top, pulled his hat down tight, hunched his shoulders, and leaned into the cold. Ben unhitched his horse, swung into the saddle, and trotted down the canyon away from town. Bluster stood on the boardwalk, whimpering into the cold night before lowering his head and following the horse's tracks in the deep snow. After a hundred yards, Ben wheeled his horse around and hissed at Bluster, clapping his hands and trying to wave the dog away. Bluster sank his haunches into the snow, hung his head, and looked up at Ben with doleful eyes. Ben continued waving and hissing before making his horse stomp and paw at the snow. Bluster didn't flinch. Ben finally shook his head in resignation, wheeled his horse back down the hill, and galloped away from town. Bluster waited for a minute and then loped through the snow after him.

Fred's team treaded softly up the snowy darkness of Jarbidge Canyon Road. The wagon wheels rolled quiet in the deep drifts and the sound of the rushing river was hushed by falling flakes. The smell of wood fires excited the horses, who sensed that the journey was nearing its end. Fred could only think about warming himself in front of a fire before sitting down to a big meal. The road narrowed and willows brushed the sides of the buckwagon. The horses chuffed, shook their manes, and came to a stop. In the dim lantern light, Fred could see a big yellow dog sitting in fresh horse tracks in the middle of the road. Fred whistled. The dog sat, unmoved. Fred cupped his gloved hands to his mouth and yelled. The snow muffled the noise and swallowed any echo. The dog continued to sit. Fred heard a clump in the back of the wagon. He lunged for the Parker gun. He felt metal against the back of his head.

A great *whoomp* thudded through the snowy night. The snow on the canyon walls briefly shuddered before the sound dampened and rolled away like distant thunder. The horses flinched and whinnied. Bluster continued to sit, still unmoved. Fred Searcy slumped forward, holding the reins. Blood rushed from a gaping wound in his forehead and a smaller hole behind his right ear. It pooled along the floorboard and dripped warm and red into the soft, white snow.

Ben Kuhl holstered his pearl-handled Colt Army .44 single-action revolver, pried the reins out of Fred's hands, and rolled the dead, bleeding body into the back of the buckwagon. He was surprised at the prodigious amount of blood. It had gotten everywhere—on his shirt, jacket, boots, and jeans. His hands were sticky and wet and wouldn't wipe clean even when he rubbed them in the snow. He drove the horses through the willows and down to the edge of the river. He dumped the contents of the satchels next to Fred's body, rifling through letters and tossing stacks of currency into the front corner of the wagon. He stuffed the money into a leather pouch and ran back through the trees to retrieve his horse. He put his boot into the stirrup, hoisted himself into his saddle, and galloped back to town. Bluster romped through the chest-high snow, trying to keep up.

The jury in Elko deliberated for only two hours. Ben had been seen with Bluster in the time leading up to the shooting. Sheriff Joe Harris had matched Bluster's paws with the prints in the snow near the murder scene. A bloody palm print had been found on one of the letters. Experts came from California to testify that the prints belonged to Ben. And with that, Ben had been found guilty of the last stagecoach robbery in the United States. He was also the first American ever convicted by using a fingerprint as evidence.

Judge E. J. L. Taber asked Ben if he wished to be hanged or shot.

"Shot," said Ben.

CHAPTER TWENTY-NINE

The best way to kill a coyote is to hit it hard on the snout with a shovel. Coyotes have long, slender noses that crack at the front of their skull in response to the slightest blow. If struck properly, the coyote collapses in a concussive daze and falls to its side, where its rapid panting causes its chest to quiver. To finish the job, the trapper places his boot on its rib cage, stomps hard, and holds his foot in place for several seconds. This cracks the coyote's ribs, punctures its lungs, and puts enough pressure on its heart so that it stops beating.

It's nasty, brutish work, but to a skilled trapper, it offers his quarry a death that, counterintuitively, is usually quicker and more humane than a shot from a rifle. And trappers never shoot their prey: It's bloody, messy, and leaves holes in the pelt.

Most people don't have the fortitude for this kind of work. Trapping a wild animal is a far different thing than hunting and shooting it from a safe distance. There's a cool detachment from placing an animal in your gun sights from anywhere between 25 and 250 yards and then gently squeezing the trigger. From a distance, it's clean, surgical, and requires only the twitch of an index finger. It enables hunters to keep their act of killing at arm's length. And if it makes them feel better, they can always attribute the animal's death to a gun and not themselves.

There is no such psychological luxury in trapping. It is an endeavor that requires the trapper to corner a chained animal, look it in the eye, and then in a quick act of hands-on savagery, extinguish the life of a creature with a rich, soft, magnificent pelt. There are no questions about who delivered the death.

My father ran a trapline in the sage-covered hills about twenty miles northeast of Winnemucca. He mostly did it for sport, but also because there had been a run-up in fur prices. Where coyote pelts had only a couple years earlier sold for around $50 each, by 1972 they commanded between $75 and $150, depending upon the quality of the fur.

It is important to know that before the men with the guns came, there were trappers. Long before the Louisiana Purchase and before Lewis and Clark, there were the French. It was they who first gave rise to the American West. The streets of Boise and Salt Lake and Reno and Missoula didn't start out smoothly paved and lined with high-rises. They started out as French and Indian trading posts, sometimes a century or more before American pioneers and settlers eventually arrived.

It was the French who had a flair for fashion. The English and the Spanish and the Dutch, by comparison, did not. And so it was left to the French to scour the rivers and creeks and woods and ranges and lakes and ponds of a pristine continent in search of exotic fur-bearing creatures that might quench the lust for such things among the capitals of Europe.

And scour they did. They were few, but they covered much ground, often working alone or in small groups. They poured into the North American interior from Eastern Canada and the Great Lakes. They followed broad, slow rivers through the Plains, made largely peaceful contact and alliances with the Indians, who knew where the best trapping grounds were, and came to the high peaks of the Rockies, which contained an astonishing bounty of beaver, fox, bear, badger, bobcat, mink, wolf, muskrat, marten, and otter. They clubbed and drowned and skinned virtually every mammal that could fetch a price. They then shipped the pelts back downstream through an intricate network of trading posts that all fed back to Hudson Bay. There the pelts were worked and tanned in factories, so called because the Hudson's Bay Company had designated their trappers as "factors," a sort of independent contractor that ran his own business. Founded by two French trappers in 1670 and backed by wealthy Boston merchants and the royal crown of England—the French secretary of state had passed on the investment, thinking there wasn't much of a future in fur and exploration—Compagnie de la Baie d'Hudson, as the trappers knew it, is the oldest corporation in North America, and one of the oldest in the world. Had the French crown backed its trappers, France's New World empire would've stretched from New Orleans to the Arctic, and the eastern two-thirds of the continent would have surely been under French dominion.

Regardless of the politics, it was mostly French mountain men who fanned out in search of pelts. They followed every river, tributary, stream, creek, and pond, pillaging each ecosystem for its fur, which was eventually delivered to European royalty, nobility, and the just plain wealthy. They found the best mountain passes, blazed the best trails, and made note of the most important landmarks. They were multilingual, and often spoke several European and Native American languages. They kept many of their trapping grounds secret in order to fend off competition. Later pioneers often thought they were the first Europeans to arrive in a particular valley, but they weren't; a lone Frenchman was almost certainly there first.

Beaver was the most prized of the pelts. It was used to make coats, trim, and hats. The thick, oily undercoat of a beaver could be crushed into a kind of waterproof felt that could be shaped into virtually any form by a hatter. Such hats were the rage on both sides of the Atlantic.

By 1850, however, the watersheds of an entire continent had been laid barren of native fauna, and the fur trade collapsed. The trappers were a transient lot; most didn't stay. They instead drifted back east, or often back to Europe. But when the men with the guns came for the buffalo and the gold and the land, they looked for the landmarks and followed the trails of the trappers who had come that way before.

Although the trappers founded few settlements and left scant evidence that they'd even been in the West, remnants of their journey can be seen in the names of the region's mountains and valleys and cities.

Trappers in present-day Idaho made note of a river lined with cottonwood and willow that snaked in deep-green contrast across a brown high-desert plateau. They called it *la rivière boisée*—the wooded river. Boise was a trapper's landmark long before it became a metropolis.

In 1820, a Frenchman set out for the trapping season in the wilderness of present-day Wyoming. He failed to show at the fall rendezvous for area trappers that year, or the next, or the next. Jacques La Remée was never seen again. Out of respect, fellow trappers began calling the nearby mountain range, peak, and river Laramie. The city came some forty-five years later.

Geographic names are often telling. They are almost always echoes from the past, revealing much about the people who traveled that way generations before.

Geographic names are also often fickle. Sometimes a landmark will be labeled with a particular name, but it ultimately won't stick; the people or the landmark will reject it.

In western Montana, five rugged mountain ranges converge, connecting a series of deep valleys to a central hub. A narrow valley to the west serves as a portal, transporting travelers in a few short miles from the Rocky Mountains to the Great Plains. It's a nearly magical intersection of two of North America's great geographic features. But for millennia, native tribes regularly fought for control of the valley, which led to lands rich in buffalo. The Flatheads, who were frequently ambushed in the narrow, forested valley by the rival Blackfoot tribe, gave it a name that translates to "the place chilled with fear." French fur trappers arrived to discover a place where human bones littered the ground and had been piled for centuries. They called it *Porte de l'Enfer*, or Hell Gate. The name stuck for over fifty years, but shortly before the arrival of a military fort and the Northern Pacific Railroad, the name of the city and valley were changed to Missoula in order to mollify current and would-be settlers.

Other times, a name will be drawn to a place, and the place just won't let go.

When my family would take summer trips to the nearby national parks in Yellowstone and Jackson Hole, the adults would snicker at the spectacular mountain range that served as an important landmark for early trappers—a beacon that could be seen for over a hundred miles, and at whose base was held one of the West's largest rendezvous.

While fishing with my grandfather on the Idaho side of the range, I could see twin granite spires rising dramatically above flat farmland and rolling foothills of light-green aspen and blue-green pine. They looked like a pair of blunt Matterhorns reaching 13,000 feet into a deep-blue sky. I was twelve.

"Why does everyone laugh when they talk about the Grand Tetons, Grandpa?" I asked.

My grandfather stood on the bank of Moose Creek, intently chewing his Doublemint gum, letting out his fishing line with his left hand, holding his rod with his right, and letting his bait float into a deep pool that swirled downstream.

"Because *Grand Tetons* means 'big tits' in French," he said, matter-of-factly, without taking his eye off his fishing line.

"No," I said with drawn-out incredulity.

"Of course. Why do you think the adults laugh?"

"But you can't have a name like that printed on a map, can you?"

My grandfather shrugged. "They tried several times to change it, but the name *Grand Tetons* just seemed to fit. No one ever called them anything else."

"Who came up with the name first?"

"French fur trappers, a long time ago."

"Why did they decide on that name?"

My grandfather shrugged again. "They were French. They were lonely. They were a long way from home," he offered.

He began reeling in his line, and then added, "If you want to give directions to have someone meet you in the wilderness, it's a name you're not likely to forget."

And they didn't forget. No one did. Not from the time of around 1806 when the first Frenchman cracked a joke to his fellow trapper about big tits. It was like a tune that won't leave your head.

In 1871, the US Congress sent Ferdinand Hayden on an expedition to officially survey the Yellowstone and its surrounding environs. Hayden and his team made the first precise maps of the region. In an orgy of hubris, expedition members stamped their names atop myriad peaks, ranges, and natural wonders. Everyone got in on the act—ornithologists, photographers, artists, wagon masters, and cooks. There was Mount Moran, Mount Jackson, Peale Island, Mount Doane, and more. Hayden, of course, saved the loveliest spire for himself, dubbing it Mount Hayden.

For sixty years, the peak was so labeled on all maps. But unofficially, the name never stuck. The big mountain sloughed it off like so much snow falling from a pine during a spring thaw. Finally, in 1931, the US Geological Survey recognized the original name, designating it officially as Grand Teton.

CHAPTER THIRTY

My father gently paddled the canoe through the glassy, cold waters of Fish Slough, a cattail-filled backwater that jutted into a meadow along the Humboldt River southwest of Winnemucca. Reeds brushed slowly along the canoe's aluminum hull as my father made his way toward the fishnet we'd laid out the night before. My father paddled from the back of the canoe; my brother Kirk and I sat near the bow. It was not yet sunrise, and our frozen breath hung in the still morning air. Pockets of snow still clung to the high cirques of the Sonoma Range, and thin ice formed in places around the reeds. It was early spring.

I leaned over the side of the canoe and grabbed a float from the fishnet we'd tied to an overhanging willow branch. My dad paddled to the other float, which had been anchored to a clump of reeds near the middle of the slough. My brother hoisted it aboard, and he and I began hauling the black net into the canoe, hand over hand, as fast as we could. At the bottom of the net were maybe two dozen fish, ranging in size from three to ten pounds. They were considered by sportsmen to be trash fish, and included carp, chub, and suckers. They thrashed and flopped furiously at our feet, filling the canoe with sounds of deep, metallic thumping.

For three straight nights, we laid the net. For three straight mornings, we made our haul. On the fourth day, my father instructed my brother Kirk and me to dig a big, round hole about four feet deep behind our vegetable garden in the backyard. We then filled a plastic garbage can about three-quarters full of the now-dead fish. My dad then placed the lid on the trash can and sealed it tight with duct tape. We put the trash can in the hole, buried it, and didn't give it a second thought for the rest of the spring or summer.

In early October, my father handed my brother and me each a shovel and asked us to remove the dirt from above the trash can—just enough so he could cut away the duct tape and lift the lid a crack. We stood back some thirty feet and watched. He then placed a glass canning jar next to the hole, handed my brother a ladle, and told him to carefully skim off some fish oil from inside the trash can. My brother was game for just about anything, so he grabbed the ladle and walked toward the hole.

"Be sure to skim from just the top," my dad admonished. "Everything has settled. Don't stir it up and get everything mixed. Also, you're going to want to crawl to the hole on your stomach, hold your breath, and reach into the trash can with the ladle from as far away as possible. The smell's going to be powerful."

My brother looked back quizzically but continued his mission without hesitation.

Lying on his belly like a bomb-disposal technician, he slowly lifted the trash-can lid with his left hand and prepared to dip the ladle with his right. He immediately let out a belching cough, sprang to his feet, and ran through the rows of dried corn before dropping to his knees on the lawn and coughing convulsively.

"Are you okay?" my dad laughed. "I told you it was powerful."

My brother's eyes watered. He was unable to talk and simply shook his head in response.

My dad looked down at me. "You want to give it a try?"

I took a step back and shook my head.

"Okay," said my dad, trying another tack. "Twenty dollars to whoever can fill up the jar with fish oil."

I looked at the ladle, looked at my brother, and ran inside the house to grab two bandanas. I wrapped them both tight around my nose and mouth. I was a decent swimmer and had trained myself to hold my breath for up to two minutes. My strategy was to ladle as much fish oil as possible before having to inhale.

I carefully surveyed my surroundings and looked to the corn stalks for any sign of a breeze. It appeared that what little wind there was that day was coming out of the west. I circled wide of the pit until I was as much aligned with the upwind direction of the feeble breeze as possible. Even then, at over thirty feet away, I got my first whiff of the fetid fish. I reflexively gagged and my stomach threatened to convulse. I stepped back and took several deep breaths. I took a final breath as deep as I could, held it, and walked as quickly as possible to the pit. I crawled the final three yards on my stomach. My eyes began to water, so I squinted tightly. I felt the urge to retch, but fought it. I dipped the ladle into the trash can, scooped it full of putrid fish oil, and poured it into the canning jar. I began to reach toward the trash can again, when I partially inhaled through my nose. I wanted to vomit instantly on the spot but resisted. I wheeled around, coughed violently, ran through the corn rows, and fell to my hands and knees, trying to recover. The wretched smell refused to leave either my nostrils or my memory. My brother picked up where I left off. It took another half-hour, but he finished the job with three additional scoops. My dad picked up the jar with gloved hands, sealed the lid tightly, and placed it in the refrigerator in the work shed behind the house.

About two dozen traps hung from nails along the shed's walls. They were mostly for rustic decoration, except for the medium-size traps. Those were for coyotes. My dad had collected the traps over the years. Some had been handed down through the family; others were much newer. They all worked the same.

In its closed position, a foothold trap has a pair of steel jaws with straight edges that clamp tight together, forming the shape of a half-moon crescent. A pair of flat, foot-long metal tongs, called long springs, attach to each side of the steel jaws. In order to make the jaws fall open and lie flat in a six-inch-diameter circle, the trapper pushes the bottom of the trap against their knee and pushes the tongs hard together. The trapper then reaches underneath the jaws and pushes up on a round metal pad about the size of a silver dollar in the center of the trap. The pad clicks onto a latch that holds the jaws open. A three-foot-long metal chain connects the trap to a metal spike that is driven into the ground to secure the trap in place.

The trapper then takes a square piece of cheesecloth or wool and squirts a dropper full of a pungent liquid on the cloth, to lure the coyote. They have an uncanny sense of smell, and depending upon conditions, can catch a whiff of skunk scent, beaver castor, deer urine, or fish oil—all of which can be used as coyote lure—for over two miles, maybe more. They are skilled predators, opportunistic scavengers, and through millions of years of fine-tuned evolution, are irresistibly drawn to the smell of death.

CHAPTER THIRTY-ONE

In December, the very cold weather came to the Humboldt. The snow, which had first dusted the high peaks of the Sonoma and Santa Rosa Ranges in October, crept down their flanks in November. Stiff winds from the northwest knocked down the last of the dry, yellow leaves that clung stubbornly to the willows and the cottonwoods. The snows came and fell deep even on the river valley floor. And when the big storm broke and the clouds cleared, the stars shone bright in a dark night sky, and the bitter cold sank from the mountain peaks and froze the river solid.

The big, male coyote trotted with quick purpose through the snow-covered sage. This was his third winter, and he'd come into his prime. His small feet pattered fast through the snow. His back stayed level, and his body seemed to glide through the brush. The cold had coaxed his coat into full, thick beauty. A deep underfur made him impervious to the bitter weather and gave him a bushy girth. A black nose sat at the tip of a long snout covered in fur of mottled gray. The gray stretched dark across his head, between his ears, down the ridge of his back, and into his tail. The tips of his tail and ears were almost black. His sides and legs were a deep tawny color, and his belly was white. If you were more than twenty feet away as he passed, you'd never see or hear him. He blended perfectly with the winter rangeland and traversed it like a ghost.

The coyote rose to a ridgeline and lifted his nose into the air. For the first time in six miles, he broke stride. He sniffed fast and deep, turned excitedly in a circle, and sniffed again. A sharp odor rode in snippets on a cold breeze. The smell was new, exciting, and irresistible. The coyote's curiosity pulled him down the hill and onto a rolling, brush-covered plain.

Beavers are trapped differently than fur-bearing land mammals. Large, square-shaped wire traps are set just beneath the surface in well-traveled waterways, or adjacent to dens. The beaver swims through, the wire clamps

shut on the beaver's body, and the beaver swims instinctively and frantically toward the bottom of the pond until it drowns. It's a cruel business,
indeed, even by eighteenth-century standards. It's also difficult, dangerous
work. Winter is the time for trapping, when the weather is cold, the snow
deep, the ice thick, and the pelts richest. In opening a continent, many
trappers died.

My father pulled a half-dozen beaver from the North Fork of the
Humboldt River in 1971. It was an expedition that gave him a severe case
of hypothermia and endangered his life.

He was in a canoe that night with a friend, checking on their trapline.
The canoe tipped, and my father fell out. Knowing it would be impossible
to pull him back into the canoe without the both of them ending up in
the water, his friend went to shore to get their truck for a rescue effort.

The water was so cold, it sent my father into near shock. He swam with
numb legs and arms through chunks of floating ice to the riverbank. But
the water was low, and the bank rose four feet above him. He clung to some
roots that dangled from the dirt walls and hoped that help was on the way.
After my father was submerged to his waist in icy water for ten minutes,
his friend returned with the truck, wrapped a rope around my dad's chest,
and hoisted him up to level ground. After stripping out of his wet clothes,
he was able to warm up by wrapping himself in a thick, wool blanket and
huddling in the heated cab of the truck while his friend sped back to town.

While it's true that the times have changed, and the days of the
mountain men have passed, it's also true that a beaver pelt is truly something to behold. They are round due to the way they're removed and are
about the size of a "saucer" sled you might ride down a snowy hill. The
color is the richest of browns—more of a nuanced brunette, a shade you'd
find on the head of a carefully coiffed model. Their underfur is a thick,
dark gray that feels like the soft down of a goose and produces waterproof
oil that gives the long guard hairs a sheen that is silky to both sight and
touch. The tips of some guard hairs are often a golden honey color that
seem to glow amber against the dark backdrop. And when the pelt is
moved under a low light, the color continuously shifts, the fur taking on
the depth, beauty, and complexity of a valuable gem. It is impossible to
hold a beaver pelt without being compelled to run it against your cheek

in a long, silken stroke. And to do so is to connect with history and to understand the nearly erotic allure that made the beaver a fashionable, coveted trapping of kings, queens, czars, and czarinas.

~

The coyote trotted swift through the sage, nose raised. He let out two sharp yips that broke the silent cold and glided above the ground as though he were being pulled forward by an invisible rope. The scent was now putrid and strong and traveled unbroken along a river of air in the steady, cold breeze. The coyote had trotted in nearly a straight line for well over a mile. The scent had flooded his being, blocked out the world, and pulled him unrelentingly forward.

And then he abruptly stopped. He waved his head in the air so his nose could take in the fullness of the scent. He was agitated, and his feet danced nervously in place. He could practically see the scent emanating from beneath a snow-covered clearing twenty yards ahead. He waved his nose in the air once more, and between the luscious aroma of death and decay, he caught faint whiffs of human. He stared at the spot and stood panting. His wariness and caution fought with his insatiable appetite and innate curiosity.

He turned right and trotted in a wide circle, his eyes fixed to the source of the scent. He orbited six times, captivated, but troubled by the occasional smell that seemed out of place. He stopped where he'd started, dropped to his haunches in the snow, his forelegs straight, ears perked, eyes focused forward. As his fur ruffled in the winter breeze, the coyote bided his time.

~

My dad came home early from work. We changed into jeans, boots, wool shirts, down jackets, and wool caps. He tossed a shovel into the bed of the old Dodge pickup with a clank. He placed the .22 rifle on the back-window gun rack, just in case. My brother Kirk, who was thirteen, was at wrestling practice. I was twelve at the time. We turned out of town and followed the two-lane blacktop that led northeast. I fiddled with the radio station but could only find country songs, car ads, and the crackle of faint, faraway stations. The tires hissed on the pavement, and the heater was on full blast. Three inches of snow had fallen overnight, and the normally brown, rolling range was blanketed with white. The morning had broken cold—into the single digits—with a biting wind from due north. But by afternoon, the clouds had thickened, the wind had shifted due west, and the temperature rose to just below freezing.

"Looks like more snow," my dad said as he lowered his head and looked out the windshield.

I scanned the sky and agreed. The gray had darkened and already swallowed the upper two-thirds of Bloody Run Peak.

The truck slowed, and my dad flipped on the left blinker even though there wasn't another car for fifteen miles. We turned onto a dirt road that was broad, white, and without tracks. The virgin snow cushioned the ride; the tires were hushed, the truck didn't rattle, and the dust didn't fly.

⸻

The coyote stood. He let out a frustrated yowl and a yip, then dropped his nose to the ground and trotted forward. He stopped after five yards, sat on his haunches, and waved his nose again in the air. He stood, trotted another ten yards, and stopped. He turned right, hung his head low, and made a tight circle. He stared intently toward the center, and the hair between his front shoulders bristled as though he were stalking prey. He warily tightened his circle until he was finally dancing just outside the source of the scent. The smell of human was also strong, but the other odor was overpowering.

He jumped excitedly on all fours and began to paw through the snow near the scent. His right, front paw scraped through the dirt, and there was a sudden metallic *clank* and a snap. The coyote flipped through the air, startled, landing on his back. He scrambled to his feet and dashed away at full speed. The trap gripped his paw, and he cartwheeled when he came to the end of the chain. The coyote snarled and growled and bit at the metal with long canine teeth. He pulled and he tugged and he yipped. He ran hard the other way and again flipped backward at the end of the chain. He rose and began running in clockwise circles, pulling his front paw against the chain.

My dad slowed to check the first trap. He left the truck idling in the middle of the road. We stepped softly toward the location, careful not to brush against the sage and leave unnecessary scent. We scanned the fresh snow for any sign of coyote and saw none.

We did the same for the second and third trap locations. As we drove over a rise, I spotted a large, brown circle that stood out amid the cover of white snow. My dad stopped the truck, and we opened both doors simultaneously with a metal creak. We walked slowly toward the trap; my dad carried the shovel in one hand, the rifle in the other.

There was carnage at the site; brown dirt and stripped sage contrasted starkly with the surrounding blanket of fresh snow. The coyote had run a circumference around the trap's center stake, and a six-inch-deep trough in the dirt had begun to take shape. All around the outside of the circle, the snow was spotted with dirt that had been flung by the coyote's frantic digging. Inside the circle, there was not a remnant of snow.

My dad handed me the shovel and said, "Do you think you can do this?"

I grimaced, having assumed I was there to just spectate.

"Can't I just shoot him?" I asked, hoping for an easy way out.

"That's not how it's done."

He held out the shovel, and I took it from him with gloved hands.

The coyote cowered and made himself small on the opposite side of the circle. I stepped forward and he jerked back, stretching the chain taut with his paw. I had a nervousness in my stomach and thought about how the coyote looked so much like someone's family dog. But as I got closer, I could see he was something different. There was a wildness in his eyes and a complete lack of connection to anything human. But still the job was hard, and I resented my father for not taking care of this himself.

I stepped closer and closer, the shovel raised forward at about ten o'clock. The coyote cowered, still tugging at the trap. He held his jaws open and all his teeth were bared. His nose was wrinkled back as though he were about to sneeze. His gaze shifted between me and the shovel that hung overhead. I stepped forward once more, and he danced sideways like a crab, never taking his eyes off me and moving away in an arc. I stepped on the chain about two feet from him. He looked up now at the shovel. I swung down as hard as I could so that he would have death without pain. The shovel reverberated with a *clunk* and the coyote dropped limp. I pressed my boot onto his rib cage but didn't have the weight or strength to finish the job. My dad slammed his boot down, and I heard the cracking of bone. The coyote's life left him, and his tongue lolled from the side of his mouth like a dog tired out from a long run.

The weather warmed, the traps were pulled, and the snow retreated up the flanks of Bloody Run Peak. On a rainy day in early March, a short, round man with a clipboard pulled up to the curb in a big, white Econoline van.

My dad led him to the work shed, opened the door, and stepped inside. From the rafters hung nearly forty coyote pelts, dangling in midair like ghosts. Their fur had been removed from their bodies and pulled inside out. The pelts had dried, and the skin was thin and papery, making a crinkling sound when handled. The fur inside was soft, and the tails hung bushy almost to the floor.

Though not as deep, rich, and plush as fur from beaver or mink, coyotes remain an important source of fur for the fashion industry. It's often used for trim on coats, gloves, and hats, in addition to full-length fur coats.

The man walked through, inspecting each pelt by hand. He made note of the color. He checked for any holes or damage. He stroked the fur and dug his fingers deep into the pelt. He made more notes and checked boxes.

When he was done, he handed my father a sheet and discussed how he had arrived at the pricing. I walked over to my coyote—which I could identify from his size and where he'd been hung—and stroked his pelt and tail one last time. He was among the largest of the lot. The man had been impressed.

We helped him load the pelts into the van, and I saw that we were but one stop on his journey. The van was loaded already with fur from at least a hundred other coyotes. The man wrote my father a check, shook his hand, and handed him a receipt. The van drove away in the rain, and I glanced over to see that my coyote had fetched $140.

CHAPTER THIRTY-TWO

Atop the White Mountains, along the border between Nevada and California, there are living trees older than written history. They grow high above what would be considered the timberline for most ranges and can be found thriving at up to 12,000 feet. Bristlecone pines cling to the fractured rock, dolomite outcrops, and slate-colored talus that clatters and slides down steep mountain cirques. They've entrenched themselves in a biotic niche that ranks among the most inhospitable on Earth.

The White Mountains are the highest and westernmost range in the Great Basin. They were thrust from beneath a great inland sea by the same tectonic forces that created all the other north-south ranges in Nevada and Utah. They begin at Westgard Pass, a 7,313-foot notch that separates the range from the Inyo Mountains to the south. A worn and rounded spine rises steadily until reaching White Mountain Peak, at 14,252 feet. The ridgeline traverses some sixty miles, terminating at 13,157-foot Boundary Peak, Nevada's highest, before plunging back to the floor of the Great Basin.

The White Mountains perch above some of the most dramatic and geologically violent features in North America. The Owens Valley to the west—flanked on both sides by 14,000-foot ranges—is the deepest in the United States. To the northwest is the Long Valley Caldera, one of the largest volcanic craters on Earth—the site 760,000 years ago of a massive eruption that vaporized entire mountains and flung a twenty-mile-diameter section of land into the atmosphere. To the south is Death Valley, a barren, scorching depression that sinks below sea level in the most arid of rain shadows.

Running parallel to the west is the spine of the Sierra Nevada—a jagged chain of 14,000-foot peaks that runs unbroken for two hundred miles, from Lake Tahoe to just northeast of Bakersfield. It is a range that lifted long ago from the earth like a drawbridge. Its western slope rises lush and gentle from the floor of California's Central Valley, wringing moisture from Pacific winds. Its dry eastern slope crashes to the Owens Valley floor in a plunge of sheer granite.

And above it all stand the bristlecone pine. They are botanic marvels that have exchanged the easy niches for a hard-won longevity. Winters are bitter, and temperatures can go as low as 50-below. The trees stay dormant much of the year and have a growing season that's a scant forty-five days. To the west, skiers call the snow "Sierra cement" because it falls wet and heavy, packing hard and deep until the spring thaw. By the time storms reach the White Mountains, the clouds have released most of their valuable cargo, and the bristlecones are pelted with flakes that are dry and light. The snowpack is thinner here, and spring rivulets and streams don't run into autumn. But with little moisture, there is not the fungus or rot that often fells giant sequoias a mere forty miles to the west.

The harsh climate, thin air, and increased solar radiation keep away most insects, beetles, or burrowing mammals that might threaten the trees' interior or roots. A thick resin courses through trunks and branches, further warding off outside intruders. The wood is so dense that it's heavy to lift and difficult to burn. Fire rarely visits the bristlecone. The trees grow in evenly spaced groves, not intermeshed forests. The ground is rocky and sparse. Should a tree be struck by lightning, fire is unable to jump through treetops, nor race through underbrush. And then there is always the wind, which can often blow a hundred miles per hour for days on end. Even in the calm of summer, breezes blow twenty miles per hour, or more. As a result, the trees often look more like driftwood than like a living pine. On the old trees, branches and trunks have been laid bare by continuous blasts of sand and ice. The exposed wood is the color of light honey with weird contours that have been smoothed and shaped by time.

In the early 1960s, a university student was researching tree rings and taking core samples near Wheeler Peak in Nevada. His tree-boring instrument broke, and the US Forest Service granted him a permit to cut a cross section of what was thought to be a garden-variety bristlecone. Upon counting the rings, he discovered that he'd murdered the oldest living thing on Earth, a 4,844-year-old ancient known as Prometheus.

In the White Mountains, a tree called Methuselah is now older than Prometheus was when it was cut down. And scientists have discovered a number of bristlecones whose ages exceed five thousand years, though they have kept their locations secret in order not to expose them to vandals or curiosity seekers. Such trees were seedlings at the dawn of the Bronze Age. They are older than Stonehenge or the Great Pyramids. Mammoths had not yet gone fully extinct. And they were already older than the oldest sequoias when Julius Caesar ruled Rome.

Bristlecone pines are extremely sensitive to weather and dutifully record any and all changes in their rings. Each tree is its own small weather station. Scientists called dendrochronologists study the trees' growth rings, aligning core samples between live trees and old, dead trunks. Thanks to the bristlecones, they've been able to build a detailed annual weather report for the Western United States that stretches back to the Ice Age. The trees' rings have documented the recent rise in atmospheric warming that will likely bring them doom. But today they still stand, high above the Owens Valley, doing what they do best, which is to continue to live, year after year after year.

In the mid-1970s, my family moved from Winnemucca to Bishop, California, located in the upper Owens Valley, when my father transferred as area manager for the Bureau of Land Management. I was a freshman and upset about leaving my friends in Nevada.

During my first week at Bishop Union High School, I was playing basketball in the gym with some classmates I'd just met. The ball bounced out of bounds and into the hands of Clay Greer, a popular kid who played on both the football and basketball teams. I walked over to retrieve the ball, which Clay was tossing up and down in his hand. He was standing with half a dozen of his football friends. I signaled for him to throw it back.

With a smirk, he cocked the ball and fired it as hard as he could into my face from five feet away.

"There's your ball," he mocked, his clutch of friends laughing as I turned away, doubled over, holding my stinging nose with both hands while blinking through watery eyes.

Clay stood his ground, chest out, backed by his gang of toughs.

In the years since, I've always regretted what I didn't do next.

And that was this: lowered my head, let out a furious whoop, charged him with abandon, slammed into his chest with my shoulder, lifted him off the ground, pile-driven him into the hardwood floor, slapped him into a full nelson, and pushed with all my might with both my interlocked hands behind his head until he thought his neck was about to snap. At that point, I'd have had him repeat after me, "Uncle. Uncle. Please, uncle, Craig. I'm sorry. Please let me go." It was something I'd learned from my brother, the wrestler.

But I didn't. And I'm sure that Clay—and guys like him—knew that I—and guys like me—wouldn't.

Instead, I reached down, picked up the basketball, and trotted back, humiliated, to my friends at the other end of the gym. Clay and his goons laughed and hurled further insults, which echoed through the gym for everyone to hear. My new friends hung their heads, embarrassed for me.

Some two decades later, I stood next to Clay at our twenty-year high school reunion, the memory of that distant event still burning in my mind as though it were yesterday.

"Hey, bud," exclaimed Clay, holding up his bottle of beer, clearly oblivious—the incident maybe less than a blip (if even that) on the dashboard of his high school experience. We clinked bottles.

"How have you been?" he continued with seemingly genuine interest. "I'll bet you're doing great. You were always a really smart guy with a great sense of humor—and a fantastic runner, too. Do you still run? You look like it. You appear to be in great shape."

Clay had done well for himself. His family had developed the Creekside Inn, which was hosting our reunion reception, and he was the hotel's general manager.

"I've been well," I replied. "And, yeah, I still run a little, but mostly just to keep the pounds off. Nice place you have here. Congratulations. And you look pretty fit yourself. What's your secret?"

"Oh, thanks," he replied. "Great question." Clay spoke with the excited tone of someone who had just gotten religion, or perhaps wanted to get you involved in a multilevel marketing scheme. He leaned in close so I could hear above the cocktail party din.

"I've been free-soloing," he said.

"Free-soloing?" I repeated quizzically.

"Free-soloing," he confirmed, before adding, "You know what that is, don't you?"

"In what sense?" I asked.

"You know, free-soloing—as in climbing a mountain by yourself without equipment."

"Oh, *that* kind of soloing," I replied, semi-relieved, given the many notions drifting through my head.

"Yeah," he continued in his low, reverent tone. "I've been going out into the wilderness by myself for a week or two at a time, and I solo-climb one or two major peaks."

"Wow, really?"

I was surprised, because even though Clay's family owned a hotel that catered to the outdoors set, the Clay I knew in high school never seemed much interested at all in fishing, hiking, or hunting.

"Yeah," said Clay. "I just love being in the outdoors by myself. It's very Zen-like. I can go, meditate, not see another human for days, clear my head, and learn to be at peace with myself. You appreciate being self-sufficient. There's nothing but you and the wilderness. It sounds corny, but you really become one with nature. You should try it."

"I don't know, Clay," I said with a tinge of worry. "One thing I've been pretty sure of ever since I was in the Cub Scouts is that it's generally a bad idea to go into the wilderness by yourself."

"Oh, no, no, no, no," he said, putting his hand on my shoulder as though he were a missionary trying to convert me. "It's not like that at all. As long as you have all the right supplies and you know what you're doing, you'll be fine. Really. I'm telling you, it's the best thing ever. It's helped me immensely."

"Yeah, but what if you break an ankle or get dehydrated? Man, it's the small stuff that'll get you."

"Yeah, and I could walk out of here and get hit by a truck. What's your point?"

Clay was beginning to get agitated that I wasn't already all in on his new religion of soloing, so I stopped playing the contrarian.

"So where have you soloed, so far?" I asked.

He lowered his voice again as though he were letting me in on a secret.

"I've done a few. Mount Tom. Red Slate. Mount Williamson."

"Mount Williamson?" I asked, impressed. "That's a serious mountain. Are you doing technical climbs or just free-climbing?"

"I've been mostly just free-climbing—rock walls and faces—but I've just started bouldering with friends out at the Buttermilks. I'm preparing for a pretty big climb on my next solo."

"And where's that?"

"Oh, I'm going next week to Evolution Valley. I hear it's really beautiful. I'm going to climb The Hermit. Do you know it?"

"Absolutely. Randy Smith, Don Pate, and I went on a weeklong backpacking trip there during high school, and I can tell you, it's really remote. It's a tough, tough hike just to get there. We went over Piute Pass and came back through Lamarck Col. I recommend that you stick to the Piute Pass route; Lamarck Col is a nightmare. You have to cross a five-mile-long boulder field. It's four hours of hopping from boulder to boulder. It'll drive you insane.

"But I'm telling you, if you get in trouble there, you're really in trouble. And The Hermit looks like a big granite thumb. I hear it's a tough climb."

"I've heard that, too," said Clay. "It sounds awesome."

I finished my beer and wished Clay the best of luck. He urged me to give soloing a shot and said that if I ever wanted to come up and give it a try, he'd give me a room at the hotel. I told him I'd think about it, but knew I wouldn't.

The big mountains in the Eastern High Sierra are different than most others. All mountains are dangerous, especially for the untrained or unwary. Weather can shift, storms can brew, directions can get mixed. A garden-variety mountain might only flash its teeth when the conditions are right; there are really only certain times that some mountains become truly dangerous.

The big granite peaks of the Sierra, on the other hand, lie in wait every hour of every day. With slopes of sheer granite and elevations of up to 14,000 feet, there is much that can go wrong for a hiker or climber. Bright blue mornings can be swallowed within minutes by roiling thunderheads hurling hail, lightning, rain, or even summer snow. Without proper gear, hypothermia is always a risk.

No, the Cub Scouts were right: The buddy system is best. It's never a good idea to go into the wilderness by yourself. The big mountains don't care if you're there to clear your head or commune with nature. They don't care if you're Christian, Jewish, Muslim, Buddhist, atheist, or soloist. You might be spiritual, but they're not. The big mountains will kill you all the same.

CHAPTER THIRTY-THREE

The first snow came to the Sierra on the last day of September. A cold wind blew from the northwest, and the high peaks disappeared into a leaden sky. The next morning was crisp and clear and still. The clouds had all vanished, and the trees of the Owens Valley and the Eastern Sierra had burst into flaming yellow against the sky's deep blue. A dusting of white covered the peaks west of Bishop, stopping at a precise line that extended level at about 9,000 feet across the whole of the range.

But the highlight of the fall season was always the first snow on Mount Tom, a massive pyramidal peak that rises equilaterally from the 4,000-foot valley floor to a height of 13,658 feet. A wall of granite fills the western view from Bishop and includes the 13,187-foot Basin Mountain, which looks like a large molar, and the 13,992-foot Mount Humphreys, which resembles a lower canine tooth. Each peak is spectacular, but it is Mount Tom that always draws the eye, commands attention, and hogs the camera lens for itself.

To understand the importance of the first snow in the Eastern Sierra is to know that in this part of the country, snow is never just snow. It is a lifeline, an economic engine, a financial institution that locks up water for six months out of the year so that it can dole it out judiciously the other six. It feeds streams, replenishes lakes, and harbors trout in clear, icy waters. It attracts those who ski, fish, hunt, hike, climb, and sightsee. And, importantly, the great metropolises of Los Angeles and San Francisco owe much of their existence to the falling of snow in the Sierra. For in the West, there is the oft-quoted saying, "Whiskey is for drinking, water is for fighting."

No entity has fought harder for its water than Los Angeles. In the early 1900s, city agents trolled up and down the Owens Valley, paying cash for farms, ranches, land, and homes. Disguised as gentleman farmers, the agents locked up the water rights for one of the world's greatest aquifers. They'd cheated, fair and square. And the people of the Owens

Valley have been bitter ever since. Today, half of the water in Los Angeles comes from this region.

And so it is that the first snow on Mount Tom is not just a photographer's delight; it is also something that fuels the economic engine of California and can reverberate through the global economy.

But during this snow season in the winter of 1976–77, the year that began with the promise of a September dusting on Mount Tom, the snow didn't come again. Not in October. Not in November. Not in December. There wouldn't be any in January. There would be a trifling snow in February, and only a little more in March. But by then, everything had been ruined. Ski resort lifts sat idle. Seasonal workers had been sent home. Hotel rooms in Bishop and Mammoth sat vacant. Fish died. Lawns turned brown in LA. And swimming pools went unfilled.

That was the year—1976—that Randy Smith, Norm Milleron, and I decided to make a winter climb of Basin Mountain.

Randy was my best friend in high school. We ran track and cross-country together. We also skied, fished, hiked, and drank beer when we could. Randy was short and wiry. He was a tenacious athlete who outworked and outsmarted just about everyone else. He was also our high school class valedictorian.

Randy and I had taken up bouldering in the Buttermilks, a geological wonderland just west of Bishop at the very foot of the Sierra Escarpment. Only we didn't call it bouldering then. This was long before twenty-year-old college guys with ponytails, tightly contoured climbing shoes, spandex shorts, and sinewy, shirtless torsos turned the Buttermilks into the climbers' version of a skate park. They coined the term *bouldering* and made it cool. We just called it "climbing rocks." Most of our friends thought we were weird.

The rocks in the Buttermilks were delivered there during the Ice Age by glaciers that sat atop the Sierra and had ground their way down steep moraines toward the valley floor. When the glaciers retreated, they littered the landscape with large, egg-shaped granite boulders that typically ranged in height from five to twenty-five feet.

It's where Randy and I met Norm. We were rock climbers; he was a mountaineer. We tagged along with him at every opportunity, pestering him to teach us what he knew. Norm had traveled the world, climbing peaks, and his list of summits was impressive. They included Mont Blanc, Mount McKinley, and Aconcagua. He was saving money for an expedition to the Himalayas.

Norm had moved to Bishop in order to keep in climbing shape and to work for the Forest Service so he could finance his forays into exotic ranges. He was in his mid-twenties and was tall, lanky, and fearless. He could splay himself against a granite wall and pull himself up with what appeared to be the greatest of ease. He enjoyed free-climbing. Randy and I would watch him quickly and delicately climb the face of a thirty-foot boulder, all the while worried that he would fall, and we would be left to haul his broken, mangled body over a mile to our truck and back to town.

As the stubborn high-pressure ridge squatted above the Great Basin, deflecting the jet stream far north and sending every storm from the Gulf of Alaska spinning through Canada and the Great Lakes, we spent several weekends bouldering with Norm, learning climbing techniques, footwork, and route planning. Normally, we'd have spent those days skiing. But there was no snow in the warm, short-sleeve weather, so we spent the time climbing with Norm instead.

That's when he looked up at the cloudless sky and said, "You know, if it's not going to snow, we should do a winter climb."

"A winter climb?" Randy and I replied. We'd never heard of such a thing. No one in the Sierra ever climbed mountains in the winter.

"Yeah," said Norm. "It's great to climb in the winter. It's really cold. Waterfalls are frozen. The insects are gone. All the animals are hibernating. It's unbelievably quiet. And it's good practice for the cold on the really big peaks in the Andes and Himalayas. Plus, you won't ever get another chance like this. These mountains probably will never again be without snow this late in the year. It's a rare opportunity."

With that, Randy and I were sold. We began making plans to summit Basin Mountain on the winter solstice, as long as the snow stayed away.

CHAPTER THIRTY-FOUR

Clay Greer stood in the ragged notch of Lamarck Col on an August day in 1998. At 12,920 feet, the whole of Darwin Valley stretched below him. The wind whistled through narrow slats of granite that spiked along the ridgeline, and Clay's thin jacket flapped loudly.

Behind him lay the farthest edge of the Great Basin. Before him was the perimeter of Kings Canyon National Park. All the precipitation that fell to his back would eventually drain into a desert flat. All the precipitation that fell to his front would find its way to the Pacific.

Clay was in the highest of the high country. The sun shone bright, and he labored to breathe in the thin air. He was far above the timberline, and everywhere the view was steep and dizzying. Below him was a desolate, boulder-strewn basin with a chain of treeless lakes, each feeding into a lower lake via a small, connecting stream. The highest lake was a milky blue from the dust of boulders that had been ground by glaciers.

Above Clay was a cluster of foreboding peaks, all of which exceeded 13,000 feet. Mount Goethe and Mount Lamarck were to his right. Mount Darwin was to his left. And the split-peak Mount Mendel was directly across the valley.

Darwin Glacier sat melting in the summer sun, less than half its original size from a century earlier. The valley reverberated with what sounded like the roar of a huge waterfall. There were no falls, however. The sound actually came from beneath the melting sheet of mountain ice. Water pooled on the surface, tumbled through crevasses, and crashed onto boulders underneath.

Five miles to the west and several thousand feet below, Clay could see a crack in the high granite basin that opened into the rich green of ponderosa, aspen, and alpine meadows. This was the upper Evolution Valley, which was known by backpackers as a mini Yosemite and one of the most scenic locations in the Sierra. It was also one of the most remote. There were few people even in the busy season of late summer, and the nearest trailhead was some thirty miles of rugged terrain away. If something happened, help would not arrive quickly. It would be at least a day's hike and a helicopter ride away.

Clay breathed deep the alpine air, shifted his backpack, and descended a steep face of loose rock that slid, clattered, and rolled downward in advance of him.

CHAPTER THIRTY-FIVE

Randy, Norm, and I hefted our backpacks onto our shoulders. The trailhead began at about 7,000 feet. Our first-day goal was to set up a base camp at Horton Lake, which was wedged in a V-shaped valley at 10,000 feet between the massive shoulders of Mount Tom and Basin Mountain.

I'd spent a lot of time in the high country but almost always in either the summer, when the meadows bloomed with alpine flowers and the hills echoed with the shrill calls of jays, or in the winter, on skis atop a deep blanket of sound-muffling snow. But never had I been to the high mountains in December with everything bare.

The severe drought was unnatural and confusing to the senses. The landscape didn't seem dormant but instead looked dead. There were leafless trees without a blanket of white beneath them. The air was dry and filled with the smell of dust that had been kicked up on the trail. The sun was bright, and the peaks were snowless and golden—just as they might look at dawn in August. But the cold was oppressive. The high-pressure ridge that had kept the storms at bay made the air still and heavy, allowing it to sink cold down the mountainsides and fill alpine valleys. The gray granite was exposed and forbidding. Streams and ponds were frosted and frozen. And the cloudless sky held no promise of change—just day after day of sun, still air, and dry, bitter cold.

We set up camp in a brown meadow amid the bare aspen next to Horton Lake. Our first order of business was to build a fire to help beat back the cold that gripped everything here. We gathered deadwood and broke branches into kindling. I stacked small sticks in the shape of a log cabin, just as my grandfather had taught me. On the outside, I placed the larger pieces of wood—again in the shape of a log cabin—with the thicker pieces on the bottom and the thinner wood on top. This formed a natural chimney that would pull air from beneath and feed flames through the center. A good outdoorsman should be able to start a campfire with one match and have it roaring within minutes.

My bare fingers were numb and clumsy. I struck the match's tip, and the sulfur flared bright. I touched the flame to the kindling. The cold wood smoldered, and smoke rose in spiral wisps. I leaned close and blew gently. Embers glowed and smoke swirled. I again blew steadily, hoping to coax fire amid the kindling. Flames burst from the smoke and danced upward. I blew hard at the base. The flames bent backward and spread to the pieces of big wood. The fire began to pop and crackle, sending sparks skyward and pushing the cold back beyond the campsite.

The ice on Horton Lake was a bluish, gunmetal gray and about four feet thick. In a normal year, the lake would be insulated and muffled beneath a comparatively warm blanket of snow that was maybe ten or twenty feet deep. But in this year of stunning drought, the ice lay thick atop the water, its surface cold, raw, and cracked. When the sun shone atop it, the ice expanded—straining, shifting, and moaning like the song of a whale. At night, when the coldest of the cold air settled in the valley, the ice contracted, sometimes violently. It bent, buckled, and snapped. The sound was startling and echoed like gunfire off the cold, hard granite of the surrounding peaks.

In a land of frozen dormancy, the small alpine lakes were unusually loud and belligerent.

<hr>

In the dark stillness just before dawn, the cold sat heavy and fierce atop the camp. Even the ice on the lake was quiet—too frozen to complain. I dressed inside my sleeping bag, pulled my wool facemask down, and stuck my head out of the tent. The air was sharp. It froze the inside of my nostrils and caused me to cough. We had no thermometer, but I estimated that it was at least 20-below.

I mustered the courage to dash to the fire ring. The cold was on me instantly and stung my bare fingers. I stacked some kindling in the fire ring and fumbled to strike a match. My fingers felt fat, numb, and useless. I dropped the first match and clumsily pulled a new one from the box. I struck the match tip three times before it flared. Fire leaped quickly from the kindling and ignited the neatly stacked branches. Sparks swirled high into the cold sky, still dark and starlit to the west. To the east, the

White Mountains roused beneath the coming dawn. The bristlecones had recorded yet another winter solstice and had made particular note deep in their trunks of the dry and the cold that had visited them this season.

CHAPTER THIRTY-SIX

Clay Greer leaned his backpack against the reddish-brown bark of a ponderosa. He stripped off his clothes and plunged naked into a deep, icy pool. The South Fork of the San Joaquin River had begun as a splashing trickle beneath Darwin Glacier. It had gathered itself through a chain of stair-stepped lakes and was now swirling swift over water-carved bowls of smooth granite amid the warm summer green of Evolution Valley.

Clay washed away the dust and the sweat before climbing atop a large flat rock and sitting cross-legged facing the sun. He closed his eyes, breathed deep the scent of meadow and pine, and felt the sun warm his face and dry his skin. He dressed, made camp next to the river, and cooked two trout he'd caught earlier in the day. The high peaks with the jagged granite were at his back. In front was the western slope of the Sierra, which dropped gentle and tree-topped for the next thirty miles until the land flattened into the rich farmlands of California's Central Valley.

There was only one big peak left as the mountains sloped down to the west. It rose solo like a big thumb of granite from above a meadow in Evolution Valley, to a height of 12,328 feet. In 1896, mountaineer Theodore Solomons described the peak as "a colossal, sugarloaf-shaped buttress of fractured granite." He wrote that it was "the advance guard of [a] host of peaks . . . so conspicuously separated from them as to suggest the name The Hermit."

The sun sank low beneath the west-slope pines and into the Central Valley. Clay meditated—a soloist alone with his thoughts—glad no people had passed on the trail that afternoon or evening. Shadows turned the forest into a dark carpet of green, above which The Hermit towered like a gold granite egg, catching the last rays of a summer sun.

CHAPTER THIRTY-SEVEN

We crossed Horton Lake just as the sun began to lift above the White Mountains. Deep, cold shadows still enveloped the valley, and the thick ice beneath our feet cracked and complained as we walked over.

We followed a small frozen creek through the pines up Basin Mountain's northwestern flank. At about 11,000 feet, the trees thinned and the timberline fell behind us. There was nothing ahead but swaths of broken, gray boulders.

Basin was technically a Class 3 mountain. That meant it required significant stamina, the use of handholds, and an occasional rope. A Class 4 mountain required technical climbing skills and the extensive use of rope. Class 5 mountains were for experts only and often featured sheer walls and extreme weather that demanded the highest level of competence and equipment.

However, we were attempting a more difficult route to the summit of Basin—one that included the ascension of an eighty-foot granite face located at about 11,000 feet. That factor, combined with the cold weather, pushed our climb squarely into the Class 4 category.

Norm paced on the ledge beneath the cliff. He eyed the granite and saw what others didn't. There were diagonal cracks in which to fit fingers, rough knobs that could serve as footholds, and the slightest of ledges that could be used for resting spots. He studied the face for twenty minutes until he'd made a complete route to the top in his head.

I got out the pitons, carabiners, and nylon climbing rope.

"I'll belay for you," I volunteered.

Norm waved me off.

"Just hand me the rope," he replied. "Once I get to that halfway ledge, I'll use it to haul up the backpacks, and then I'll anchor you and Randy. Once we're all on the ledge, I'll free-solo to the top and we'll repeat what we did on the bottom half."

Randy and I were stunned.

"You're going to climb that without a rope?" I exclaimed.

Norm cocked his head and looked up. "Yeah. It's not that hard."

"But what if you fall on the second section?" I asked. "Randy and I will be stuck on the ledge with no way to get down."

"Oh, don't be such a baby," Norm chided.

I tried to talk him out of the plan, but Norm was already hugging the granite wall ten feet above me before I could begin to make my case.

"If you fall," Randy hollered after him, "I'm leaving you here."

Randy and I looked up, shook our heads, and stepped to the side so that Norm wouldn't take either of us with him. The view upward was frightening. The view down was dizzying. Talus swept steep for over three hundred feet down to the tree line.

Randy looked down and then back to me.

"So when he falls, do you think he bounces and stops fifty feet below us, or will he keep rolling until he hits those trees?"

I looked at Norm, who was now forty feet up a sheer cliff without any support or safety equipment. I looked down at the slope below and shook my head.

"Fifty feet," I said definitively.

"No way," said Randy. "He's not stopping until he hits those pines."

I took a deep breath and nodded, conceding the possibility that Randy was right. Regardless, we were both angry. It's one thing to take risks with your own life. It's quite another to risk the lives of those around you.

The red-and-silver climbing rope bounced down the cliff and landed in a coil at our feet. Norm leaned his face over the ledge, gave the rope a waggle, and hollered with some self-satisfaction, "Come on, you big pansies, get a move on."

CHAPTER THIRTY-EIGHT

Clay scrambled up the boulder-strewn slope above Evolution Lake, taking the northeast route to the summit of The Hermit. He wore only climbing shoes and tight cargo shorts that came to his knees. The ethos of free-soloing called for a minimal footprint and an avoidance of climbing equipment. Less was always better.

The sky was clear and the day was relatively hot for the high country. Clay's bare torso glistened with sweat as he passed 11,000 feet. He still had the stout build, tight abs, and broad shoulders that had made him a starting guard on our high school basketball team twenty years earlier. His hair was black and curly and clung in wet strands to his forehead.

The Hermit was a Class 3 mountain with a number of challenging but manageable routes to the summit. But Clay wasn't interested in the merely challenging. He wanted something that would test all his senses, all his strength, and all his skill. He wanted to feel fear and then overcome it. He wished to skirt death and thus feel alive.

Clay reached the point in the route where he could've followed a long traverse upward to the summit. Instead, he dropped to the base of a cliff that rose sheer for a hundred feet directly beneath the peak.

He looked up, studied the possible routes, and smiled. In the tight-knit world of free-soloists, others had climbed this face without equipment. They'd made diagrams and notes of available routes, handholds, and danger spots. Clay had received them in e-mails, printed them out, and committed their every detail to memory.

So with the confidence of a bullfighter, he dug his fingers into a large diagonal crack, balanced his toes on a knob, and pulled himself skyward. He followed the crack some fifty feet and made his way to a narrow ledge, where he rested. With Evolution Valley spread beneath him, it was good to be alone and alive in the Sierra.

The granite wall became less sheer and fissures laced the rock, providing Clay with solid footing and ample handholds. He looked up and never down—moving always forward, refusing to retreat, and keeping his momentum going. There was ease and efficiency in movement, strain and static in pausing. Most of the danger from exhaustion came from too much stopping and starting.

Clay was twenty-five feet from the top when the fissures grew narrow, the rock grew smooth, and the wall pitched ever steeper. He grabbed a protruding handhold, pulled himself upward, and could feel the granite bending back, near vertical. This was the danger point all the free-soloists had circled. It required strength, finesse, and a literal leap of faith to ensure that you could quickly find a suitable toehold with your right foot, thus enabling you to make a crossover move to safety.

Clay felt for a toehold with his left foot and could find only the slightest of cracks into which he thought he might be able to wedge the rubber tip of his climbing shoe. He debated whether he should make the move or not. Fear welled up inside him. He cleared his mind and focused on the task at hand. It wasn't yet too late to step down and traverse sideways to safety. But once he'd committed to the move, he was all in; there would be no turning back.

He considered long and hard but became agitated because he'd now lost momentum due to indecision. With that, he jammed his left foot hard into the crack and pushed up with all his remaining strength. He lunged crossways, grabbed the knob he'd been eyeing with his right hand, and then let go with his left. His right foot searched for a toehold, too, but was left dangling. Ensconced tight in its rubber climbing shoe, the foot scuffed at the granite, groping blindly to detect a bump or a notch or a crack. His left hand searched for a suitable hold, too. It gingerly prodded the stone with fingers eager to grip any imperfection but could feel only smooth rock.

Clay was left splayed in an awkward diagonal, with his left foot low and right hand high. He pressed his cheek against the cliff and looked down for the first time in desperate hope that he might spot the toehold that had eluded his foot. But he couldn't see beyond his shoulder, and his foot was on its own.

Clay held on. Sweat dripped into his eyes and streamed down his back. His right forearm trembled and his left calf burned. He thought about screaming, but there was no one to hear and certainly not enough time for help to arrive. He closed his eyes tight and refused to give in. His left foot wobbled and slipped with a jolt. He dug all ten fingers hard into the granite and began to move down with only a slow, scraping slide. But the wall fell away, and Clay succumbed to a cartwheeling plunge down the hard granite face.

In the cirques to the west, the sun beat relentlessly on high-altitude glaciers. The San Joaquin River gathered the meltwater and raced over granite ledges, across meadows, and beneath trees, whose tops swayed and whispered through the eons. Stains of blood and sweat were smeared across the rock face where Clay took his last breath. His body lay broken in the boulder field below. High above loomed The Hermit, towering solo into an impossibly blue Sierra sky.

CHAPTER THIRTY-NINE

Aside from Norm's harrowing free-climb, the ascent of Basin Mountain was proceeding with monotony. We trudged from boulder to boulder, the thin air and the cold slowing us down considerably. We'd carefully mapped out the ascent and had calculated times for each stage. As we approached the summit, we were over an hour behind schedule.

A slab of granite rose steep for twenty feet like a ramp, then flattened at the top of Basin Mountain. We each made an easy scramble up the slab and stood clustered on the summit. Far to the northwest, we could see the Yosemite Valley and Half Dome. Beyond the White Mountains, we could see the Great Basin roll eastward in range after sage-covered range. To the south were the big fourteeners, peaks over fourteen thousand feet high—Mount Whitney, Mount Williamson, and North Palisade. To the southeast were Telescope Peak and the Panamint Range, behind which Death Valley dropped to below sea level. Directly below were the Owens Valley and the flat grid of Bishop. We strained to see if we could pick out our houses.

I stuck my head over the eastern edge of the summit where a sheer wall made a vertiginous drop of over five hundred feet into a boulder-filled basin. A forty-mile-per-hour wind blasted straight up the rock face but fell still when I took three steps back. The temperature was well below zero, and I could feel the wind beginning to suck warmth from the core of my body. In spite of the spectacular view, all I could think about was getting back to camp and building the mother of all infernos.

After five minutes, Randy and I looked at each other and pointed downward. It was time to go. We slid down the granite slab and turned to wait for Norm to follow. I looked up and his head popped over the summit ledge.

"I'll be a few minutes," he yelled. "I want to read my Bible."

"What?" Randy yelled back, wanting to make sure of what he'd just heard.

"My Bible," Norm hollered, waving into the wind a small, thick edition bound in burgundy leather. "I like to read it on mountaintops. I feel closer to God."

Randy and I looked at each other and shook our heads.

Randy yelled skyward, "Well, be sure to tell God you're in a hurry. It's getting late."

I looked at my watch. It was 2:00 p.m. on the shortest day of the year. Randy and I sank to the ground, huddling shoulder to shoulder with our backs to the granite slab that led to the peak.

Norm sat hunched, the Bible held open on his knees, the whole world stretched out below him. A weak sun moved low across the sky, offering little warmth and migrating toward the jagged crown of Mount Humphreys. Sunset was at 4:36 p.m. Darkness would come around 5:00, and the deep, bitter cold would soon follow. The flat, stumped prominence of Basin Mountain lorded atop miles of boulder-strewn slopes, and the peak grew more dangerous with each passing minute.

CHAPTER FORTY

The first snow came to Mount Tom, the poplars stood tall and yellow in Round Valley, and Steve Wiswell decided it would be a good day to rob a bank.

Steve was a high school friend and had been voted class clown. But he'd since taken a job as a long-haul trucker, developed a taste for methamphetamine, and all the humor had left him. He was now on the cusp of fifty, and the promise of youth had long faded.

He opened a dresser drawer, pulled out two pistols, and held them up to the mirror. In his left hand was a chrome-plated Ruger Blackhawk .44. In his right was a Glock 9mm.

They were different guns from different times. The Ruger was a classic six-shooter. It had a long, silver barrel and revolving cylinder. Its polished, walnut handle was dark, rich, and smooth. A medallion the size of a dime was imbedded into the right side of the handle and depicted the Ruger logo—a black phoenix with its head in profile and its flaming wings held high. The gun was heavy and substantial. It was designed and developed in the 1950s by two Connecticut gun enthusiasts working out of a small machine shop. They had conceived it during the height of the Hollywood Western craze on television and in the movies. The gun makers were disappointed that Colt Manufacturing had let a bit of the Old West die when, at the outbreak of World War II, the company had ceased producing the iconic Colt Single Action Army .45 that had been favored by so many gunslingers, on-screen and off-, since 1873. Bill Ruger and Alex Sturm had a hunch that Americans might still treasure and covet a link to history, so they, too, could own a gun that paid homage to one that might have been used by Wyatt Earp, Jesse James, or Butch Cassidy.

Their hunch was right. Americans did. They purchased Ruger six-shooters in droves, and a major new gun company was launched.

Steve liked the Ruger because it was immediately recognizable, inducing fear and commanding respect. He could flash the Ruger to any teller in the bank, and they would know instantly that he was not a man to be trifled with. The Ruger also had sentimental value. It was as old as he was and had been given to him by his grandfather. If he were going to go out in a blaze of glory, he may as well hold in his grip a connection to someone he loved.

He then held up his right hand and considered the Glock. It was a marvel of smooth, sleek engineering. Developed by an Austrian curtain rod engineer who had never before set foot in a gun factory, the Glock famously outperformed all other handguns by a wide margin in 1980 when the Austrian Army was seeking to upgrade its firepower. Gaston Glock, the curtain rod engineer, wasn't restrained by the shackles of history or tradition. As such, he was free to experiment with lightweight polymers and innovative metal components. He ultimately created a gun that was remarkably light, tremendously accurate, and comparatively affordable. The Austrian Army placed a large order, followed by the American FBI, DEA, and major metropolitan police forces. The American public loved the gun, as well. It had a low price point and was modern, black, and cool. But best of all, it wasn't constrained to a mere six rounds. It had a magazine capacity of between seventeen and thirty-three bullets, all of which could be fired in rapid succession.

Steve was torn. He'd concluded that the Ruger Blackhawk would be more intimidating to a bank teller. However, the Glock, with its ample magazine, would be better suited for a shoot-out with the police.

Steve jammed both guns into the front waistband of his jeans and grabbed two boxes of ammunition. He decided to do some target practice on his way to the robbery. Perhaps he could settle his indecision by having a shoot-off between the Ruger and the Glock. He pulled a case of Coors from the refrigerator in the garage and slid it onto the passenger seat of his Dodge Ram pickup.

He popped open a beer as he pulled onto the two-lane asphalt of Highway 6, which ran lonely beneath the towering slopes of the White Mountains. He had little concern about getting stopped by the Highway Patrol for either an open container or a DUI. If that happened, it would just save him some trouble and a trip into town. He would just as soon have a shoot-out with the cops on the side of the highway as he would in a bank parking lot.

He sped toward Bishop from his home near the Nevada border some thirty-five miles away in the tiny town of Benton. After three beers and twenty miles of driving, he slowed to turn left onto a dirt road. He traversed a broad, green field of fresh-mown alfalfa. Rectangular bales lay evenly spaced in rows, representing the final cut of the season. He followed a creek that had come from a steep mountain canyon, at whose base cottonwoods spilled yellow onto a brown desert floor. He came to a split-log fence that ran along the trees and pulled to a stop.

Steve placed his three empty Coors cans atop fence posts, along with another three cans that were full. He opened his truck's tailgate and set down his guns and boxes of ammunition. He loaded the ammo, popped open a fresh beer, and watched the foam as it bubbled from the top, slid down the can's side, and splashed in sudsy drops to the dusty ground.

He held the beer in his left hand down by his waist as he raised the Glock level in his right. He squinted with his left eye and aligned the nub of the front sight into the notch of the back sight so that both pointed true to the Coors can, some twenty yards away.

Steve squeezed the trigger.

Pop cracked the gun with barely a kick.

The can sat still atop the fence post.

Steve lined up the sights again.

Pop-pop-pop-pop-pop-pop-pop-pop went the gun.

The can jumped and somersaulted backward off the post, its aluminum shredded with bullet holes.

The creek burbled and the cottonwood leaves shimmered.

Steve stared at the gun, then squinted. He liked its efficiency, but there was something lacking.

He took a long swig of Coors and set the Glock back on the tailgate.

He picked up the Ruger and bounced it up and down in his hand so he could get a feel for its heft and weight. Its barrel was several inches longer than the snub-nosed Glock, and it gleamed silver in the sun.

He took another swig of beer and raised the Ruger toward the fence. He cocked the trigger with his thumb and aligned the gun sight toward one of the full cans of Coors. He squinted and slowly squeezed his index finger.

The gun leaped backward and Steve's arm raised high above his head. The sound of the shot raced up the steep, narrow canyon and roared like thunder in the mountains. The beer can exploded in a splash of foam. Steve closed his eyes, breathed deep the scent of alcohol and gunpowder, and smiled.

Perhaps today wasn't such a great day to rob a bank, he thought. Not when the first snow had fallen on Mount Tom and the poplars stood tall and yellow in Round Valley. No, bank robbery would have to wait. There would be better days to commit mayhem and carnage in the weeks and months ahead. Steve gave a hop and sat on the open tailgate of his truck. He looked up and felt a rare moment of peace. Staring at the blue autumn sky and listening to the breeze riffling through the gold trees, he could just make out the silhouettes of bristlecones perched high on the ridges of the White Mountains.

CHAPTER FORTY-ONE

"Shit," said Randy. "I'm going up to get him. If he won't come, we're heading down without him."

I slapped my gloved hands together in a futile effort to maintain warmth in my fingers and nodded in agreement. We'd been yelling at Norm for the past twenty minutes, but he simply ignored us. He'd been on the summit in biblical reverie for nearly an hour.

Randy spidered back up the granite slab and returned with Norm a couple minutes later. Everyone looked at their watches, glanced up at the sun, and then gauged the route down.

"Three o'clock," said Norm. "How come you guys didn't come get me sooner? I get really lost when I read my Bible on mountaintops. I had no idea it was so late."

"You didn't hear us yelling?" complained Randy unsympathetically.

Norm ignored him and continued, "All right, guys, we need to hustle. We have to get to that rock face before it gets dark; otherwise, we won't be able to safely descend it. So let's go as fast as we can without anyone making a mistake and getting hurt."

I didn't ask what would happen if we weren't able to make it to the wall by sunset. I didn't really have to. I knew it wouldn't be good and would involve a great deal of cold.

But that possibility was far away. Though fear had begun welling up inside me, I pushed it out of my mind and focused on hurrying down the mountain.

Surprisingly, the descent of a mountain can in many ways be more difficult than the ascent. We hopped from boulder to boulder in a race against the sun, turning frequently to track its progress toward Mount Humphreys. We moved through the boulder field and down the slope much more slowly than we'd expected. Even though we were all athletic and in great shape, there's a certain speed limit to these things, and we'd already hit it.

The sun hovered above Mount Humphreys, and we stopped to watch it sink beyond the Pacific Crest. Shadows fell and the whole world turned gray.

Fear was something we all felt but had left unspoken, just as you'd refrain from mentioning seasickness to others when on a boat in the ocean, or chatting about plane crashes with your seatmate as the jet is on the runway, preparing to take off. We all knew we were in trouble; there was nothing more to say about it. I began running scenarios in my head, and none of them were good.

If I had to spend the night on the side of a mountain at 12,000 feet in 30-below weather, would I live? Perhaps. I had numerous layers of clothing specially designed for the outdoors. But without wood to make a fire or any shelter other than exposed rock, it might be difficult to hang on until morning. The more immediate question was how many fingers or toes would I lose? My hands and feet were already numb. I'm sure that Norm and Randy were running similar scenarios and thinking comparable thoughts.

Norm pulled out a topographical map, and we all studied it.

"That knob just to our left is 11,800 feet. At the rate we're going, there's absolutely no way we make it to the wall in the next twenty or thirty minutes. It'll be pitch-black by the time we get there. We'd just never make it down that face in the dark."

Norm pointed to a saddle in a ridge about three miles to the west.

"We can cross this boulder field, climb up to that saddle, and drop down into Upper Horton Lakes. There's a hiking trail there somewhere that we can connect to. It'll loop us around to the base of Four Gables and then drop straight back to our base camp."

Randy and I studied the terrain and the map.

"Holy crap," said Randy. "That's nearly eight miles. We're not going to make it back to camp until after midnight."

"And that's if we don't run into a cliff on the other side of that ridge," added Norm. "It looks pretty steep on the map. If we do, we'll be stuck there until morning."

"Have you ever been that way?" I asked.

"No," replied Norm.

"I have—not to that ridge, but I've been fishing at Upper Horton Lakes. There's a small lake up high and a bigger lake below. The problem is that there's not really a shoreline to hike around because there are cliffs on both sides of each lake. We'll have to walk across the ice, which shouldn't be a problem. The trail picks up at the mouth of the big lake. It's a two- or three-mile hike back to our camp from there."

Everyone nodded and silently agreed with the plan.

"Get your flashlights out," Norm advised. "You're going to need them."

We began hopping from boulder to boulder, making our way slowly to the ridge in the distance. And then the darkness came, followed by the deep, gripping cold. We followed our flashlights, which seemed small and feeble against the enormity of a night so black. There was no moon, and the Milky Way glimmered sharply overhead. The absence of stars was the only way to tell where the sky ended and the mountaintops began. Behind us, Basin Mountain—that unassuming, flat-topped peak that stood in the shadow of the glamorous, photogenic Mount Tom—was poised to kill us.

We made it over the ridge at nine p.m. and began a steep descent into the Upper Horton Lakes basin. Danger lurked everywhere in the cold night. A simple slip, twisted ankle, or loose boulder would mean doom to our Plan B. A night on the mountain would then be a certainty.

But there were no cliffs on the other side of the ridge, just steep rugged terrain that took hours to descend in the dark. I hadn't been able to feel my feet since just before sunset, and my fingers now burned with pain from the cold. I ignored both and just focused on keeping moving.

We reached the small lake at eleven p.m. We were deep in a narrow alpine valley above the tree line. To the immediate west, a massive ridge rose two thousand feet straight up. It was invisible in the night, but it blotted out the stars, and we could sense its looming presence. I stepped onto the ice and it cracked and popped, the sound bouncing between granite walls and into the sterile, cold night.

"Wait," said Norm before I took another step.

He stomped his foot several times, and the ice sounded hollow.

"There's no water holding up the ice," said Norm, his suspicion confirmed. "I've seen this before. The surface here probably froze in September, but then because of the drought, most of the water in the lake drained out. It's hollow underneath and can collapse easily. If you fall, you'll either land on some rocks or in some water. You might die from the fall, or you might die from hypothermia."

Norm stomped his foot again on the ice.

"It's pretty thick. It should support one person at a time. But we're going to have to crawl across one at a time on our hands and knees to distribute our weight. Randy's the smallest. He should go first."

"No way," Randy protested. "You were the one reading the Bible for an hour. You go first."

Norm said nothing. He got down on his hands and knees and began shuffling forward. He turned back and said, "When I get about halfway across, the next guy should go. Keep everything spaced by about fifty yards."

The ice made loud, terrifying pops beneath me, and the dead silence of a mountain winter was shattered by noise that sounded like sporadic gunshots.

We made it across the first lake and hiked down to the much larger lake, which was probably three hundred yards across. It, too, had a layer of three-foot-thick ice suspended over a hollowed, mostly drained lake.

Norm led the way. The cracks beneath me were louder and more ominous. This lake was bigger than the first, which meant that if the ice were to give way, the fall would be farther, the water deeper, and the results deadlier.

I shuffled across the ice holding my flashlight ahead of me in my right hand. Norm was about two-thirds of the way across, I was just over halfway, and Randy was about twenty yards behind me. The only thought in my head was of the huge fire I was going to build as soon as we got back to camp.

A crack erupted in the ice from shore to shore and sounded like cannon fire. A *whump* of air reverberated over me, and a great roar echoed off the mountain walls. The back third of the lake had collapsed just behind Randy's feet. Several acres of ice with all its tonnage had collapsed fifteen feet into jagged, broken heaps atop boulders and water on the lake's drought-stricken floor.

Randy screamed and sprinted from out of the dark behind me. I got up and started running in a full sprint side by side with Randy.

Norm yelled, "Stop! Stop! Don't panic."

But it was too late. Randy and I weren't spending a second longer on the ice.

We sprinted to the lake's edge, where there were trees and a well-maintained hiking trail. Randy and I kept running. We jogged the final two miles with our flashlights to the base camp.

I struck a match, held it to the kindling, and watched the flame come alive. I encouraged it and stoked it and fed it piles of dead pine. By the time Norm had arrived, the flames were jumping eight feet high and sparks swirled toward the stars. The intense heat pushed the wall of cold back toward the dark. Across the frozen lake, high above the ridge, Basin Mountain stood unassuming but deadly beneath the Milky Way.

CHAPTER FORTY-TWO

The last big storm of the season slammed the Sierra. Winds howled, snow blew, and heavy, gray clouds descended almost to the Owens Valley floor, pulling the curtains shut on the high peaks where the storm raged through the day and into the night.

To the east, the bristlecones stood stout. The snow there fell cold and dry, blowing hard across the ridges and shrouding the ancient trees behind blinding sheets of white. Another winter was in its last throes. It was but one of five thousand and soon would come a new season.

Steve Wiswell was sullen. He'd been sitting at home all morning, drinking beer and watching news on cable TV as the wind rattled his windows and blew down his fence. Over the previous two days, the storm had dropped six inches of snow in his front yard and several feet in the mountains. But the clouds had begun to break, revealing an eager March sun.

Steve looked outside and could see the snow already melting on the road's blacktop.

Today, he thought, *would be a good day to rob a bank.*

He wrote a note to family and friends and left it on the kitchen table. He threw on a blue sweatshirt, a yellow ball cap, and sunglasses. He grabbed both his guns and boxes of ammo. He hopped in his pickup and raced down Highway 6. His truck was buffeted by winds that blew crossways over the road. It was clear overhead, but clouds clung stubbornly to the high ranges on the east and the west.

Steve turned right onto Highway 395 and drove slowly down the Main Street of Bishop. He pulled into the parking lot of Chase Bank, located only a few blocks from the high school.

He tugged the bill of his cap low, pushed his sunglasses tight, and strode through the doors. He walked up to a young, blonde teller, pulled up his sweatshirt, and showed her the Ruger Blackhawk .44. Her eyebrows lifted, and she silently reached back to open some drawers. She slid $2,300 in stacks of twenties and hundreds across the counter. Steve scooped the bills into a plastic shopping bag and calmly walked out the door. He drove slowly from the parking lot, turned right on Main Street, and casually drove north on 395.

He stopped at the Paiute Palace Casino less than two miles away, walked in, presented his Paiute Palace Players Card, and received $10 in free chips. He sat at a 21 table, a grocery bag full of cash beneath his stool, and played $100 a hand. With both his Ruger and Glock set snug in his waistband, he felt like Wild Bill Hickok the day he achieved immortality in a Deadwood saloon for getting shot while holding a poker hand of aces over eights.

He played cards for four hours and waited for the police to storm the casino with guns blazing. The dealer shuffled and dealt, shuffled and dealt, shuffled and dealt. Steve got drunk, bored, and disappointed. It appeared no shoot-out was forthcoming.

Steve shoved $300 in chips toward the dealer as a tip, picked up his grocery bag, and shuffled out of the casino. He hopped in his truck and drove lonely down Highway 6 to his home in Benton.

He set his guns on his dresser and dropped onto his bed, dejected that there had been no blaze of glory. He stared at the guns and contemplated the merits of each. Either could certainly do the job. The Ruger was louder and heavier and stronger. The Glock was light and efficient. But with the Ruger, he worried about dishonoring his grandfather, so he picked up the Glock.

Steve walked to the field behind his house. The skies had cleared, the sun had just set, and snow blew in pink wisps from the peaks of the Sierra. To the east, the White Mountains had faded in shadow, but the bristlecones on the high ridges were freshly crowned in white and now glowed purple in the gloaming.

Pop went the Glock in the twilight.

Steve staggered back, not dead, and stood stunned with blood running down his forehead. His knees wobbled, so he sat in the snow beneath some sage. The last rays of sun shone on the high, sharp point of Boundary Peak, its fresh snow the color of salmon. Steve slumped forward, blood oozed from his wound, and then the sun set fully.

CHAPTER FORTY-THREE

It was the best of times, it was the worst of times, it was the age of wisdom, it was the age of foolishness, it was the epoch of belief, it was the epoch of incredulity, it was the season of Light, it was the season of Darkness, it was the spring of hope, it was the winter of despair, we had everything before us, we had nothing before us, we were all going direct to Heaven, we were all going direct the other way—in short, the period was so far like the present period, that some of its noisiest authorities insisted on its being received, for good or for evil, in the superlative degree of comparison only.
—CHARLES DICKENS, *A TALE OF TWO CITIES*

On an exposed, windswept plateau, high above Mono Lake, there lived the Bad Man of Bodie. Unfortunately, for the residents of the gold-rush town in the Eastern High Sierra, he was but one of many, many bad men.

Gold was struck in Bodie in 1859 by one Wakeman S. Bodey, a respected Poughkeepsie, New York, merchant who'd kissed his wife and children good-bye in 1849 to seek his fortune by sailing past two continents, around Cape Horn, and back north to San Francisco. For a decade, he tramped the goldfields of California with nothing more to show for his efforts than several gold nuggets and a few small pouches of placer. He traversed the Sierra in hopes of finding better luck and untrammeled ground in the high country east of Yosemite.

In the late summer of 1859, he struck a large vein of gold on an exposed, treeless hilltop at an elevation of 8,379 feet. It was an unlikely place for a city of 10,000, which it eventually became when the gold boom peaked. Winter temperatures dropped to 35-below. Winds howled at up to a hundred miles per hour. Snow sometimes topped two hundred inches for the season. But people will put up with a lot for $1 billion of today's dollars in bullion.

Bodey was so ecstatic with his find that he decided against returning to Sonora on the mild western slope of the Sierra to wait out the winter. Instead, he set up camp next to his mining claim and trekked to Monoville, a nearby trading post, to purchase supplies that would carry him through until spring. On his way down the mountain, he was swallowed by a blizzard and not found until April.

In spite of Bodey's mishap, the prospectors came, and a town sprang up in the harshest of locations. To add insult to Bodey's injury, a sign painter misspelled his name, and no one bothered to change it.

After the prospectors came the mining companies, the saloons, the brothels, and the men with guns. In Bodie, a town with over sixty saloons, everyone was armed, and the law cowered.

Residents of Bodie never questioned anyone's right to carry a gun, either concealed or in the open. It was an inalienable right. Samuel Clemens, who later became known as Mark Twain, did some prospecting in Bodie before drifting to the nearby silver town of Aurora, where he took his first job as a writer for the *Esmeralda Star* newspaper. Of the Colt Navy Revolver he'd strapped to his waist, Clemens said, "I wore the thing in deference to popular sentiment, and in order that I might not, by its absence, be offensively conspicuous, and a subject of remark."

Contrary to what might be assumed, Bodie was not completely lawless. It was fully staffed with a sheriff and deputies. There was a courthouse with plenty of judges, prosecuting attorneys, and defense lawyers. And business was brisk. But in a milieu where everyone was armed and a person could make a claim of self-defense based on a mere scowl, a sideways look, a harsh word, or a drunken punch, convictions were hard to come by. The courts and the culture upheld the Old West code of "No duty to retreat." During Bodie's worst stretch of violence, there were over seventy shoot-outs in the small mining town. Over forty men were arrested for murder. All claimed self-defense. Only seven cases went to trial. Six resulted in acquittal. The single conviction was hung on a town drunk who had beaten a woman to death in public with his bare hands. He might have fared better had he used a gun.

A vigilante group composed of Civil War veterans sprang up with the ominous name of Bodie 601. No one is quite sure what the "601" stood for, but it was presumed to be "six feet under, zero trial, one rope." Oddly, vigilantism arose not due to the absence of a legal system but because of its presence. Since anyone with a gun could claim self-defense, there were cases of acquitted gunmen who'd shot victims for little reason, point-blank. In these particularly egregious cases, an impromptu gallows would be quickly erected during the night. The following morning, townsfolk would find the acquitted person hanging in the street with a calling card pinned to his shirt that read only BODIE 601.

CHAPTER FORTY-FOUR

The plateau upon which Bodie perched was ideal for hunting sage grouse. Ample grasses and meadows grew between clumps of sage, which were unusually stunted and didn't impede the springtime strutting of showy males.

But it was late October, and we hadn't come for sage grouse; we were out for trophy buck. My dad's GMC four-wheel-drive rumbled up the dirt road that cut through the sage and across the level hilltop. A plume of dust rose from behind but did not linger. It was caught by the wind that always blew here and swirled quickly to the east. In the distance, clusters of buildings slumped and sagged. The unpainted wood had taken on the complexion of the land, becoming weathered with streaks of silver, gray, and brown. Tailings were heaped high on the slope behind the abandoned town, a remembrance of when the earth had yielded riches. To the left, tombstones of marble and slate and wood did their best to hold back both time and the elements so they could respectfully tell of those who had bravely ventured to the end of the world only to die of disease or cold or cave-in or bullet. Few tombstones told the story of old age.

To the north of Bodie is Potato Peak, one of the least-imposing 10,000-foot mountains one is ever likely to encounter. Its slope rises gently behind Bodie and can be easily walked. The summit is steep for fewer than ten yards.

We followed a dirt road around its western flank and the country opened to wide benches of yellow aspen and narrow valleys of green meadows. We stopped below a high ridge whose spine ran for over a mile down to a meadow that was bisected by a creek. The ridgeline was bare except for a few boulders and bunches of bitterbrush, which was like catnip for deer.

We surveyed the scene and tried to think like a buck.

"If I were a deer," my dad said, "I'd spend my time in this glade, where there's plenty of shelter. I'd come up for this bitterbrush, which you can see has been eaten back, and I'd go down to that meadow for water and grazing."

I agreed. It was remarkable deer country.

"Let's do this," my dad suggested, revealing his plan. "I'll swing wide right of the aspen and then hike down about two miles to that meadow. You hike up to that big rock on the top of the ridge and wait. I'll come straight back up the hill through that aspen grove. If there are any deer there, they should get pushed out. They'll cross that ridge right in front of you. Just be sure to sit quiet and be patient."

I hiked fifty yards uphill, put the strap of my gun on my shoulder, and climbed up the back of the rock. It had a flat top about six feet across. On its front, there was a ledge where I could comfortably put my feet while I sat about six feet off the ground.

I settled in and figured that it would take my dad at least an hour to complete his circuitous hike. I was facing due north, and a steady breeze was blowing toward me. I was upwind, and any deer downrange would likely never detect my presence.

The high peaks of the Emigrant Wilderness, about twenty miles to the west, were already covered in snow. The big bucks typically liked to stay in the highest of the high country for as long as possible in order to avoid the hunters. But the autumn snow had driven them down this season, and that boded well for my prospects.

The hillsides were covered with swaths of yellow aspen, broken only by green stands of pine and brown ridges of sage. Several thousand feet below tumbled the East Walker River, named after Tennessee mountain man Joseph Rutherford Walker, who came this way in the early 1830s. Having set out from Fort Hall, just outside Pocatello, he established the California Trail by blazing across Nevada along the Humboldt, crossing the Sierra and reaching San Francisco from an overland direction. He returned via a more southerly route over a high pass that bears his name. He then dropped into the mountain valley below me. Along the way, he became the first white man to lay eyes on Yosemite.

The breeze whispered. All else was silent. My gun, a .30-06 with a deep-brown walnut stock and a telescopic lens, lay crossways on my lap. I watched and waited, watched and waited, watched and waited.

CHAPTER FORTY-FIVE

Thomas Treloar had fallen 225 feet down a mineshaft in the Comstock and lived. He came to Bodie with a slightly damaged brain, and his writing had deteriorated to a scrawl. But he was from Sithney in Cornwall, on the southwestern tip of England, where they had mines as large as any in the world. Young Cornish immigrants were prized throughout the West for their know-how, work ethic, and fearless ways beneath the ground. Treloar was thrifty, owned a house, and was well-off. He knew that he was stalked by death in Bodie and had purchased a $1,000 life insurance policy for that eventuality. He worked for the Standard Mining Co. deep in the Fortuna Lode.

Johanna Lonahan was from Chicago. As a young woman, she found romantic prospects in the Midwest lacking. She boarded a train in 1878 for San Francisco. There she heard stories of fabulous wealth east of the Sierra, where miners were rich and women were sparse. She and a female friend boarded a stage for the fifty-hour trip to the rugged outpost of Bodie. Their hope was to strike gold indirectly through betrothal with well-to-do bachelor miners.

Joseph DeRoche was a Canadian carpenter from the French-speaking provinces of the East. He found work in Bodie hewing timbers for the mines and hastily assembling hotels and houses, saloons and stables. He'd known the Lonahans of Chicago and had called on Miss Johanna in the years before they'd both come west. In fact, it was DeRoche who'd first written Johanna about Bodie and who'd sent her the stagecoach fare to come visit. They were on-again, off-again lovers. But DeRoche was a spendthrift and a bit of a cad; Johanna was wary.

Instead, the dependable Treloar caught her attention, and in spite of his dim wit, she agreed to marry him.

Patrick Reddy was a big Irish miner, stocky, strong, and full of bluster. In 1864 in a saloon in Virginia City, he took exception to comments made by a small man with a dull mind. Reddy stood, encircled by fellow drinkers of whiskey, and thundered eloquently about the muddled thoughts of his diminutive acquaintance. Men laughed and raised a toast to their brash Irish friend. Reddy smiled and held his shot glass high. The small man drew his Colt Army .44 and blasted Reddy in the arm, just below the bicep.

His humerus shattered and his arm amputated, Reddy had been rendered useless as a miner. He spent days assessing his new lot in life and concluded that there would be little disadvantage in practicing the law with one arm. In the mining towns, there was always plenty of trouble, and arguing never ceased. Men argued over horses. Men argued over women. They argued about land, about claims, about gold. They argued about honor and cards and killing. And anything that couldn't be settled with fists or knives or guns usually fell to the attorneys and judges and courts. It was good to be a lawyer in the Old West, and Reddy made himself into one of the best. He read stacks of books, worked as clerk of the court, and was admitted to the State Bar of California. He first practiced in San Francisco and then Mariposa, before becoming perhaps the most important man to know in Bodie.

He cut an imposing figure in the courtroom, with his booming voice and pinned-up sleeve. And in spite of his unfortunate brush with a gun, he defended vigorously its use on the frontier. He was a friend of the gunman, cleverly crafting courtroom defenses and cutting state prosecutors to ribbons with eloquent speeches about liberty, freedom, honor, self-defense, and "No duty to retreat." No slight was too small nor alibi too flimsy upon which Reddy would gladly build for his client a bedrock of logic, a fortress of fact, and an unbreachable moat of legal theory. No gunman was ever prosecuted on Reddy's watch, and they paid handsomely for the privilege. Some paid more often than once. There was no better place in all the world to practice such an art than in Bodie.

CHAPTER FORTY-SIX

The breeze still whispered, the aspen still shimmered, and nothing had yet stirred along the open ridge.

I picked up the gun, pressed the butt to my right shoulder, lowered my cheek against the stock, and scanned with my scope for any movement. Large, sharp images jiggled and danced into view. I moved the scope slowly along the tree line and could see nothing of interest. I placed the gun back across my lap, and my eye was drawn to motion below and to my right. A pair of fawns moved silently from the glade of aspen. They meandered toward me, nibbling at bitterbrush as they approached. I breathed slow and quiet. I resisted the urge to rub an itch on my nose. The fawns had been born in the spring. They were still reddish, but their white spots had all but vanished. They walked side by side and periodically would rub their long necks together. When one fawn stopped to nibble a tender shoot, the other would immediately investigate, pushing its sibling away by swinging its neck like a crane. The fawns stopped just beneath me. If I had been a mountain lion, lunch would've been guaranteed. I remained silent and motionless. I knew that the fawns wouldn't be alone and would likely be trailed by a doe or even a big buck. If they spotted me, though, they'd leap with a start, flash their white tails, and alert the others in their herd.

A dun-colored doe slipped silently from the trees and caught up with her offspring. While the young deer seemed oblivious to their surroundings, the doe was not. Her long ears continuously perked and turned, listening for any out-of-place sound. Her head perpetually swiveled and darted—her big, dark eyes looking for motion and her nose sniffing for danger. She instinctively did not like the path the fawns had followed.

I strained to breathe shallowly and to blink my eyes slowly. The tip of the doe's ear flicked back and forth just below my boot. She lowered her head, dropped down into the aspen on the other side of the ridge, and the fawns followed closely along either flank. Within a month, the doe would go into estrus and take a mate. The fawns would then be on their own, their mother no longer available to nudge them along should they linger beneath a dangerous ledge.

A buck emerged from the trees about twenty yards downhill from where the fawns had crossed. I counted two points on the left and three on the right. He was still young, likely eager to mate, and thus following the doe. However, his prospects were limited due to his youth and small antlers. When the rut began in late November, he would surely be driven away by older bucks with much larger and more dangerous racks.

I slowly and gently lifted my gun to my shoulder and propped my left elbow on my knee. The buck's head didn't dart and turn like the doe's. It carried the weight of antlers and swung with a purpose. He raised his head and flared his nostrils. He'd perhaps caught my scent, or maybe that of my dad. I stopped breathing and didn't blink. The buck lowered his head and grazed on some bitterbrush. I slowly placed my cheek on the gun's stock, closed my left eye, and found the buck in my scope. I raised the crosshairs to just behind its shoulder blade. The scope jiggled at first and then steadied. I exhaled slowly and calmly held the crosshairs in place. I then lifted my head so I could watch the buck without the scope. He continued on his way, free to pursue the doe in hopes of perpetuating his genes. Though it would've been a very easy shot, we were hunting in an area in which bucks were to be three points or more before they could be taken. This young male was saved by a single point on his left antler.

CHAPTER FORTY-SEVEN

A full winter moon hung high overhead and snow-covered Potato Peak glowed a bluish-white beneath a black sky. Thomas Treloar stomped down Lowe Street, crunching through snow and muttering in his deep Cornish brogue. The clear air was frigid, and the steady wind was biting. His ears were numb, and his nose was red, but his lips kept moving in anger.

He burst through the doors of the Mono Dancehall and glowered at the crowd in anger. His Smith & Wesson Schofield Revolver was strapped to his hip and at the ready. The piano music was loud as he picked out his wife, spinning with glee in the arms of her on-again Canadian lover.

Treloar pushed through the crowd, grabbed his wife's fair arm with his thick miner hand, and pulled her along behind him. DeRoche followed. Treloar turned and glared, stroking the handle of his gun. The crowd parted, and DeRoche put up his hands and stepped backward. Treloar spun, dragged his wife outside, and stomped back down the middle of Lowe Street. His wife pulled away, said she was cold, and walked with a friend a block behind her husband.

Treloar stomped onward, snow crunching loudly beneath his boots. He reached the intersection of Lowe and Main Streets. The streets were deserted, the moon shone bright, and the thermometer read 20-below.

Treloar paused to wait for his wife and heard a click behind his left ear. DeRoche had cocked his British Bull Dog pocket revolver. He squeezed the trigger, and the shot echoed both ways up Lowe and Main. The .44 caliber slug pierced the Cornishman's skull, flattened as it traveled through his cranium, and shattered his right, front forehead, leaving an exit wound almost the size of a fist.

Treloar dropped to his knees, fell to his face, and bled in a large, dark pool on the moonlit snow.

Even in Bodie, there were limits to when and how to kill. And it seems that DeRoche had exceeded those bounds by committing a number of faux pas.

Shooting an unsuspecting man from behind was considered an act of cowardice.

Shooting a person in the middle of Main Street was an egregious display of violence. Shooters should have the good sense to keep gunplay confined to saloons or back streets.

Carrying on in public with a married woman and then shooting her husband when confronted was bad form.

Shooting a handicapped or mentally impaired man was frowned upon, especially when that man was well known and well liked.

Yet DeRoche still might have wriggled his way free from the debacle had he not committed one final cardinal sin: He had killed a Cornishman. And that was something from which he might not escape without some airtight logic.

Over a third of all miners in the Comstock and the Eastern Sierra were from Cornwall. Known as Cousin Jacks, they were clannish, highly skilled, and ran most of the big mines. Pick a fight with one Cornishman, and you may as well pick a fight with them all.

A posse found DeRoche a few days later holed up at a nearby sawmill owned by a fellow French-Canadian. They dragged him back to Bodie and court immediately convened. DeRoche claimed that it was Treloar who had drawn first, and that when DeRoche had grabbed his arm to stop the assault, Treloar accidentally shot himself. Such fables of self-defense, no matter how thinly constructed, usually worked in Bodie. And with the great Patrick Reddy by your side, it was impossible to be con-victed for a shooting offense. DeRoche asked for the big Irishman but was told he'd have to choose different counsel. Reddy had agreed for the first time to work for the prosecution in a shooting case. In a preemptive strike, the Cornish miners had likely pooled their resources and turned the Irish barrister against DeRoche.

"Hang me now, hang me now," DeRoche declared with woe.

And so they did. The Bodie 601—composed of town fathers and leading merchants—couldn't wait for the wheels of justice to turn. Nor, it seems, could they bear to risk an acquittal based upon self-defense. Of course, Reddy made an impassioned plea for patience; lynching was bad for his business.

Before the trial could begin its second day, the Bodie 601 met during the night. At the intersection of Lowe and Main, workmen placed a large wooden tripod typically used for hoisting wagons up for repair. They hung from it two nooses—one for DeRoche, and one for Johanna. They reviewed the particulars of the incident and voted that DeRoche should indeed be hanged. They passed a ballot on the fate of Treloar's wife. Her neck was saved by one vote. They put her on the next stage to Virginia City instead.

DeRoche was marched up Bonanza Street in chains, prodded onward by men with pistols and shotguns. He wore a calico shirt and light-colored pants. The moon shone and lit the way toward death. The crowd reached the intersection of Lowe and Main. DeRoche was marched up a platform, and his head was placed in a noose. Clouds gathered and the moon grew dim. A light snow began to fall. DeRoche was asked if he had any final words.

He replied: "I have nothing to say, only, 'Oh, God.'"

The platform dropped from beneath him. His neck snapped with a jerk. His body danced above the street, snow dusting his calico shirt.

A man on a horse pinned a note to the deceased's shirt that read ALL OTHERS TAKE WARNING. LET NO ONE CUT HIM DOWN. BODIE 601.

CHAPTER FORTY-EIGHT

Small clouds spilled over the Sierra Crest and whisked across the sky. They cast shadows that raced over hillsides in patches. It had been fifteen minutes since the deer had passed. I watched a cloud blot the sun and darken the ridge. Moments later, the light returned, and the aspen along the tree line shone bright.

A glint caught my eye. I looked downhill and stared at a spot beneath a mountain mahogany, which grew about eight feet high. I focused intently, and amid the branches, the glint flashed again. And then like an illusion that had just been revealed, it appeared. I could see the form clearly where only moments before there'd been nothing. It was like he'd been conjured out of thin air. He was the biggest buck I'd ever seen, sitting regally and without care in the shadows of a gnarled tree. His color matched perfectly the tone of the sage and mahogany. His huge antlers blended with the branches, and it was impossible to tell where the tree ended and he began. Millions of years of evolution had perfected his ability to hide in plain sight.

My heart pounded, my respiration quickened, and my hand trembled. I tried to calm myself, but I began to shake harder. I slowly pulled back the bolt on my gun, careful not to make a jarring click or metallic clank. A fat, brass-cased bullet rolled into the chamber. I pushed the bolt forward and locked it into position. My index finger clicked a metal pin to the left, releasing the gun's safety. As slowly as I possibly could, I lifted the gun to my shoulder, pressing my cheek to the stock and closing my left eye. The magnified view in the scope wobbled wildly. The buck was well over two hundred pounds and had at least six points. My heart pounded and caused the view in my scope to jerk with every beat.

I estimated his distance at 250 yards. It was certainly possible to get a clean shot from that far, but it would take considerable skill, and the way I was shaking, I had little confidence in my ability.

The buck was old and smart. He knew it was hunting season and made sure to bed down during the day when hunters roamed. He moved around only at dusk, dawn, or in the night. He let the small bucks meander after does and knew that when the rut came, he would run them off—if they hadn't already been shot—and have his pick of the herd. He'd been sitting patiently beneath the mahogany for the entire time I'd been on the rock, perhaps aware that I was there but confident enough in his own stealth that he didn't think of me as a threat at such a distance.

I convinced myself I needed to get closer in order to take a reasonable shot. I slowly crawled to the back of the rock, careful not to give myself away through the loud scuff of a boot or the clink of metal. I climbed to the ground, and in a low crouch, worked my way carefully down the ridge by slowly and silently ducking from sagebrush to sagebrush. After about a hundred yards, I lifted my gun over a two-foot-high boulder, raised my head, and found the buck in my scope. He seemed relaxed and unwary. I put the crosshairs on him and rested the gun's barrel on the rock. I managed to keep my breathing steady but had begun to perspire. Beads of sweat rolled down my forehead and into my eyes. I looked down the hill and saw another boulder about fifty yards down the ridge. I convinced myself that if I could make it there undetected, the shot would be a sure thing. I became greedy.

I got on my hands and knees and crawled slowly through the brush. For the final twenty-five yards, I got on my belly and army-crawled, using my elbows and splayed knees. I could see the buck easily now without a scope. Just as I reached the boulder, he swung his head up and froze. I held my breath. Perhaps he'd heard me. I waited two minutes, barely breathing and hardly moving. The buck relaxed. He lay on his side with legs tucked beneath him, his thick, powerful neck easily holding his antlers high. I slowly lifted my gun above the rock and laid it level. I raised my head, looked down the scope, and placed my right index finger on the outside of the trigger guard. I didn't have a clear shot at his heart, so I settled the crosshairs on his right, front shoulder. I slowly moved my finger from outside of the trigger guard and lightly touched it to the trigger. My heart pounded. With each beat, I could see the crosshairs jiggle from left to right. I exhaled. The big buck jumped to his feet, startled. I looked up from behind the scope to see what had happened. Perhaps he'd smelled me. Perhaps he'd had a vague sense of danger and was just nervous. His ears twitched. He stood still and broadside.

I found him again in the scope and lowered the crosshairs to just behind his right shoulder. It was an opportunity for the shot of a lifetime. I had been overthinking things and taking too much time. In nature, a killer must be swift, silent, and decisive. Now was the time to act. This chance might never come again.

I moved my finger to the trigger. I exhaled.

The big buck sprang out of view. Shocked, I tried to follow him, but it is nearly impossible to hit a moving target at a distance with a scope. The deer had bounded fifteen feet in a single jump from a standing start. He landed at the edge of the aspen and then leaped high into the air again. He disappeared into the trees, sounding like a boulder that had gone bouncing and crashing down the side of the mountain. Every two seconds I could hear the loud rhythm of him landing and leaping. The sound carried sharply up the ridge and echoed through the hills. He bounded for at least a mile until the sound became faint and there was nothing but the breeze.

I sat stunned, with a pit in my stomach and my eyes blank with despair. I knew instantly that if I hunted for all of my remaining years, I would not likely ever again be a hundred yards from such a buck, with my scope on its heart and my finger on the trigger.

My dad emerged from the aspen grove. I raised my barrel to the sky, flicked on the safety, and walked with shaky knees to meet him.

"Holy crap," he exclaimed. "Did you see that? Jesus, he was huge. I barely saw him through the trees; he was going about forty miles an hour. Where'd he come from? Weren't you able to get a shot off?"

I didn't want to admit that I'd blown the game-winning layup.

"Yeah, I saw him. He was on the ridge the whole time under that mahogany. I didn't have a clear shot, though, and had to crawl to another rock for a better position. He got startled and then bolted. He was a six-point."

"Damn," my dad said, looking in the direction of where the deer had escaped, "that would've been a heck of a trophy."

I looked to the ground, dejected.

He put his hand on my shoulder and said reassuringly, "Hey, it's not a big deal. Don't worry—you'll get another chance."

We both knew that likely wasn't true.

And it wasn't. That was my last deer hunt with my dad—the final time I traipsed through the sage, clambered up rugged ridges, walked through the aspen, looked at the bitterbrush, and tried to think like a buck.

I moved to San Diego the following September to attend college and left my guns at home. I haven't been deer hunting since.

But I often think of that day when the clouds scudded overhead, the breeze blew in my face, and the great buck stood in perfect silhouette before me. And I'd like to say that, looking back, I'm glad that the buck was able to bound through the aspen, live another season, battle challengers with his trophy antlers, mate with his hard-won harem of does, and preserve his genetic majesty for all time.

But I'd be lying. The sting of that moment never leaves. Most of me is still a hunter. And in those quiet moments when I get a chance to replay the events in my mind, I am always silent and swift, steady and certain. I calmly place the crosshairs behind the buck's shoulder. I exhale slowly and squeeze the trigger steadily. The buck flinches, drops to his belly, and lets his heavy-antlered head fall to the side. The loud *crack* rockets down the hillside, rolls over the aspen like thunder, and fades into the valley first found all those years ago by Joseph Rutherford Walker. The clouds scud overhead, the breeze blows in my face, and the gun is light in my hands.

CHAPTER FORTY-NINE

I fell in love with Robin Wentworth on a warm July evening in Bishop.

In all my years before or since, I have never fallen harder. I have never fallen farther. I have never fallen so completely. That is how it often is with first loves. Especially when they bloom suddenly, unexpectedly, on a warm summer night—a night in which juvenile tedium lay behind and the intoxicating possibilities of the adult world stretch endlessly ahead.

The day had been hot. A pale sun beat down on the valley floor, its rays reflecting off the bone-colored alluvial sand and decomposed granite. The air had begun to bake dry by mid-morning, smelling of dust, sage, and heated rock. By afternoon a silver sheen shimmered above the ground in the distance as the heat intensified. Thermals of air spun and twisted sky-ward, and all across the valley, a half-dozen dust devils danced. But as the hour grew late, Mount Tom cast its long shadow, the fearsome sun sank behind the jagged peaks of the Sierra, and the night was welcomed with relief. The sky grew dark, a band of stars glimmered bright overhead, and as the evening continued, a river of cool air sank from the mountaintops and settled among the willows, cottonwoods, and alfalfa fields. For a seventeen-year-old who'd just graduated high school and would be leaving to attend college within four weeks, the night buzzed with excitement and promise.

Robin leaned against the counter of the Fosters Freeze, a local burger joint, and took my order. After, I turned to join a group of friends.

"Craig," she called out as I walked away.

I stopped and looked back. Her eyes twinkled, her smile flashed, and her brown hair shone beneath a spotlight. She was fresh, beautiful, and smart. I was surprised she knew my name, let alone that she would take the time to both address me and smile at me. She was one of the most popular and renowned girls at our school. She was a prom princess and a champion skier. I'd only had one class with her in four years at Bishop High, and I doubt she even knew I'd been in the room. At school, she hung out with a couple of cheerleaders and was often gone for days at a time, traveling the country for ski races. She was a member of the US Junior National Ski Team and had just returned to Bishop after four weeks of downhill race training in the Chilean Andes, where it was winter. Her boyfriend the previous year had been Mike Elliot, a tall, handsome athlete who'd been drafted right out of high school by the Cleveland Indians.

"I really liked your graduation speech. I thought it was beautifully eloquent. My dad thought it profound. My mom asked, 'Robin, who is that boy?' They couldn't stop talking about it."

I was frozen. Half coming, half going—unsure of what to do next.

I could only nod.

She smiled, nodded back, and pirouetted to take the order slip to the cook.

A short time later, my number was called, and I returned to pick up my meal. Robin was waiting, smiling, holding a plain white bag containing a hamburger and fries.

"I hear you're going to San Diego State," she said.

I nodded again, still unsure of what to say to a girl I knew about but didn't actually know in the slightest.

"I'm going to Western State University. That's in Gunnison, Colorado. I'm going there to ski. Too bad we'll be so far apart."

I nodded some more and grabbed the bag. She held onto it tight, refusing to release it to me, determined to have a conversation.

"Aren't you going to miss the mountains? I love the mountains. I couldn't imagine ever living away from them."

I nodded yet again, looked into her eyes, and my heart fluttered. The world fell away, and there was only us.

"Yes. I'll miss them."

She smiled, almost mischievously, looking like a girl—almost a woman—who was used to getting what she wanted.

We both held the folded top of the bag, studying each other intently, smiling. My knees wobbled, a warmth radiated through my chest, and my face grew flushed. Her beauty was breathtaking to me, and I thought I could see affection behind the twinkle in her eyes.

It was only a moment—the most fleeting of encounters, as seemingly delicate and ephemeral as the summer night's breeze that blew cool across the valley, perfumed with only the slightest hint of sweet alfalfa that had been freshly mown that afternoon in a faraway field. And yet it was eternal. I would never forget. I would remember and replay it for all my years.

Robin released her hold on the bag. I backed away slowly and turned to join my friends. I sat at an outdoor table, reached in the bag to grab my hamburger, but instead felt a piece of folded paper. My friends talked about a keg party out at the river that they'd heard about. It was supposed to start around ten. I carefully unfolded the paper beneath the tabletop as my friends continued to talk. I could immediately see the neat, looping handwriting of a girl, written with a red pen: *I need a ride home. I get off at 9:30. Love, Robin.*

I slowly folded the note closed. I could hear my friends chattering, but to me it was distant background noise. I breathed deep and steady through my nose. My heart pounded. I thought about Robin's eyes, smile, and straight, bouncy hair. I then knew why she'd held the bag for that extra moment. She had a plan. I had none. I was at least two moves behind on the chessboard. My mind raced. I searched for meaning. I held the note beneath the table, carefully unfolded it again, studied the penmanship, admired the graceful curves, and stared at the word *Love*.

Okay, maybe I was three moves behind.

"Collins," barked Steve Peters, my track teammate and the school's star miler. "Let's hit it. Party at the Crow's Nest. Shit, you haven't even eaten yet. What? Are you saving that for later? 'Cause I'll help you with those fries right now, if you want."

I slid the entire bag over to him.

"Uh, I'm not that hungry. I need to head home. I've got to get some sleep. I've been out late every night this week, and six a.m. comes awfully early."

I didn't dare tell them about the note from Robin. That would incite near pandemonium, not to mention a number of playfully obnoxious comments to Robin and anyone else who might be listening.

"Oh, you big pussy," said Randy Smith. "C'mon. When have you ever worried about getting enough sleep? You can do that later. It's not our fault you work at a golf course."

"Nah," I said. "These guys can go with you in your truck. Have a beer for me."

"Oh, we will," said Steve. "Thanks for the burger."

—◦—

I sat in the empty parking lot behind the Fosters Freeze in my powder-blue Datsun 510, a zippy four-door sedan I'd purchased three months earlier for $500, used. A wall of cottonwoods, which lined Bishop Creek, towered in front of me, their leaves rustling a greenish black, catching only glints of light from the streetlights and passing cars on Main Street, fifty yards away. All four windows were rolled down. I had no air-conditioning. On my cassette player, I kept playing, rewinding, and playing again the Patti Smith song, "Because the Night." I'd been waiting for Robin for over half an hour, and I'd replayed it about eight times. I couldn't stop thinking of her. Every few minutes, I would unfold the square piece of paper, tilt it toward the faint light emanating from a distant streetlamp, and study each letter and curve for clues. The music seemed deep and profound for the moment. I hung on every word. In my mind, the lyrics, written by Bruce Springsteen, had seemingly been fine-tuned just for me, and just for this occasion.

"Because the night belongs to lovers . . ."

Indeed.

The back door to the Fosters Freeze swung open at 9:38. Robin ran across the parking lot toward my car, bouncing happy with every step. She'd changed into a pair of jeans, a white T-shirt, and white canvas sneakers. She held her folded Fosters Freeze uniform—a blue-and-white-striped dress with a name tag—in her right hand. At the last second, it occurred to me that I should be a gentleman and open the car door for her. I jumped out and began to stand, but she arrived quickly, flung the passenger door open, plopped down on the bucket seat, and tossed her uniform in the back. She leaned toward me, placed her hand gently on my forearm, and smiled.

"Thanks for waiting. I had to change," she explained loudly over the deep bass of the music. She reached toward the cassette player, unimpressed at my music selection, and turned down the volume.

"Here, I brought this," she said, holding up a cassette of the new Rolling Stones album, *Miss You*. She ejected the Patti Smith tape, handed it to me dismissively with her left hand, and clicked in the Rolling Stones with her right. She turned the volume back up, and the car was filled with the thrumming of a disco-blues beat.

"That's better," she smiled, resting her hand gently on my shoulder. "I love the Rolling Stones. Let's go."

I pulled up to Main Street and put on my left blinker.

"No, turn right," she pointed.

"Don't you live up Line Street, near me?"

I'd been friends with a couple of guys who'd hung out with her older brother and had been to her house previously a handful of times—not that she'd have ever noticed.

"Just turn right," she assured me.

I flipped my turn-signal lever in the opposite direction and pulled slowly into traffic. Most of the people on the road this time of night were just passing through. Bishop's Main Street was actually Highway 395, which used to run from the Mexican border near San Diego all the way up to Canada on the eastern Washington border. That was before Interstate 15 cut off the southernmost portion of the route in the high desert just east of Los Angeles. Highway 395 ran parallel and about 150 miles inland from Interstate 5, which connected the great metropolises of the West Coast—Seattle, Portland, Sacramento, Los Angeles, and San Diego.

But where I-5 was glitz and glamour, with travelers who were all going somewhere fast, 395 was rural, lonely, and a world apart. Bishop was the only city of consequence between LA and Reno. There was a twenty-five-mile-per-hour speed limit through town, as well as only two stoplights—each placed strategically on the city's north and south entrances. The big semi trucks would slow after a fast haul across the deserts to the south or the long downhill mountain grade to the north. Their air brakes would blare and their gears would grumble loudly with each downshift as they approached the city limits. RVs would pull into gas stations to refuel—families tumbling out, stretching, and then racing to be first to the restrooms. Passenger cars going north would typically pull into Fosters Freeze for a quick meal on the go. Cars going south would pull into Schat's Bakery, a local institution favored by Angelenos, who couldn't get enough of the fresh-baked squaw bread and made a point of purchasing a half-dozen loaves at a time to bring home.

And, of course, there was always a parade of outdoorsmen in campers and pickup trucks. They would stop in the morning for coffee and breakfast at Jack's Waffle Shop before making a sojourn to Brock's Sporting Goods to stock up on fishing supplies and to get tips from the owner, Jim Brock, who made it a point to know every stream, lake, river, and any other body of water in the Eastern Sierra. When it came to information on where the fish were biting, no one had better data than Mr. Brock, who spent all day, every day, talking to fishermen who were both coming and going.

We picked up speed as Main Street jogged west through the Paiute Indian Reservation, with its cold-water streams and open meadows, which passed by our side windows, cool and dark in the night. When William Mulholland, the powerful head of the LA water agency, sent his henchmen north in 1905 to pose as ranchers and farmers who would buy over 85 percent of all private land in the Owens Valley, and the accompanying water rights, Angelenos were unable to get their hands on Indian land. And so, the Paiute Reservation just north of Bishop is lush with free-flowing water, while the rest of the valley is mostly dry and sage-covered.

Robin and I each held a hand out the window and could feel alternating waves of cool and warm air pass by. Mick Jagger wailed in a false country twang about the girl with the faraway eyes while the summer night rushed through the open windows, its low roar competing with Ron Wood's pedal steel guitar and Keith Richard's backup vocals. Street signs leading into the reservation glowed a reflective white in the headlights and had names like See-Vee, Tu-Su, and Pa-Ha.

I shifted gears and accelerated as we exited the city limits. The night air roared, and the Stones were muffled. Robin and I rolled up the windows and the Stones burst back to life. The countryside grew impossibly dark as we headed north up Sherwin Grade, which led over a mountain pass and into the high country of the Eastern Sierra. There was no moon, and clouds of stars shone white against an ever-darkening sky.

I turned to Robin to check if this was still where she wanted to take us. She smiled, picked my hand up off the stick shift, and held it tight atop her leg. I pressed my foot steady on the gas pedal. The Datsun strained as it climbed the steep grade, its engine whining to maintain sixty-five miles per hour. I had no idea where we were headed. I only knew that it was late, we were alone, and the car was hurtling into the black. But I was certain that if Robin had asked me to keep driving up 395—through Bridgeport, Carson City, Alturas, Pendleton, Spokane, and on into Canada—I would have. I'd have just held her hand, kept my foot down, and taken the car as far as it would go.

Only two days earlier, my father had taken me to dinner at Whiskey Creek, a restaurant that passed as the fanciest in Bishop. We ordered prime rib. We talked of college, he told me I should get a part-time job, and we reviewed names and phone numbers of his friends I could call if I ever got into serious trouble. He had taken a promotion with the Department of the Interior and was moving for two years to Washington, DC, 2,500 miles away. When we were done with dinner, we stepped outside and stood next to his car. There were no tears. He didn't cry. Neither did I. He only shook my right hand and clasped my shoulder tight with his left. He gave me a strong handshake—a grown-man's handshake—and I gave him a strong handshake back. He told me that he was proud, and that if I worked hard, good things would come to me. He hopped into his car, turned onto Main Street, and drove north on 395. I watched his taillights as long as I could until I lost them in traffic.

I was to stay in Bishop with some family friends until school started in San Diego in late August. I had a room in the back of a large house and could come and go as I pleased. For the first time in my life I felt free and grown-up. I could make decisions without being questioned or second-guessed. I had no curfews or restrictions. If I wanted to hop in my car and drive north into the mountains on a dark, moonless night with a beautiful girl, for the first time, there was nothing to stop me.

We'd gone about thirty-five miles. The air was cool and smelled of pine. A road sign appeared for an exit to Hot Creek.

"Turn right, here," Robin said.

I exited the highway onto a dirt road that wended through the sage. The Datsun rattled and bounced as I tried to carefully navigate away from any large rocks or deep ruts. Behind us, dust billowed red from the glow of the taillights. Ahead, light washed over the sage, painting them a ghostly white. On either side, there was nothing but dark. Robin turned off the music so I could concentrate as we drove eerily forward. To the left, we came to a dirt parking area occupied by half a dozen cars.

"Have you ever been to Hot Creek?" Robin asked cheerfully, her secret plan revealed.

"Sure, lots of times."

"Really?" she asked, disappointed. "When?"

"With my dad, fly-fishing. This is one of the best trout streams in North America."

"No," she laughed, relieved. "Have you ever been swimming here in the hot pools?"

"Swimming? No. Have you?"

"Of course. Lots, after skiing at Mammoth. It's great to come here when there's snow. Everyone tries to keep this place a secret. It's supposed to be locals only. No flatlanders allowed. Remember that."

"I certainly will."

We were parked on a bluff about twenty feet above the creek. Columns of steam billowed white in my headlights before vanishing into the night. I turned off the engine, cut my lights, and Robin and I stepped into an inky black. It was the kind of darkness that people who live in cities have forgotten. I couldn't see my feet.

Robin held my hand, and we shuffled and felt our way down a path that led to the creek's edge. The broad stream burbled, and we could hear the sound of an occasional voice floating out of the dark and across the water.

"I didn't bring a swimsuit," I observed in an almost-whisper.

Robin laughed low.

"You're not supposed to bring a swimsuit to a hot pool," she said. "I was at ski races in Norway and Sweden. I don't think those people know what swimsuits are."

"Okay," I answered, willing to give it a try.

I gently kicked off my shoes and slowly pulled my shirt over my head. I stared down at my jeans, which I could barely see. I pulled the buttons open and began to slip them off. I heard a splash as Robin stepped into the creek. She'd disappeared into the dark, but I could hear her swishing through the water as she waded to the far side. I finished undressing, leaving my clothes in a pile, and shuffled gently, barefoot, to the creek's bank. The smooth, black water undulated beneath me. I stepped in slowly, keeping a hand on the bank. The water was icy and came to my waist. I leaned into the current and began wading.

"Over here," Robin said in a loud whisper. "I found a spot."

I kept wading in the direction of her voice until I could feel pulses of warm water mixing with the cold. A hand grabbed mine and pulled. The water was nearly up to my chest. I bent my knees, lowered my chin to the surface, and glided toward the pulling hand. Plumes of hot water welled up from the creek bed, steam rose, and the air smelled faintly of sulfur.

Robin grabbed both my hands, and we faced each other in the dark.

"Hold your breath and go underwater with me," Robin said.

I closed my eyes, and together we sank beneath the surface.

I could hear clacking from the pebbles on the creek bed that jittered beneath my feet. I could hear the deep rumble of a geothermal spring. My body shook from the confluence of water and a vibrating earth.

We rose to the surface, our hair stuck flat and wet to our heads. I blinked water from my eyes but didn't dare let go of Robin's hands. We used the balls of our feet to bounce buoyantly in unison in the water.

"So, Craig Collins," Robin asked. "How come you never asked me out?"

"Me?" I was taken aback. I fumbled to formulate an answer. "I didn't know you wanted to be asked out," I offered as a defense.

"You boys are so dumb," she chided. "I came to one of your track meets. You won. You looked amazing."

"I didn't win," I corrected. "Steve Peters won. He always wins. He's one of the fastest milers in the state. I came in second. I always come in second."

"Well, maybe I didn't go to watch Steve Peters. I just saw that you were way ahead of everyone else. After the meet, my girlfriends and I hung around so we could talk to a group of you runners, but every time I said something to you, you just looked past me and made stupid jokes with your buddies. And then I kept trying to get your attention at graduation, and you just mostly ignored me. And every time you came to Fosters Freeze, I made a point of personally taking your order and being extra nice."

I was stunned and felt guilty for committing a litany of crimes, none of which I was remotely aware.

"So now summer is almost over," she complained, "and we have only a month before we have to go off to school. You should've asked me out sooner."

"Well," I said, squeezing her hands reassuringly, "a month can be a long time. Hemingway said you can sometimes live a whole life in a single day."

Robin bobbed in the water, thought for a moment, and smiled at that notion.

"What else did Hemingway say?"

I laughed. "He said a lot of things, like, maybe, 'If you're going to run in Pamplona, don't worry about the bulls, just be sure you're faster than the other guy.'"

We bobbed in silence.

Robin gazed at the sky. "Wow. Look at the stars. I've never seen them this bright."

I looked up and studied them. The Milky Way draped itself across the darkness in a cool, white, blazing band that stretched from the nearly invisible Sierra Crest to the White Mountains far to the east.

"That's because we're at a high altitude, the air is dry, we're far from any city lights, and it's cloudless and moonless. This is how the sky always was for our ancestors. That W-shaped cluster over there is Cassiopeia. She was a Greek goddess banished to circle forever around Polaris, the North Star. And that, of course, is the Big Dipper, part of Ursula Major, the bear constellation. It has two stars that point to Polaris, so you can always find it. And over there are three stars in a perfect line—Orion's Belt. He's a hunter. His belt contains a star, Mintaka, that always rises in the true east and sets in the true west, no matter where you are in the world.

"So," I concluded, "that way's north, that way's south, that way's east, and that way's west. The Owens River's over there. Lake Crowley is over there. Mammoth Mountain is over there. Convict Lake is over there. And Bishop is back there."

Robin stared up in wonder.

"Who taught you all that stuff?"

"I don't know. My dad and my grandfather, maybe. It's important to always know exactly where you are, so you don't get lost."

"And where, exactly, are you, Craig Collins?" Robin asked, her voice low and soft.

"I'm right here with you," I answered in a whisper so low I wasn't sure I'd said it.

She pulled me close. I wrapped my arms around her and kissed her softly at first. Her breasts pressed slippery against my torso. She opened her mouth, and our tongues found each other. We bobbed in tandem in the water and kissed without concern for time. We pulled away, touched noses, and stared into each other's eyes. We kissed again. And again. We finally stopped when Robin hugged me tight, placed her chin over my shoulder, and stroked the back of my head with her hand.

She turned slightly and whispered ever so softly into my ear, "Do you love me, Craig Collins?"

I didn't hesitate. I said the only true thing I could.

"I do."

We bobbed once. We bobbed twice.

I turned my head and whispered, "Do you love me, Robin Wentworth?"

"I do."

Above us, the Milky Way blazed. Starlight glimmered faint on Hot Creek's glassy, black surface. Mintaka drifted ever west. Cassiopeia orbited coldly around Polaris. In the Sierra, Crystal Crag towered in the blackness like a granite sentinel. Below, in the waters of Crystal Lake, a small stream began its journey, tumbling over boulders and into Lake George. It rushed past the south flank of Mammoth Mountain, an old volcano, dormant for now, but still given to rumbles and belches of steam. It picked up tributaries, gathered speed, and dropped into the treeless depression of the Long Valley Caldera. In the springtime, snowmelt atop the nearby Mono Craters had seeped through the porous, volcanic soil, settling in a large, underground reservoir atop a scalding dome of granite, heated by magma that had been pushed upward from deep beneath the earth. The pressurized water expanded, jetting through fissures that opened into a streambed, over which ran the cold, alpine waters that had first begun beneath Crystal Crag.

Around us, all this swirled. For we were the center. All that mattered.

The ride home was dark and quiet. Robin laid her head on my shoulder and slept while I drove. I rolled slowly into her driveway and gave her a soft kiss good-night.

The world is always confusing, calamitous, and sometimes cruel. But in the many days and years since, in my life, I know this: There was only a time before Robin, and then a time after.

The following day was exactly the same as the previous.

The sun rose hot over the White Mountains. By mid-morning the air had once again been baked dry and smelled of dust, sage, and heated rock. By noon, the sun was pale and high overhead. A sheen of shimmering heat could be seen blanketing the valley floor. The hot air rose, and dust devils danced by the dozens.

And yet for me, everything was different. My alarm rang at 5:30 a.m., and I bounced out of bed. I ate a bowl of cereal over the sink, grabbed an apple on the way out the door, hopped into my Datsun, and drove to my job at the Bishop Country Club, a nine-hole golf course with a commanding view of the Sierra just off 395, to the south of town. I spent all morning in the growing heat atop a red Toro mower, cutting grass on the tee boxes and around the fringes of each green. The big machine rumbled, blades whirred, my seat vibrated, and puffs of white mower exhaust mixed with the smell of fresh-cut grass.

I played and replayed each word, each kiss, each caress from the night before. More than once, I drifted off-line and mowed in areas where I shouldn't have. I heard a chunk near a green, followed by the yell of an angry golfer. I had a bag of found golf balls in a pouch behind my seat. I gave him two new ones and apologized for ruining his lie. At 11:30, I steered the red Toro back to the maintenance shed behind the clubhouse, lumbering along the ninth fairway's edge. I maneuvered into the open bay door atop a concrete floor. The mower filled the big garage with a roar. I cut the engine and there was silence. I hopped down, neck sweaty and flecks of grass sticking to my calves and forearms. My ears rang slightly from the engine's morning-long rumble.

Doc was the golf club's head greenskeeper. He was a round man with a round face and round glasses. He was a wizard at fixing any machine and could look at a patch of grass and tell whether it needed water, fertilizer, or spray to kill the cutworms. He stood in the back of the garage, cleaning a long metal part with a rag. He smiled at me—his cheeks round and rosy—pointed toward a bench with his piece of metal, and said, "Your lunch is over there."

I was puzzled, having planned to order a sandwich and chips from the clubhouse.

Two workers, both in their mid-twenties, sat hunched in chairs near the shed's entrance, eating sandwiches over paper lunch bags that sat at their feet on the concrete floor.

I walked toward the bench and could see a thatched basket.

One of the workers let out a long whistle.

"Mmm-mmm. Do you know that fine, young lady who brought you that?" he asked. The workers turned to each other and laughed. "Because she surely was a looker. As cute as cute can be. You just missed her. You certain you know what to do with a lady like that? 'Cause if you don't, feel free to ask. I can give you some pointers. Or even take her off your hands if she's too much."

The workers laughed again. Doc smiled, not interrupting his work with the machine part.

I opened the basket and in it lay a roast beef sandwich made with two thick slices of homemade bread. There were fresh-baked oatmeal-raisin cookies and a slice of blackberry pie. A red Coke can stood in the corner, its cold metal sides beading with moisture. Tucked between the sandwich and the cookies was a carefully folded piece of pink stationery scented with perfume. I removed it, unfolded it slowly, and turned my back to the two workers. I immediately recognized the long, looping, graceful letters, and my heart fluttered once more at the sight of them.

Dearest Craig,

I hope your morning was as wonderful as mine. I can't stop thinking of the stars. I hope you're thinking of them, too. Enjoy the lunch.

Love,
Robin

P.S.—Stop by my house after work, if you like, and we'll go for a swim. You can borrow a pair of swim trunks from my brother. See you soon. (I hope.)

⸺

After work, I pulled into the driveway of a ranch house with a large, white-barked birch tree in the front yard. I rang the doorbell. A dog barked.

"I'm back here," Robin yelled from the backyard. "Go around the side and through the gate."

I unlatched the gate and saw Robin next to the pool—in a bikini, drying her hair. I swung the gate wide and she ran to me, hugged my neck, and gave me a long, deep kiss. Her face was still wet, and her bikini made two dark, damp marks against my shirt.

"Sorry," she said. "It was so hot, I couldn't wait. I had to jump in and cool off."

She stepped back and inspected me up and down. I was sweaty from being in the sun all day and covered in dirt and grass clippings.

"Look at you," she said. "You've been working. Go inside; the bathroom's on the right. I set out some swim trunks for you. Go ahead and rinse off in the shower. My parents won't be home 'til around five."

Afterward, I walked back outside, and Robin was standing at the edge of the pool with an outstretched hand. I grabbed it, and she pulled me to her. We kissed for several minutes.

She then stepped back and said, "C'mon, let's dive in together."

Holding hands, we dove in tandem. After rising back to the surface, we both kicked our legs and settled into a stroke. She swam gracefully, athletically, effortlessly. I churned and splashed to keep up, but fell farther behind with every stroke. By the third back-and-forth lap, I was hopelessly behind and stopped at the edge of the pool where we'd begun.

We got out. She poured us glasses of iced tea. We sat holding hands in adjacent lounge chairs.

"So, Craig Collins, we have thirty days to live a lifetime. I counted. Let's start by you telling me everything about yourself."

"Everything? Geez, it's not that exciting."

"You know what I mean. Where are you from? Where were you born?"

"Well, I'm from a place you've probably never heard of."

"Try me."

"It's in Idaho."

"Really? You're kidding. I'm from Idaho."

"No. Seriously?"

"Yes. Where's the place you think I've never heard of?"

"Pocatello."

"Pocatello?" She sat upright. "No way. Really? You're from Pocatello?"

"Wow. So you've heard of it?"

"Heard of it? I was born there."

"Really? Pocatello? You were born in Pocatello? Man, what are the odds? That's hilarious."

"Hilarious? It's amazing. What's your sign? What month were you born in?"

"Libra. October. You?"

"Oh my God," she said, shifting to her knees. "This is getting intense."

"Why? When were you born?"

"October." She held my hands, looked in my eyes, and said, "Okay, what day?"

"You first," I laughed.

"The seventh."

"Oh, man," I said as I leaned back. "You wrecked it. I'm the fourteenth."

She laughed. "No, that's still amazing. What are the odds? We were born in the same hospital a week apart."

She looked into my eyes and in a low voice said, "It's like we were meant to be. It's in the stars."

I kissed her, then stood and made a running dive into the pool. She gave chase. We swam several more laps before I conceded. I got out and stood by the pool to wait. She glided to the pool's edge, grabbed the concrete lip, and began to pull herself out.

She looked down and gasped, "Oh my God, Craig—what happened to your foot?"

I turned, embarrassed, and walked over to the lounge chair, where I sat down and hid my foot beneath a rumpled towel.

Robin toweled off and sat next to me on my chair.

"No, really. What happened?"

"Nothing. I don't want to talk about it."

"Oh, come on. You have to now."

"No, really. I really don't."

"Oh, I'm sorry," she said, lying down next to me and putting her head on my chest. "You don't have to talk about it if you don't want to. I didn't mean to embarrass you."

She caressed my neck and ran her fingers through my hair.

"That's okay," I said. "It's just something I never really talk about, and I don't like people to see."

"I understand," she said, giving me a peck on the cheek and stroking my shoulder.

There was a long silence.

"Was it awful?" she ventured.

I didn't answer.

She gave me a deep, passionate kiss and nibbled on my ear before whispering, "You can tell me."

"Okay," I said, giving in. "I shot myself in the foot."

She bolted upright.

"You what?" she blurted, surprised and almost laughing.

"I shot myself in the foot," I confirmed.

"Holy crap," she laughed excitedly. "I've never met anyone who's been shot. That must've really hurt."

"See, this is why I never tell anyone."

"Oh, poor baby," she laughed. "I didn't mean to hurt your feelings. It's just that it's so interesting. How did you do it?"

"A hunting accident. It was a thirty-thirty deer rifle."

"It's a miracle you still have your foot."

She reached her hand slowly toward the towel. I grabbed her wrist and stopped her.

"Oh, c'mon," she complained. "I want to see. If we're going to be lovers, I need to know everything about you."

She kissed me deep, wrapped her leg around my waist, and pressed her breasts hard against me. She lowered her mouth to my ear and whispered, "Please?"

I sat up, and she lay down on the lounge chair in the opposite direction, with her feet toward my head. She removed the towel, and I winced. I'd never allowed anyone other than a doctor to closely study my foot.

She softly kissed my knee and ran her hands slowly down my calf. She gently rubbed my foot as she studied the part that had been shot.

My heart pounded, and I felt queasy. I hated even thinking about my foot.

"So it went in here?" she softly asked.

I nodded.

"And came out here," she concluded. "Poor baby."

She kissed the top of my foot, and I relaxed. She turned, sat astraddle my waist, lowering to kiss me again in thanks for sharing something private and painful.

"Tell me more about yourself, Craig Collins," she said.

"Tell you what?" I replied. "How 'bout you let me take you out on a proper date tonight. I'm thinking Whiskey Creek at seven."

"Wow. Whiskey Creek? That's fancy. You sure you can afford it?"

"Afford it? Heck, yeah. I have that incredible job mowing greens at the golf course, remember?"

She laughed. "Yes, Craig Collins, who shot himself in the foot with a deer rifle, I would gladly be your date tonight."

"Oh, wait. What time do you have to be at work?"

She laughed again. "Well, let's just say I wasn't cut out for the food service industry."

"What? You were fired! How do you get fired from Fosters Freeze? You must've been really bad at what you did."

"No, silly. I quit."

"You quit? Why?"

"Why not? There wasn't much of a future. Plus, how can you expect to be able to fit a whole lifetime into thirty days if you have to split your time with Fosters Freeze?"

I kissed her nose and pressed my forehead against hers.

"I'm going to go home, catch a little sleep, shower, and change. I'll be back at a quarter to seven to pick you up."

The next morning, the sun rose hot over the White Mountains. And the next morning. And the next. And the next.

Robin and I were inseparable. We went on day hikes into the Sierra, picnicking at Granite Lake, atop a large, warm boulder, from which we dove repeatedly into the glacier-fed waters. A couple times a week, we drove to Hot Creek and swam beneath the stars. We had lunch at Mammoth Lakes and window-shopped at the stores. We rented a boat at Lake Sabrina and floated, mid-lake, beneath the towering granite peaks, the only vessel without fishing poles dangling over the side. On the days I worked, she brought me lunch, which we ate together during my break on the grass beneath a giant weeping willow. We drove for miles, aimless, along the many dirt roads and two-lane highways that wended through the region, just talking, listening to music, and holding hands. I told her everything I could think of about me. She told me everything she could think of about her. We spoke mostly of the past and the present and did all we could to avoid the future.

And we kissed. We kissed atop boulders. We kissed in Hot Creek. We kissed in Mammoth. We kissed in the middle of Lake Sabrina. We kissed in restaurants. We kissed in her pool. We kissed in my car.

Yet the days passed. And, again, the sun rose hot over the White Mountains. In late afternoon, Mount Tom cast its long shadow. And when the evening grew late, a river of cool air sank from the mountaintops and settled among the willows, cottonwoods, and alfalfa fields. In the night sky, Mintaka drifted west, and Polaris pointed north.

My alarm rang at 5:30 a.m. I pulled myself out of bed and dressed slowly. High atop the Sierra Crest, a cold breeze—the first of the season—blew through the passes and cols and swirled down the steep slopes and over the granite boulder fields. The sun was much later rising than it had been in July, and so the breeze pushed to the valley floor, sweeping across meadows and streams, making the cottonwoods shudder.

I stepped outside and rubbed my arms briskly, surprised by the chill. The sun had not yet risen, and I needed headlights to drive. I made my way east on Line Street. Ahead, the White Mountains stood in dark silhouette. There would be no hot sun rising today, not with this cold breeze rushing across the valley floor, the first full hint of autumn. Instead, the sky above the mountains was a pale blue in the coming dawn. A half-moon had set long ago. The sun was late in arriving. And so Venus, the morning star, seized the fleeting opportunity, shining bright above the bristlecones, briefly the most brilliant object in the heavens.

During my lunchtime break, Doc handed me an envelope with my last paycheck. He thanked me for my hard work and said that if I wanted to come back next summer, I was welcome. He gave me the rest of the day off since I was leaving for college in less than forty-eight hours.

I rushed to see Robin, eager to squeeze something from every remaining minute we had left together. She would be leaving at sunrise the next morning, her parents driving her to Colorado for school. I'd be leaving the following day for San Diego.

In my Datsun, we ascended the narrow road that snaked steeply along Bishop Creek, rising from 4,000 to 9,000 feet in just over fifteen miles. I noticed that small puffs of clouds had gathered around the tops of Mount Tom and Mount Morgan and grew concerned about a possible afternoon storm. The big mountains were volatile, and the slightest shift in weather could trigger wind, lightning, rain, or even snow, no matter the time of year.

For the first time since our initial trip to Hot Creek, Robin was sullen and didn't speak. She simply held my hand and leaned her head against my shoulder.

We stepped out of the car in our short sleeves, and the cold breeze bit at our bare arms. I grabbed a blanket from the trunk, and we ran to the boat dock. There were fewer than half a dozen boats on the lake, fishing for trout, and the dock manager pointed to the clouds billowing over Lamarck Col and Mount Darwin in the distance.

"If those clouds get much bigger or closer, be sure to hurry back in. Don't hesitate," he warned.

I nodded, and Robin wrapped herself in the blanket while I sat in the back of the small boat, cranking the throttle and steering toward a far cove. Small waves chopped against the bow, and the ride was much rougher than during our previous trips to the lake.

We crossed the water, and I stopped beneath a sheer granite cliff, atop which several small pines bravely clung. Robin shared the blanket, and we lay down in the boat, using life preservers for pillows.

We stared up at the blue skies and Robin said, "That's autumn. Can you feel it?"

"Yes."

"The aspen will turn yellow up here in only two or three more weeks."

She put her head on my chest and clung to me tightly. We drifted, and there was no sound except the hush of the cold breeze across the water and the lapping of waves against the hull.

"I'm sad," she said much later.

"I know," I answered, stroking her hair. "Hemingway said, 'You expected to be sad in the fall. Part of you died each year when the leaves fell from the trees.'"

"There you go with Hemingway again," she said, her hands clinging to my shirt. "He makes me even sadder."

We closed our eyes and drifted. After another while, Robin whispered to me, "So, do you think we did it?"

"Did what?" I asked.

"Lived a lifetime in a month?"

I smiled. "I think so. Don't you?"

She gave me a long, deep kiss before whispering, "Yes."

I looked up, and the blue sky was gone. Dark clouds had blown in quickly, high overhead. Out of the corner of my eye, I saw a blue spark several miles away on the jagged teeth of Lamarck Col. I sat up and told Robin we had to hurry back. We'd drifted to the farthest point from the dock, which I could now barely see.

I grabbed the plastic handle on the side of the engine that dangled from a nylon rope and gave it a yank. The motor started with a gurgle. I scanned the lake and could see that we were now the only boat on it. I pointed the bow toward the dock, held the outboard's tiller, and twisted the throttle full. The bow lifted, the boat chopped hard into the small, windblown waves, and the underwater propeller churned the dark water white. Robin sat in the front, the blanket covering her head and wrapped tightly around her body.

A bolt of lightning slammed bright and blue into the mountainside above the boat dock. Thunder shook the air and made Robin flinch. Clouds descended quickly, and the dock vanished behind a dark sheet of gray. A gust of wind blew hard into our faces, and the boat slowed, its motor straining to make headway. Just beyond us, the lake surface splashed beneath a sheet of advancing raindrops. The wall of water walloped us, with driving raindrops that fell big and cold, stinging our faces and my bare arms. Lightning crashed with a stomp into a big lakeside pine, sending a shock wave across the water's surface.

As we neared the boat dock, I worried about the lightning. A figure stood on the dock, barely visible in the rain, awaiting our arrival. I swiveled alongside him and tossed the coiled rope that was attached to our bow. He helped us onto the dock and admonished me for not paying closer attention to the weather. I apologized as we jogged down the dock, just before Robin and I broke into a full run to my car in the parking lot.

We hopped in, slammed our doors shut, and listened to the big drops pinging on my roof and hood. Robin and I looked at each other, both cold and soaked, and began to laugh.

"Holy shit," I said. "That was stupid."

"I thought for sure we were going to get hit by lightning," she said. "I can't believe we just did that."

I started the engine, turned on the heater, and we shivered and kissed.

"I suppose I should take you home."

"No," she said. "Not yet. I don't have to be back until dinnertime. Our friends have a cabin just down the road in the aspen above Bishop Creek. I know where the spare key is hidden. They wouldn't mind."

We drove a short distance down from the lake and turned onto a dirt road that led through sage and pine, before crossing a narrow bridge to a glade of aspen beneath the steep mountainside. Swollen by the downpour, Bishop Creek thundered through the canyon, angry and white. A row of about six rustic cabins sat amid the woods. Robin pointed out the one that belonged to a family friend.

I parked the car beneath a big ponderosa, and we made a dash through the rain. Robin turned over a flat rock next to an aspen alongside the cabin and held up a silver house key. We stood on the rough-hewn log porch while Robin fumbled with cold fingers before she was able to unlock the door. The place was small, for summer only, and came with just a living room, kitchen, and bedroom. Upon seeing the fireplace, I grabbed some newspaper from the basket near the hearth, crumpled it, and stuffed it beneath the grate. I carefully stacked kindling atop the paper and went out to the porch to get an armful of split logs. I pushed a lever to open the flue, struck a wooden match, held it to the paper, and watched the glow turn rippling bright. I blew gently on the flame, coaxed it into the kindling, and listened as the crackle grew into a roar. I placed three split logs atop the blaze, blew hard at the base of the flame, and the room brightened with light, sound, and warmth.

"We need to take everything off," Robin said, "so our clothes can dry by the fire."

We shed all and carefully draped items over the fireplace screen and mantle. I jumped on the couch beneath a heavy quilt while Robin lifted open the window. She climbed under the blanket, lay on top of me, and we listened to the rain patter loudly on the roof and in the trees. We kissed. Our bodies grew warm, and the shivering stopped. A gust blew into the side of the house, and the rain pelted hard in sheets against the outside wall. A white lace curtain lifted to let the wind in, the cloth dancing and fluttering as it rose. The gust blew at the fire, which brightened and hissed back. The wind swirled once around the room, then twice, before settling and releasing the smell of wet trees, chimney smoke, and autumn.

"I love you, Craig Collins," Robin moaned.

"I love you, too," I whispered.

———

I awoke, and the cabin was dim and silent. The fire was done crackling, the wind done blowing, and the rain done pattering. I was by myself on the couch, and I looked to see Robin, wearing my much-too-big shirt, staring out the window at the creek rushing by. I pulled the quilt from the couch, stood behind her, and wrapped the blanket tight around us both. She was crying.

"Shhhh," I said. "Shhhh. Everything's going to be all right."

"No, it's not," she sobbed. "No, it's not. You're going to San Diego, and I'm going to Colorado, and we're never going to see each other again."

"Yes, we will," I said. "I promise."

She turned and held me tight, pressing her head against my chest.

"Come to Colorado with me. Come to Colorado. You'd love it there. There are aspen stands for miles. And you should see it when they turn yellow. You've never seen such a place. Come to Colorado. You can go to school there. Don't leave me."

I stroked her hair and felt her sobs heaving against me. She looked up at me, her eyelashes wet and tears streaming down her face.

"You better write me, Craig Collins, you hear? You better write me every day."

"I will," I promised.

"Because I'll write you every day, and I'll count the days until Christmas break."

She squeezed tight and added, "I love you, Craig Collins."

I squeezed back and said, "I love you, too, Robin Wentworth."

And then we both cried uncontrollably.

It felt like dying.

But it wasn't.

The storm passed, and a breeze blew gentle. The white lace rippled again in the window, and the embers glowed in response.

Robin and I did write each other every day, sometimes twice. We called every Sunday, and we counted down the days until Christmas break, when we spent five glorious weeks together—one in San Diego while I finished my finals, one in Bishop to visit her parents over Christmas, and three in Colorado, where it was cold and white and just as beautiful as Robin had promised.

CHAPTER FIFTY

Through the town of Ketchum flows the Big Wood River, which rushes south from its origins near Galena Summit in the Boulder Mountains before spilling into a man-made reservoir that sits atop a massive, sage-covered lava bed comprising the Snake River Plain. Beneath the hard-crusted earth are catacombs of hollow lava tubes, cavernous chambers, cracks, fissures, and porous ash. Water from rivers like the Big Wood and the Big Lost, which runs parallel and to the east, falls as though through a trapdoor, into a great labyrinth concealed beneath the surface of the hardened lava rock. The water seeps underground, flowing downhill and south, until it reaches a 250-foot wall of sheer basalt, carved over eons by the Snake River. There, the springwater from northern rivers gushes from the canyon side in a bubbling spray of foamy white before settling into cold pools on the valley below and then draining, finally, into the Snake, on its way to the sea.

In the Hagerman Valley, the canyon-side water is called Thousand Springs. The valley floor is lush, and the spring-fed ponds attract an abundance of waterfowl. It's also what attracted Gene Van Guilder on a crisp autumn morning in late October of 1939.

Van Guilder, thirty-four, was a publicist for the Sun Valley Lodge near Ketchum, which had opened, alongside the nation's first destination ski mountain, nearly three years earlier. An affable, talented writer and an avid hunter, Van Guilder had helped to garner publicity for the Lodge by wooing Hollywood, convincing actors like Gary Cooper, Claudette Colbert, and Clark Gable to sojourn in central Idaho to ski, dine, play, and be photographed. The strategy worked, and the property received national and international acclaim.

But Van Guilder's biggest coup came in the fall of 1939. That's when he convinced Ernest Hemingway to come for the hunting, and the writing.

Hemingway had been spending most of his time in Cuba. But he'd been working recently on a novel about the Spanish Civil War, set in the

Pyrenees. He felt Sun Valley would provide better inspiration than the Caribbean. The region was home to one of the largest Basque populations in the United States. Each fall, Basque sheepherders would drive huge flocks of sheep—the largest in America—out of the alpine meadows of the Sawtooth Range and into the Wood River Valley, where they would be loaded onto trains at the Union Pacific terminus in Ketchum before being shipped by rail to market.

The mountains of central Idaho had always reminded Hemingway of the Spanish Pyrenees. And he liked the notion of being able to write in the mornings and hunt in the afternoons. His quarry included deer, rabbit, duck, geese, pheasant, quail, and chukar. He'd also previously acquired a fondness for the area from the many stories told to him by the poet Ezra Pound, a fellow expat in Paris and Idaho's most accomplished writer, who'd grown up just down the road in Hailey.

And so Hemingway came. Van Guilder set the writer up in Suite 206 with his journalist girlfriend and soon-to-be wife, Martha Gellhorn. Papa took to calling the Sun Valley Lodge "the Glamour House," doing some of his most important work there, specifically, most of the writing, editing, and polishing of his opus *For Whom the Bell Tolls*.

Van Guilder spent much of that September and October hunting with Hemingway. He arranged trips, served as guide, and made sure the writer was engaged, relaxed, and productive.

One night in late October 1939, Van Guilder asked Hemingway if he'd like to join some other hunters and him for a sunrise duck hunt at Thousand Springs. Hemingway declined, as Van Guilder suspected he might. He was engrossed in his prose, and even though it was a Sunday, the writer didn't want to break his morning regimen at the typewriter.

The sun rose over acres of just-harvested farmland. Miles of potato fields lay plowed, expanses of broken clods and dirt. Corn stalks stood brown and dry, rattling in the slightest of breezes. Van Guilder sat hunched in a canoe that was tied to a willow and tucked surreptitiously behind some reeds on the canyon floor. The Snake River rolled a few yards behind him, and a network of spring-fed ponds bubbled in front. It was Indian summer. The sky was cloudless, the wind calm, and the temperature was expected to surpass 60 degrees, a rarity this late in the fall. Van

Guilder could barely see his breath and felt hot in his long johns, wool shirt, and canvas hunting jacket. Decoys bobbed on the clear-water pool.

As daylight spread, flocks of mallards could be seen as small silhouettes against the pale blue of the morning sky. Van Guilder rolled his wooden duck call between his palms, cupped it lightly, and held it to his lips.

Kaaanc, kaaanc, kanc-kanc-kanc, called Van Guilder in two high, drawn-out notes followed three quick notes in descending volume.

Kaaanc, kaaanc, kanc-kanc-kanc, he continued. *Kaaanc, kaaanc, kanc-kanc-kanc.*

The calls blew clear and loud into the October sky and echoed off the basalt cliffs, where the springwater hissed through cracks in the sheer walls.

Kaaanc, kaaanc, kanc-kanc-kanc.

Kaaanc, kaaanc, kanc-kanc-kanc.

A flock appeared about a half-mile west and appeared to be heading away, south.

Kaaanc, kaaanc, kanc-kanc-kanc.

Kaaanc, kaaanc, kanc-kanc-kanc, Van Guilder pleaded.

The lead duck veered toward the call, and the flock lowered beneath the canyon rim.

Kaaanc, kaaanc, kanc-kanc-kanc.

Kaaanc, kaaanc, kanc-kanc-kanc, Van Guilder called excitedly.

The ducks, about thirty in all, approached single file, wings beating, necks outstretched. The lead mallard, a male, flew out of the canyon shadow and into the morning sun. He locked his wings and prepared to land, his head shining an iridescent green, almost purple, in the sunlight. The ducks flew left to right in front of the three camouflaged hunters. The lead duck skimmed his outstretched webbed feet on the water's surface before gliding to a stop and settling atop the pool near the wooden decoys. Another duck landed. Then another. And another.

The two hunters to Van Guilder's left took aim.

Pa-hoom.

Pa-hoom, pa-hoom, pa-hoom, went their shotguns, the sound thudding against the canyon walls.

Two incoming ducks folded their wings and made spiraling plunges into the pond, landing with adjacent splashes. A black Lab bolted from beside the willow and charged toward the water. The trailing ducks awkwardly aborted their landings. They unlocked their wings and began flapping frantically.

The hunter to Van Guilder's immediate left spotted one such duck. From a sitting position, he pulled the gun's butt snug to his right shoulder, closed his left eye, and looked down the bluish steel barrel. He placed a small bead near the muzzle into his view, aligning it with the moving duck. His shotgun, a beautiful Browning over-under 12-gauge with a burled-walnut stock, began left and swung in tandem with the duck's movement to the right. The hunter, his index finger gently atop the trigger, began to squeeze. But the duck dipped behind some reeds and the hunter was forced to hesitate, though still tracking the bird with the bead atop the barrel. Three other ducks trailed close behind.

Van Guilder picked one out, stood quickly, and pulled the butt of his gun to his shoulder. The lead duck rose above the reeds, the hunter to Van Guilder's left still tracking. The hunter placed the bead about a foot ahead of the duck's bill and squeezed gently on the trigger, just as an unexpected object came into view.

Blue smoke and birdshot roared from the gun's muzzle. The sound thudded against the basalt cliffs and echoed into the crisp, blue sky. The mallard, his head gleaming green, beat his wings furiously, rising high above the river valley, cresting the canyon rim, and disappearing into a bright autumn sun.

And Van Guilder, the man who'd coaxed perhaps America's greatest living writer to the wilds of Idaho, and, once there, encouraged him, befriended him, supported him, and nurtured him—the man who perhaps as much as anyone had helped to midwife a great American novel that would resurrect Hemingway's flagging career, and most certainly help land him the Nobel Prize—was shot.

Van Guilder was struck in the left side of his back with about five hundred lead pellets traveling nearly 900 miles per hour in a tight, round pattern about the size of a coffee-cup saucer. The pellets tore through skin, muscle, and cartilage. They crushed rib bones with blunt force and left a wound area in which his blue-and-black-checked wool Pendleton shirt was tattered and mashed into shredded muscle that had the consistency and appearance of bloody hamburger. Narrow strips of white long johns dangled from the wound, but the cotton wicked the blood and quickly turned a bright crimson.

Van Guilder felt like he'd been hit in the ribs with a hard swing from a baseball bat. Air was knocked from his lungs. He tried to say, "You shot me, you shot me," but he had no breath. His hunting companion cried out in panic, "Gene, Gene. Oh, God! Oh, God!" The other hunter kept his cool, untied the canoe, and began digging his paddle deep into the water.

Van Guilder was alert and understood fully what had just happened. He lay down on his stomach in the canoe and waved with his right arm for his fellow hunters to get him to a doctor. Both hunters were now paddling hard and in tandem. They maneuvered the canoe into the slow but strong current of the Snake River, aiming for their pickup truck on the far bank. The black Lab—duck in mouth—swam dutifully after the departing vessel. The dog entered the open water without hesitation, churning through the current, but being carried far downriver. The hunters' arms burned and their chests heaved, but desperation pushed them onward.

They slid through the reeds and the lead hunter jumped out, splashed through knee-deep water, and pulled the canoe onto the bank. They carried Van Guilder to the truck and placed him facedown on the flat metal bed in the back.

Still, Van Guilder was alert. He tried to say, "I'll be okay, I'll be okay," but was now wheezing and only able to mouth the words. He began spitting up blood, and it was then that his hunting companions were certain he wouldn't be.

The Lab, who'd made it to the bank, trotted through the tall grass toward them, focused only on returning a duck to his master—oblivious to panic, mayhem, and impending death.

The hunter who'd shot Gene knelt next to his friend in the truck bed. He talked calmly, assuring him that a doctor would be there shortly and that all would be well—even though now they both knew this was a lie.

The other hunter fumbled for his keys. A duck—dead, limp, and wet—plopped at his feet. The Lab, huffing and drooling and looking up with a tired, lolling tongue and black, eager eyes, waited for a pat on the head and a word of excited encouragement in exchange for his heroics with the duck. But none came. His master unlocked the door, wrenched it open with a loud, metallic creak, and pulled up on the dog's collar, signaling it to leap into the cab—which it did. The dog whimpered dolefully for the duck that had been left unappreciated on the ground.

The hunter started the engine and raced toward the dirt road that rose in a diagonal up the side of the canyon before leveling over the south rim and connecting with a narrow paved road that traveled straight, without a turn or the bother of a middle stripe, through the harvested fields of potato, corn, and wheat, before finally nearing an intersection where stood the small farm town of Buhl. There is perhaps no place as quiet as a Mormon community in the middle of the fields on a Sunday morning after the harvest is in. Into this the truck sped—engine roaring, tires sibilant, and horn blaring into the Sunday silence like that of Gabriel.

The truck rattled into the parking lot of the sole gas station, which was closed. The horn wailed and wailed and wailed again. In the rearview mirror the driver could see an old man, trotting bowlegged in jeans and a white T-shirt, along the side of the road.

"Call a doctor, call a doctor, a man's been shot!" yelled the driver. The old man turned back, before even reaching the truck, and trotted bowlegged back to his house two doors away. The doctor, who was neither Mormon, nor Catholic, nor Lutheran, and so was at home, answered.

In the truck bed, Gene gurgled and gasped, and gripped with terror the man's hand who'd shot him. Bubbles of blood now frothed from his mouth and began pooling on the scuffed and scratched metal upon which his head lay. Then his hand went limp, his lungs filled with blood completely, his torso convulsed, and his eyes froze wide and dull. The doctor arrived only in time to declare Gene Van Guilder dead.

His friends and family were shocked and traumatized. Hundreds gathered for his funeral, held just down the street from the Sun Valley Lodge, in the small Ketchum cemetery that served as a final resting place mostly for families of miners, ranchers, and farmers. The day was warm, the sky cloudless and blue. The Big Wood River rippled cold, carrying yellow leaves dropped by the cottonwoods that lined its banks. Bald

Mountain, where the new ski slope had been built, stood majestic, its flanks ablaze with yellow aspen, standing in contrast amid pine forests of deep green. Van Guilder's horse, Sunday, stood beside the gravesite. Van Guilder was lowered into the ground in a silver coffin with his saddle, bridle, blanket, hat, and gun.

Hemingway stood and spoke. Of his friend, he said:

When I heard that Gene had died, I could not believe it. I cannot believe it now. Yes, technically he is dead. As we all must be. But the thing he gave to those who knew him was not a thing that ever perishes, and the spirit of Gene Van Guilder is not a thing that will perish either.

Gene loved this country. He had a true feeling and understanding of it. He saw it with the eyes of a painter, the mind of a trained writer, and the heart of a boy who had been brought up in the West, and the better he saw it and understood it, the more he loved it.

He loved the hills in the spring when the snow goes off and the first flowers come. He loved the warm sun of summer and the high mountain meadows, the trails through the timber and the sudden clear blue of the lakes. He loved the hills in the winter when the snow comes.

Best of all, he loved the fall. He told me the other night riding home in the car from pheasant hunting, the fall with the tawny and gray, the leaves yellow on the cottonwoods, leaves floating on the trout streams, and above the hills, the high, blue, windless skies. He loved to shoot, he loved to ride, and he loved to fish.

Now those are all finished. But the hills remain. Gene has gotten through with that thing we all have to do. His dying in his youth was a great injustice. There are no words to describe how unjust is the death of a young man. But he has finished something that we all must do.

And now he has come home to the hills. He has come back now to rest well in the country that he loved through all the seasons. He will be here in the winter and in the spring and in the summer and in the fall. In all the seasons there will ever be. He has come back to the hills that he loved, and now he will be part of them forever.

In spite of this tragedy, Hemingway kept writing at the Sun Valley Lodge through the fall and into the start of winter before returning to the tropical warmth of Cuba. But he'd been smitten with Idaho. He returned the following fall, again for the hunting and the writing. It was then and there that he finished *For Whom the Bell Tolls*, submitting it to his publisher and creating an international sensation when it was released for publication in late 1940.

Hemingway returned to Ketchum in the fall for nearly each of the next twenty years. Many Hemingway scholars believe that it was he who loved the fall, best of all—that the eulogy he'd written for his friend Van Guilder was actually a foreshadowing, a premature eulogy for himself. Perhaps. Perhaps not. Whatever the case may have been, it was clearly a piece of heartfelt prose from a man—an ambulance driver in the killing fields near the trenches of World War I—who understood deeply and profoundly the knee-buckling grief that descends after the sudden, senseless loss of a young man shot by a gun.

Scholars have written stacks of dissertations puzzling over what Hemingway may have been looking for in Idaho. The vanishing frontier? The killing of birds and mammals as a means of confronting death? The fall season and the coming winter as a reminder of life's transience? The anonymity among unpretentious Idahoans? A tranquil place where he might recapture the magic and power of his youth? A small town with good bars and clean, well-lighted places where a man could drink with friends and not be judged or bothered?

All have been suggested. The answer can never truly be known.

Regardless of what the case may have been, Hemingway loved Idaho—the mountains, the seasons, the streams, the woods, the hunting, the writing, the people. And as the years wore on and his body and mind began to flag beneath the ravages of his youth—the war, the shrapnel, the lost friends, the safari plane crashes, the concussions, the hard drinking, the travel, the broken marriages—he began to worry about the loss of his most prized possession: his ability to write.

In *A Moveable Feast*, which Hemingway edited and completed in Ketchum, he takes a swing at his Jazz Age rival F. Scott Fitzgerald in a passage that many scholars, again, describe as another possible self-eulogy: "His talent was as natural as the pattern that was made by the dust on a butterfly's wings. At one time he understood it no more than the butterfly did and he did not know when it was brushed or marred. Later he became conscious of his damaged wings and of their construction and he learned to think and could not fly any more because the love of flight was gone and he could only remember when it had been effortless."

Hemingway returned to Idaho in 1960 for good. He purchased, north of Ketchum, a house nestled amid the cottonwoods and aspen along the banks of the Big Wood River. He'd been diagnosed with depression and had been recently treated at the Mayo Clinic in Minnesota with electric shock therapy. It's certainly not surprising what happened next. At that point, he was just another depressed American male with a gun.

The warm weather had long since come to the Wood River Valley by July 2, 1961, though snow could be seen still clinging to the cirques and north-facing slopes on Galena, Silver, and Boulder Peaks, which stood blue in the distance. The buds of the cottonwoods, willows, elm, and birch on the valley floor had unfurled fully, and the valley was transitioning from the delicate, new green of spring to the lush, dark green of summer. On Mount Baldy, the ski runs twined their way from the mountain peak, through stands of aspen and pine, their broad corridors covered now with green meadows dotted with the blue, yellow, and red of blooming penstemon, black-eyed Susans, and crimson clover. In the house amid the aspen and cottonwood, the Big Wood River raced by, rushing and rippling. A warm breeze blew across the cold water and riffled the white curtains inside an open window early on a promising Sunday morning.

In the basement, a man, who now appeared much older and frailer than he should at his age, unlocked a storage room. On the far wall was a gun rack. The old man ran his fingers over the soft, polished wood of each gun's stock, as well as the cold, blue steel of each gun's barrel. He settled on an old favorite—a side-by-side double-barreled pigeon gun made by W. & C. Scott & Son of Birmingham, England. The gun was nearly as well traveled as the old man, having gone with him for duck hunts in Italy, safaris in Africa, and skeet shooting in Cuba. For the old man, the gun seemed appropriate and well suited for the task—a last, best good friend.

The old man pushed heavily up the steep basement steps, arriving in the foyer of his mountain home, breathing hard. He stood at the large picture window where a patch of morning sun had made the tile warm beneath his bare feet. He watched the white-linen curtain in the open window lift slowly and flutter down softly. The summer breeze carried whispers of the Big Wood River, melodious and mesmerizing.

The old man pressed a lever and breeched the gun. He pulled two shotgun shells from the pocket of his robe. His hands trembled. In his younger years, he could've deftly slipped a shell in each chamber, snapped the breech shut, and lifted the gun to his shoulder in the time it took for another pheasant to rise and take wing amid the brown of a late-autumn wheat field. But his fingers were stiff and swollen. He fumbled for a time, finally sliding each shell into the base of each bore. He slowly lifted the barrel, and it took some effort before he was able to close the gun with a mechanical *click, click.* His unsteady thumb pulled back the hammer of the right barrel. It, too, settled into place with a *click, click.* He did the same with the left barrel. *Click, click.* He ran his hand over the well-worn but still ornate Damascus barrel that had been forged with twisted steel by a skilled British gunsmith maybe sometime shortly after World War I.

He looked out the window and admired once more the summer morning. The river rippled shallow, maybe thigh-high in front of his house. But the water pooled, deep and clear beneath the big cottonwood just downstream. There he could see mayflies just above the slow, swirling pool, their wings a haloed silver as they danced in and out of the shafts of morning sunshine. He imagined that the pool likely contained a big brown trout like the one he'd caught there before. The fish had probably been there all morning, feasting on the mayfly hatch, its body and tail waggling in rhythm with the flowing water, its blunt, drab-green head just beneath the surface.

The old man thought of how, on another day, if he were not as tired, he might have put on the waders that hung from a peg near the back door and picked his way, gingerly, into the clear, rushing water, careful that his feet not slip on the round river stones beneath. Of how he would have whipped his fly rod, letting the whistling line drop from the sky, gently landing on the river's surface, just above the pool, so that the current could take the feathered fly—a black Western Quill—and float it surreptitiously and irresistibly just above the big trout's nose. He thought of how exciting the first few hard tugs would be, and of how the brown would have fought mightily, jumping, splashing, his sides flashing silver in the sunlight above the river. He could hear the trout sizzling in an iron skillet atop the stove and could smell the side dish of cubed potatoes, chopped onions, and bell pepper—cooked also in a skillet—and what a fine Sunday breakfast that would've made. But all that would've been on another day.

Both barrels exploded into the old man's mouth. A flock of blackbirds in the front yard jumped and took flight. A blast of fire and smoke and birdshot crashed through the bottom of the old man's skull, removing most of his brains and the top of his cranium. He dropped backward, the gun fell forward, and the Damascus steel clattered hard near his feet.

The old man lay dead, his blood pooling bright and deep ruby red across the white stone floor. The mayflies danced silver above the downstream pool. The white linen lifted in the window, and a breeze carried whispers of the Big Wood River, which raced ceaselessly by, rushing and rippling, melodious and mesmerizing.

CHAPTER FIFTY-ONE

On a sunny February day in San Diego, I decided not to write to Robin for the first time since we'd started college. It wasn't because I was tired or because I was forgetful or because I was busy. It was simply because for the first time in our relationship, I was rational. I thought about the future. And not just the future of tomorrow or next week or next month. I thought about the future that stretched into next summer, next fall, next year, five years, ten years. I was headed in one direction and Robin in another. We were on divergent paths, and any rational person could see that no amount of letter writing, *I love you*s, or pledges of eternal fidelity would change that.

After I ceased writing, Robin ceased, too. One week passed. Then two. I mustered up courage and made the inevitable call that I'd been avoiding. I calmly explained our dilemma. I told her that it would be foolish and impractical to spend the next four years of our lives living remotely, communicating by letter and phone, only to see each other in the summer and at Christmas. Plus, there was the additional fact that we were so young. There was a big world out there, with lots of other people. It seemed too early and a bit illogical to make a lifelong commitment at the age of eighteen. And with that preamble, I told her this: We should part. There were tears on both sides of the phone, but not as many as I'd expected. I hung up and sat there thinking, proud of my maturity and eager to explore my new freedom.

During the following week, I went to class, I studied, I took tests. I shrugged and shook my head at all those who'd ever written or sung about the deep pain of ending a true love. After my last class on a Friday afternoon, I stopped by Monty's Den, an on-campus pub that viewed the drinking age of twenty-one as more of a guideline than a rule. I saw Don Pate, my friend from Bishop, and his roommate working on a pitcher of beer. I sat down. They poured me a glass. Then another. Then another. Don asked me what I'd been up to.

"I broke up with Robin," I replied—casually, confidently.

"You *what?*" Don blurted.

"Yeah, I broke up with Robin. The long-distance thing got to be too much. It was time."

"Are you out of your mind? Do you know how many guys would trade places with you? Man, you're an idiot. You'll never find anyone as great as her. And she really loved you, too. You were lucky. I can't believe you."

I sat, stunned.

Don was right. What the heck was I thinking? I had to fix this. I had to make it right. I had to put the broken vase back together again.

In a panic, I ran home to my apartment, drunk. I burst through the door, grabbed the phone, and dialed Robin's number. Her roommate answered. Loud music played in the background. I could hear people talking and laughing.

"Is Robin there?" I asked.

"Oh, hi! Is this John?" she yelled, not recognizing my voice above the din of the party in her dorm room.

"Sure," I said dejectedly, my heart aching. I pulled the receiver from my ear and was about to hang up.

"Oh, hey. Are you and your friends still heading over to that party at the Lazy J?"

I grimaced, embarrassed to tell her that this was Craig, not John.

"Uh, sure," I replied, just wanting to hang up and end the conversation.

"Oh, that's great. Robin should be back from class any minute. She'd kill me for saying this, but she really thinks you're cute. She has the hots for you, you know. Tell you what, when she gets here, I'll bring her to the Lazy J. We can play pool and have a couple beers. But you should really make a move on her. You two would make a great couple."

" 'Kay," I said, defeated.

"Great. We'll see you in a little bit," she yelled.

I hung up and spiraled into depression.

The following morning, my phone rang. I answered and heard Robin yelling at me for causing her so much embarrassment. I apologized. I told her I was an idiot, and that I only wished her the best in life. There was silence on the phone. A minute passed. Then two.

"Okay," she finally said, her anger gone, her voice soft and sincere. "You take care of yourself, Craig Collins. Go out there, work hard, and chase all those big dreams you have. I have no doubt you'll catch them. And just know that I'll always remember you and hold a place in my heart for you."

"You take care of yourself, too, Robin Wentworth. You're an amazing person. I wish you only happiness. And if you're ever in trouble, just call, and I will come, 'tho' it were ten thousand mile.'"

And then we hung up. We never spoke again.

I went back to studying for a class in British literature and opened my book to a poem by Robert Burns. I could hear my professor reciting it in his lively Scottish brogue.

> O my Luve's like a red, red rose
> That's newly sprung in June;
> O my Luve's like a melodie
> That's sweetly play'd in tune.
>
> As fair art thou, my bonnie lass,
> So deep in luve am I:
> And I will luve thee still, my dear,
> Till a' the seas go dry:
>
> Till a' the seas go dry, my dear,
> And the rocks melt wi' the sun:
> I will luve thee still, my dear,
> While the sands o' life shall run.
>
> And fare thee well, my only Luve
> And fare thee well, a while!
> And I will come again, my Luve,
> Tho' it were ten thousand mile.

The rains came in early March and didn't let up for days. Cold, wet storms swept out of the Gulf of Alaska, and sheets of water—the likes of which

I'd never seen before in the arid Mountain West—pelted my apartment window in relentless, wind-driven torrents. I sat in my room—alone—reading, studying, working. The pain was deep, dull, and surprising. And it, too, came in relentless torrents.

But time passed, as it always does. The rains stopped. An orange tree blossomed just outside my apartment. The sun shone, and a warm ocean breeze wafted through my open window, carrying with it the blossoms' near-intoxicating fragrance. I breathed deep and smiled.

Some friends coaxed me into joining their intramural softball team. We played a game on a Friday afternoon in Aztec Bowl. By the final inning, the sun sat big and low on the horizon. I smelled of sweat, dirt, and grass stains. Across the street, a band played on the balcony of the Delta Upsilon fraternity. Dozens of college students laughed, talked, and drank in the yard below. After the game, my softball teammates and I marched over to the frat party, dirty uniforms and all, paid a dollar each to get in, and were handed plastic cups, which we filled with beer from a keg.

I stood by myself in the corner of the yard and blew the foam off my beer, which landed in splats near my feet on the trampled grass and mud. The band played a Rolling Stones song, and I felt a pang, thinking again of Robin. I gulped my beer and looked up to see a petite blonde with a button nose and cute face squeezing through the crowd, her beer cup held high.

"Hey, you're in my British lit class, aren't you?" she shouted above the music.

"Yeah, I recognize you. You usually sit up near the front, right?"

"Uh-huh. So, what do you think of Dr. Kehler? Who knew that poetry could be so engrossing, right?"

"He's pretty amazing. I've never heard anyone read poetry like that. When he starts reciting something, you can't help but be in a trance. When he reads aloud, you can hear a pin drop. It's remarkable. So, who's your favorite poet?"

"I can't seem to get enough of Wordsworth—Keats, too, for that matter. You?"

"Oh, you're a romantic, I see. Well, I was big on Robert Burns at first, but now I've got to go with T. S. Eliot."

"Eliot? C'mon, he's not even British. He was born in St. Louis."

"Yeah, but he moved to London and became a citizen of the UK. They claim him as their own. It's not that different from Babe Ruth. He started out on the Red Sox, but ended up a Yankee."

"Okay. So why's he your favorite?"

"His writing is just so dark, unusual, and complex. I tend to agree more with his worldview."

"So you're the tall, dark, and complex type, is that it?" She laughed and gave her bobbed hair a shake.

The band pounded on, the sun sank in the nearby Pacific, and the night air was warm and humid, smelling of the ocean, orange blossoms, beer, and mud. We talked of literature, philosophy, life, and love. She told me of how homesick she'd been when she first moved to San Diego in the fall. I told her of how I'd been miserable in the rain. Every twenty minutes or so, I would take both our cups, push through the growing crowd, and get a refill of beer at the keg. We talked for two hours. I was much taller, and as the party got louder, I had to bend down to hold my ear near her mouth. We leaned against a fence, and she draped her bare arm around my neck as she spoke. We kissed—in the corner, against the fence, oblivious to the people in the yard behind us, with the band still pounding, and the air still smelling of ocean, orange blossoms, beer, and mud. I caressed her neck and her back and held her tight. It was then that the pain lifted. And it was good again to be eighteen and in college.

◆━◆

Hemingway was right: You can live a lifetime in a day. And he was probably also right about the doom that awaits young love. But that's no matter.

As it turns out, Cassiopeia, Polaris, and Mintaka do not revolve around two lovers, no matter how passionate they may be. The earth doesn't rumble just for you. And the sun doesn't rise and set for your pleasure. There is much in the modern world to conspire against young love—or any love, for that matter. Eventually, white-hot passion must be put aside, and the yoke of daily living must be taken up. It is unavoidable. And in that manner, the sun, the moon, the stars—they'll always have their way.

The day I left Bishop, I packed everything I owned into my Datsun 510 and drove south on 395. I looked steadily in my rearview mirror. Every so often, I would take a quick glance at the highway ahead and then go back to studying the mirror. I knew the import of the moment. I knew that it would never come again. I wanted to be sure not to miss it and to be able to remember it always. Bishop sat green amid an expanse of sage. The Sierra Crest rose sharp in the morning sun. As I drove up the grade toward Wilkerson Ranch, the familiar peaks began to disappear from view. First Mount Humphreys. Then Basin Mountain. And, finally, Mount Tom. I dropped over a rise, and the green of Bishop fell out of sight. I took my eyes off the mirror and focused on the road ahead, which stretched for miles down the Owens Valley, across the Mojave, and on to San Diego.

From the time I was young, I always wanted to see what it would be like to live on the other side of the divide. To live in a place where not everyone knew my name. To get away from the lonely two-lane highways that stretched from nowhere to nowhere. To travel in a hurry, up and down the I-5. To do big, important things. To go to Paris, to Tokyo, to London. To find things that couldn't be found in Bishop or Winnemucca or Pocatello. I would be the first Collins in at least six generations not to live on the frontier at the edge of the wilderness. My blue Datsun raced down the Owens Valley, the desert to my left, the Sierra to my right, my future out somewhere far ahead. To me, it never felt like I was leaving; it felt like I was going home.

CHAPTER FIFTY-TWO

A small creek, not much bigger than a rivulet, tumbles over rocks, beneath the chokecherry that overhangs its banks, and wriggles away from its place of birth just below the north slope of 12,156-foot Younts Peak in the Absaroka Range of northwestern Wyoming. *Absaroka* means "Children of the Large-Beaked Bird," and is the name the Hidatsa people of the Upper Missouri gave to the Crow of the Yellowstone Valley.

From there, the creek connects with other nondescript mountain waters, flowing to the north and the west, pushed by snowmelt and mountain springs into the shadows of the Grand Tetons and past the phantasmagoric land of the Yellowstone with its cauldrons of bubbling mud, scalding pools of morning-glory blue, and spraying steam of thunderous geysers.

The water is gathered in a large lake atop the Yellowstone plateau, from which flows what could now be called a true river. As it is funneled into the 1,000-foot-deep Grand Canyon of the Yellowstone, it crashes over a 109-foot drop before, a quarter-mile farther, plunging furiously over another drop of 308 feet, nearly twice the height of Niagara. The falls were first reported and drawn on a map by famed mountain man Jim Bridger in 1846, though the French fur trapper Baptiste Ducharme had visited them regularly in the 1820s and 1830s. Of course, for millennia before that, the pounding waters were no secret whatsoever to the Children of the Large-Beaked Bird.

The Yellowstone then snakes north into Montana, emptying from its cradle in the Rockies and traveling eastward across the Upper Great Plains, where it gathers other waters from other streams in other mountains—the Bighorn, the Tongue, the Powder.

After almost seven hundred miles, the Yellowstone flows into the Missouri just across the Montana border in North Dakota and just upstream from Lake Sakakawea, named in honor of the Lewis and Clark Indian guide, a name given her by the Hidatsa people and meaning "Bird

Woman." From there, of course, the Yellowstone becomes part of the big waters that flow broad and deep and south until they swirl black and slow beneath towering cypress, gum, and magnolia in a land that would have been as foreign to the Hidatsa and the Crow as the Absaroka Range first was to the French and the English.

And from that first drip, drip, drip of melting April snow just beneath Younts Peak, the waters of the Yellowstone are united with the Gulf Stream, where, perhaps, thousands and thousands of years hence, they will again find their way to another snowbank beneath another pristine peak amid another mountain range on another continent.

My great-grandmother died and is buried on a bluff overlooking the Yellowstone River; her son, my grandfather, was just five at the time. My great-grandfather, too, died and is buried on the same bluff overlooking the Yellowstone River. My grandfather was just ten when he became an orphan.

My grandfather spent the first two years of his life in a raucous gold town high in Jarbidge Canyon, Nevada. But the rest of his childhood was spent on a ranch along the Yellowstone, where he was raised mostly by a committee of older sisters, cousins, uncles, and aunts. There, he learned to ride, fish, hunt, explore, rope, and shear sheep.

When my grandfather was thirteen—the same age I was when I shot my foot—"he got on a horse and rode off," as my great-aunt Edna, his sister, used to say.

And here are some of the places he rode off to: Chamberlain, South Dakota; Kalispell, Montana; Thermopolis, Wyoming; Blackfoot, Idaho; Logan, Utah; Ely, Nevada; Grand Junction, Colorado.

My grandfather was barrel-chested and strong, even as a teen. He had thick, powerful forearms and could work a sheep shear better than just about any adult. He had several metal shears from the old days hanging in the shed behind his house. My brother and I would try to work them, but we would have to use both hands and strength from both arms. My grandfather could shear all the wool from a single sheep in about five minutes, cutting with his left hand, maneuvering the animal with his right, and muscling it with his torso and legs. It was hard work for tough men. But a talented sheep shearer could make good money in those days in the West and was always in high demand.

The summer before I shot my foot, my brother Kirk and I got into an epic fight. We'd been staying with our grandparents in Pocatello, where we regularly visited cousins and multitudes of other relatives. The fight started innocuously early in the morning after my grandfather went to work at the Union Pacific rail yard. To this day, neither my brother nor I know what started the fight. But that didn't matter. The battle raged through mid-morning, well past the lunch hour and into the afternoon. It mostly involved name-calling, shoving, yelling, slamming of doors, running through the nearby park, and an occasional punch in the shoulder or ear. The battle ebbed and flowed, and whenever it spilled into my grandparents' small home, my grandmother, who had raised two boys of her own but had never quite figured them out, became hysterical in her attempts at brokering a détente. By the afternoon, she had washed her hands of the whole affair and was reduced to admonishing us in a high-pitched, worried whine, "Wait 'til your grandfather gets home, wait 'til your grandfather gets home."

My grandfather always walked through the door at 4:30 p.m. every weekday, like clockwork. At 4:15 p.m., all hostilities between my brother and me ceased. We both sat down at the kitchen table and began working quietly and intently on model cars that we'd been building. We figured that our eleventh-hour cease-fire would mask the tumult of the day, appease my grandmother, and throw my grandfather off the scent.

The front door opened, my grandfather stepped in, and my grandmother buried him with a barrage of run-on sentences and breathless excitement.

"Louie! Louie!" (She called my grandfather Louie for reasons only she and my grandfather knew.) "You have to do something about the boys I've tried everything but they don't listen to me and they've gotten too big for me to handle they've been running in and out fighting and yelling nonstop oh dear oh dear I just don't know what to do they've been slamming doors and I've asked them to stop but they don't listen they don't listen and I thought one was like to kill the other Louie you have to do something."

My grandfather didn't say a word. He simply did what he always did after work. He put his lunch pail away, washed his face, combed his hair, and made himself a plate of salami, cheese, and hot chili peppers. He went to the refrigerator, opened a Coors, and sat in a chair on the back porch. But after a few minutes, he went downstairs to the basement and came back with two pairs of boxing gloves that had belonged to my dad and his brother. He waved us over without saying a word, asking us each to stick out a hand. He placed the red gloves on us, tightened the laces, and looked us both in the eyes.

"Okay, you want to fight—then fight."

He motioned for us to go down the porch steps and onto the lawn beneath the spreading branches of the huge black walnut tree.

My brother and I stood face-to-face with boxing gloves dangling at our sides. For some reason, having an adult command you to fight under their supervision sapped the battle of all excitement, anger, and urgency.

I looked up dolefully at my grandfather.

"But Grandpa, we don't want to fight."

He stood up, took off his wide leather belt, gave it a frightening snap, and set it on the porch rail for effect.

"You've been fighting all day, so now finish it," he commanded.

I raised my gloves. Kirk raised his. Gone was all animosity. We both felt embarrassed and foolish.

My grandfather snapped his belt again.

I gave my brother a halfhearted punch in the arm. He punched me almost apologetically in the nose. I punched him in the chest. He snapped his right glove into my left ear. My eyes welled with tears, and I turned to my grandfather, again pleading, "I don't want to fight."

My brother lowered his gloves in agreement.

My grandfather laughed and motioned us to the porch.

As he untied my gloves, he said to me, "You know, you're taller than your brother now, but he's going to end up bigger than you, and you'll wish you hadn't antagonized him so much."

"But he started it," I said reflexively.

"That doesn't matter. It doesn't take a tough guy to start a fight, but it does take a tough guy to walk away from one."

"It doesn't do you any good to be tough here," he added, pointing to my bicep, "if you're not tough here," he said, pointing to my head. "And no matter how tough you think you are, there's always someone tougher."

"How about Muhammad Ali?" I protested. "There's no one tougher than him."

My grandfather pulled my gloves off and shook his head.

"Even Muhammad Ali. Somewhere someone is training right now to beat him. It'll happen. No one is champ forever."

I believed him. My grandfather spoke with the authority of someone who knew these things deeply. I could imagine him walking into a bar in Helena after a long day of work and there being no doubt among the others who the toughest man in the establishment was.

"Did you ever fight, Grandpa?" I asked.

"Yeah, a few times," he said. "But then I figured out that no matter where I went, there would always be someone tougher. After that, it doesn't make any sense to fight. I just learned how to walk away. It takes a tough guy to do that. That's the kind of tough guy you want to be," he said, poking his finger into my chest. "Now go in and apologize to your grandmother."

❧

Amid the crumpled, treeless hills—halfway between Winnemucca and Elko—twin plumes of steam used to billow eerily above a sage-covered plateau that stretched toward the horizon. It is among the loneliest of lonely spots in the Great Basin. Some years ago, a geothermal power company drilled into the earth beneath the plumes and managed to fracture the intricate mechanics that had produced geysers and fumaroles in such an unexpected place. After an eon of lording over a seemingly infinite expanse of sage, the twin plumes of steam are no more.

But that is now. This was then.

The place is called *Beowawe*, pronounced bay-uh-WAH-wee. It's a Paiute word meaning "the gate" and refers to a pair of hills that nearly pinch together before creating a valley that widens to the west. We used to watch as we drove by for the plumes of steam—off in the distance, far south of the interstate—so we could stare, mesmerized, at the white pillars that billowed upward, twenty or thirty feet, before dissipating into the sky. A large green sign would appear alongside the freeway, with a white arrow pointing toward the steam and almost daring you to slow and turn south onto a gravel road. To the side of the arrow was that word: BEOWAWE. Whenever you read it, you couldn't help but say it.

"Beowawe. Beowawe. Beowawe."

"That's where I almost died," my grandfather would say whenever my dad drove past the site on our way from Winnemucca to one of our favorite fishing spots along the North Fork of the Humboldt River. "Had the train continued on to Elko, none of us would be here right now."

My grandfather had been shearing sheep in the Central Valley of California during the depths of the Great Depression and was making his way back home to Pocatello. He'd thought about spending twelve of his hard-earned dollars to buy a train ticket, but that seemed frivolous when it was so easy to hop a freight car. So hop one, he did.

They called it "riding the rods." On most boxcars, parallel metal rods, about a foot apart, hung from the undercarriage on either side. A freight hopper—and they were legion in the Great Depression—could lie atop the rods as though they were a metal hammock, cantilevered about a foot above the rail bed. It was neither stylish nor comfortable, but it was certainly an inexpensive way to get from point A to point B.

The Union Pacific freight train left the rail yard in Sacramento with a metallic jolt that rippled from the engines up front before clanging from boxcar to boxcar to boxcar. My grandfather lay beneath a rectangular car that swayed softly and reverberated with a rhythmic *ch-ch-chunk, ch-ch-chunk, ch-ch-chunk*. He'd jammed his duffel bag between the rods and had laid his head back on an elevated wooden slat. He was reasonably comfortable as he skimmed just above the rocks that served as ballast for the track bed, before sloping down and away from the steel rail, just to my grandfather's left. To his right, the ground was a blur. But when he lifted his gaze toward the horizon, a panorama would drift endlessly by.

It was February, and the cold of the Sierra crossing had surprised him. He'd planned to get off in Reno and grab a hot meal, but the train didn't stop. Instead, it sped urgently through the high Nevada plateau and into the deep cold of a winter night. By the time the lights of Lovelock swept by, my grandfather was cold—as cold as he'd ever been. For the trip, he'd worn long johns, jeans, two flannel shirts, a heavy canvas jacket, a double pair of wool socks, leather work boots, leather gloves, and a wool cap. And still the cold wicked heat from his body like a determined thief. As the train sliced through the still of the night, the wind nipped and probed and found ways inside a pant leg or up a sleeve or down a collar. His feet and hands were at first in excruciating pain but then grew numb and leaden. The cold became like a vise; it pressed hard against my grandfather, and he could feel the life being squeezed out of him.

Ch-ch-chunk went the train. *Ch-ch-chunk, ch-ch-chunk, ch-ch-chunk.*

The train was likely scheduled to go on through to Salt Lake City, my grandfather thought, over four hundred miles to the east. There, a rail-yard worker would find his frozen corpse. Perhaps the train might stop in Winnemucca, seventy miles away, but most likely it wouldn't. The next stop after that might be in Elko in two hundred miles. But that wouldn't do him any good, my grandfather thought, because he couldn't hold on any longer and would probably be dead in no more than two hours.

Ch-ch-chunk went the train. *Ch-ch-chunk, ch-ch-chunk, ch-ch-chunk.*

My grandfather shivered and waited, shivered and waited, straining to keep his eyes open. He could see the lights of distant ranch houses, which signaled the coming of Winnemucca. He pulled his knees to his chest and every muscle shivered and ached.

But the train barreled through Winnemucca, the lights of the town and its station flickering by—so close, but so despairingly far.

Ch-ch-chunk went the train. *Ch-ch-chunk, ch-ch-chunk, ch-ch-chunk.*

And once again, he was plunged into the deep, desolate cold of the Nevada night. His last hope gone, my grandfather closed his eyes and let the sleep come.

He sank into the cold fog of a dream. And there he would've remained, never to return, but for the screech of metal wheels on steel tracks, which jolted his senses and caused him to stir.

Ch-ch-chunk went the train. *Ch—ch—chunk, ch—ch—chunk, ch——ch——chunk.*

The boxcar shook and rattled and wobbled to a stop. My grandfather strained to lift his eyelids. He unfurled himself painfully, first stretching his arms and legs, all of which had gone completely numb. Stiff and cold, he turned his head to the side and could see a land that was otherworldly. A full moon had risen high overhead. The sage stood silver above a snowy blanket of bluish white. In the air, a dull whiff of sulfur mixed with the sharp cold. He peered into the distance and could see a few dozen yards from the tracks twin pillars of steam, billowing skyward—hot, thick, and white.

Beowawe, he immediately thought.

And then he struggled to whisper thankfully through near-frozen lips, "Beowawe. Beowawe. Beowawe."

Here a water tower stood beside the tracks—a place where steam engines often stopped to get replenished. My grandfather rolled off the rods and dropped to the ground. He staggered to his feet and stood wobbling with his duffel bag, trying to focus on some ranch-house lights that glowed yellow and warm against the blue-white cold. The lights were maybe a mile down a snow-packed dirt road through the sage. He leaned into the cold, stumbled forward, and listened to the snow crunch and squeak beneath his boots. The only other sounds were those of the train engine and the geysers, each huffing and huffing into the moonlit night. He arrived at the ranch house, cold, numb, and near death. The rancher and his wife had seen train men like him before. They wrapped him in a blanket, set him by the fire, and fed him hot soup and homemade bread. He stayed for three weeks, splitting wood, mending fences, and herding cattle. And then, my grandfather's debt sufficiently paid, the rancher gave him a ride to Elko so he could continue his journey.

That singular event some forty years earlier now bound us all together—my grandfather, my dad, my brother, and me, as we drove past the mysterious plumes of steam in the desert—and formed an unbroken chain from father to son to son. And so it is that history cascades through the ages and that the customs, the thoughts, the knowledge, the sense of place, and the sense of self come to reside in you, the son of a son of a son of a son.

All because a train stopped in Beowawe.

Beowawe. Beowawe. Beowawe.

Because of my father—and his father, and his father, and his father—I was given a gift and came to know the wild in a deeper, richer way than most. It was no surprise, then, that a .30-30 Winchester fell into my hands at such a young age. Destiny, it seems, is not as mysterious as we sometimes think.

My grandfather died on a late winter day in Pocatello in 1981. I was in college in San Diego when I heard the news. My father had just relocated to Susanville, California, northwest of Reno, for his job with the BLM.

He left for Pocatello immediately, opting to drive the back roads, those two-lane highways that stretch for mile after lonely mile through empty, sage-covered rangeland punctuated by solitary pine-dotted mountains. He stopped in Alturas, a remote ranching-mining-lumber town situated near the nexus of California, Oregon, and Nevada. There, he found the Niles Hotel, a block-shaped building made of hewn granite with a boardwalk behind a facade of delicate wooden columns that supported a balcony featuring a flourish of wrought iron.

The hotel had been built by a Jay Niles around the time my grandfather was born. Niles had traveled as a child with his father and mother from New York, crossing the Isthmus of Panama and sailing to San Francisco, where the father had hoped to find riches in the goldfields. Those dreams never materialized, but the young Niles was able to extract bounty from the West, eventually finding prosperity in timber and construction. Just off the lobby stood a saloon that invited all travelers from all walks. It looked much then as the day it had been built. My dad pulled up a barstool, ordered a beer, and atop the deep, rich, long mahogany bar that had been imported from the East, he wrote on a notepad a eulogy for my grandfather.

And here it is. Listen:

"The best years are gone," said one old buckaroo.

"Yeah," said the other. "But you saw more of them than I did."

"Everybody that's ever rode has been bucked off," quipped the older gent.

And so the conversation continued at the end of the bar with words of bygone days flowing freely with the drinks. Their memories became more vivid as they reminisced on the good old days out on the range, and they ordered another round.

They were in their element—surrounded by an ornate, full-mirrored back bar, well stocked with whiskey. Western lore adorned the walls in the form of big-game mounts and Charlie Russell prints. In the corner, a potbellied stove burned bright, filling the room with warmth and an earthy scent of smoldering juniper.

It was all there—the atmosphere of the West—the cocky, Stetsoned buckaroo, the coveralled hired hand, the Indian from the nearby reservation.

Somewhere my dad was there—he belonged to this fraternity of Western folks—sharing experiences, lending a hand, just being one of the boys.

But there comes a time when the bartender sets them up for the last time, when one more for the road is no more, when not much more can be said.

The sun has set, and the last gate has been closed. My dad lived as he died—he left no burdens, he left no debts.

—"He Belonged," by Ben F. Collins

CHAPTER FIFTY-THREE

The buzz saw snarled and rattled in the yard
And made dust and dropped stove-length sticks of wood,
Sweet-scented stuff when the breeze drew across it.
And from there those that lifted eyes could count
Five mountain ranges one behind the other
Under the sunset far into Vermont.
And the saw snarled and rattled, snarled and rattled,
As it ran light, or had to bear a load.
And nothing happened: day was all but done.
Call it a day, I wish they might have said
To please the boy by giving him the half hour
That a boy counts so much when saved from work.
His sister stood beside him in her apron
To tell them "Supper." At the word, the saw,
As if to prove saws know what supper meant,
Leaped out at the boy's hand, or seemed to leap—
He must have given the hand. However it was,
Neither refused the meeting. But the hand!
The boy's first outcry was a rueful laugh,
As he swung toward them holding up the hand
Half in appeal, but half as if to keep
The life from spilling. Then the boy saw all—
Since he was old enough to know, big boy
Doing a man's work, though a child at heart—
He saw all was spoiled. "Don't let him cut my hand off—
The doctor, when he comes. Don't let him, sister!"
So. But the hand was gone already.
The doctor put him in the dark of ether.
He lay and puffed his lips out with his breath.
And then—the watcher at his pulse took fright.
No one believed. They listened to his heart.
Little—less—nothing!—and that ended it.

No more to build on there. And they, since they
Were not the one dead, turned to their affairs.

—"OUT, OUT–" BY ROBERT FROST

CHAPTER FIFTY-FOUR

"Mr. Collins," fifteen-year-old Bryan Goebel declared, "Chris tells me you shot your foot. Is that true?"

Oh, God, I thought to myself in exasperation. *The secret's out. Now I've got to talk about* this *again*.

I was on a day hike with my son Christopher and his best friend. They'd known each other since birth; Bryan's mom and my wife worked together and were each pregnant at the same time. Our families lived a couple blocks apart. I regularly took the boys out for treks through Mission Trails Regional Park, a large, chaparral-covered open space on the northeastern edge of San Diego. I was almost fifty now and hadn't fired a gun in over twenty years. But I still enjoyed the outdoors and tried to instill in my son a sense of wonder and respect for nature, only without all the shooting. I had also developed a wariness for guns and made sure to keep my son as disinterested as possible in them. So here I was, straining to keep pace with a pair of energetic teens. They scampered up the hillsides like quail and bounded over the ridges and down the other sides like deer. After a couple hours on the trails, my shirt was drenched, and I had to stop frequently to guzzle water from a plastic bottle.

"You can't believe everything you hear," I goaded Bryan.

"See, Chris," Bryan said, "I knew there was a reason I didn't believe you."

Christopher leaped to his own defense, "Dad, c'mon. You know it's true. Tell him."

Bryan's mom was fanatically antigun. She wouldn't let Bryan accompany Christopher and me to certain movies if they depicted any gun violence. And despite Bryan's pleadings, she wouldn't dare let Bryan go with Christopher to any of the local paintball parks. Out of respect for the wishes of Bryan's mother, I always tried to steer away from any gun talk, though Bryan knew I was knowledgeable on this topic and would frequently press me. But I certainly didn't want to send Bryan home so he could regale his family at the dinner table about the story of how I shot my foot. It already bothered his mother that I sometimes called Bryan "Jason Bourne," after the super-violent super-spy played by Matt Damon in the movies. With his buzz cut and buff physique, Bryan, who'd grown handsome and athletic, was a spitting image of the actor Matt Damon.

But Bryan was relentless.

"C'mon, Mr. Collins. Tell me what it was like. Did it hurt? What kind of gun were you using?"

"Nah," I deferred. "Your mom would kill me."

"No, she wouldn't," Bryan protested. "She's softened about guns lately. In fact, my dad just started teaching me to shoot with his Weatherby two-fifty-seven rifle."

My eyebrows rose. "What? Your mom let your dad take you shooting?"

"Yeah, it's pretty cool. We've been going to the firing range about twice a month. I'm only allowed to touch the rifle there."

"Wow. I'm surprised. I thought your mom was pretty entrenched on that topic."

"Well, she is. But my dad sort of talked her into it."

"Okay. So, are you a good shot?"

"Yeah, pretty good. I like the Weatherby best. It has a pretty good kick to it, though. So, what about your foot?"

I shrugged and gave Bryan a short version of the story.

"Holy cow," he exclaimed. He possessed a curiosity and excitement about guns that Christopher had never shared. Even when Bryan was four or five, his mother had worried about his intense interest in guns. I told her it was no big deal. Just about every little boy I knew growing up had an interest in guns. "You're lucky they didn't have to amputate. So, can I see your foot?"

"Nah."

"Oh, c'mon," pleaded Bryan.

"No, you can do without seeing my stinky old foot. Just let it serve as a warning to be careful with guns."

"Oh, I am. I've already taken a gun safety course."

CHAPTER FIFTY-FIVE

Remnants of a tropical storm had drifted north into San Diego from Baja. It had rained on and off throughout the day but had begun to clear in spots by late afternoon. Thunderclouds bunched over the mountains in the east, rising dark over the city.

My wife and I were attending an open house on an evening in early October at my son's high school. Parents were herded from one class to another to meet teachers and ask questions about the courses and their kids. Everywhere there was hope. Future dreams of college and careers hung in the air like the humidity.

As we shuttled outside, I looked up at the eastern sky and saw a double rainbow blazing against the dark backdrop of an ominous thunderhead. All the parents stopped, gathered in bunches, and pointed upward. And then the rain burst from the clouds, and we scattered.

Bryan and Christopher attended different schools. Christopher was a sophomore at Scripps Ranch High School, and Bryan attended his dad's alma mater, St. Augustine High, or Saints, as it was known colloquially around town.

Saints was a football powerhouse in San Diego County. They had a big rivalry with Cathedral Catholic, and both schools sent a bounty of athletes to play at places like USC, Nebraska, and Stanford.

Bryan played on the freshman team at Saints. He was athletic, strong, and quick. But he was comparatively small. It's difficult to impose your will on the opposition when you're only five-foot-six and playing against guys who will soon fill roster spots on top-twenty college teams. Bryan was not invited to try out for the team his sophomore year. He was crushed. So was his dad, who'd played football all four years at Saints and still reveled in the rivalry with Cathedral.

Fresh from his defeat on the gridiron, Bryan turned his attention to romance. He asked one of the prettiest, most popular girls at the nearby Our Lady of Peace all-girl campus to the homecoming dance. She said yes. Bryan was elated. Then she said no. She'd decided to attend instead with one of the guys on the football team. Bryan was crushed again.

Bryan's mother confided this to my wife. Bryan seemed depressed, so she got him an appointment with a psychiatrist. He went to his first appointment and said it helped a lot. The counselor was going to be on vacation the following week but advised Bryan and his mom that they'd pick up as soon as he returned.

In a private, post-session discussion with the psychiatrist, Bryan's mom expressed her deep concern over her son's zeal for guns. The counselor advised her that she was being overprotective. It was his opinion that Bryan was a typical American boy, and, as such, his interest in guns was nothing more than a healthy curiosity. Nonetheless, when she returned home, Bryan's mom sat with her husband and demanded that he get rid of the rifle. He agreed and told her that he'd make arrangements to do so.

A few days later was Bryan's sister Caitlin's tenth birthday. Bryan's mom came home from the office, gave him a hug, and asked him how his day was. He hugged her back, said his day was great, and told her about a funny thing that a kid had said in class. His mom laughed and told him to do his homework. She took his sister out on a quick trip to the store to pick up a cake, candles, and balloons for the small celebration the family was planning later in the evening.

Bryan sat at the desk in his room to write an essay. He typed one sentence on the computer, then two. He thought about the Weatherby .257. He typed another sentence, and then a paragraph. He thought about the Weatherby .257 again. And then he typed another paragraph. But the Weatherby .257 wouldn't leave his thoughts.

He abruptly pushed his chair back, tromped downstairs, found the stepladder in the garage, and brought it to his parents' room. He set the ladder on the ground in his parents' walk-in closet, banged it open, and slammed the hinges with the palm of his hand to lock them into place. He gently climbed the ladder, got to the top, and slowly pushed open the hatch door in the ceiling. He pulled himself into the attic, with its exposed 2x4s and pink fiberglass insulation. It wasn't quite dark in the attic, but the air was heavy and dank and still.

Caitlin ran excitedly into the party store. She was very precise about making sure that the napkins, candles, and balloons were all color-coordinated. She had the clerk bring her several samples before making a final selection.

———

Bryan stepped from 2x4 to 2x4, which were aligned in rows about two feet apart. He ducked beneath crossbeams and made his way to a back wall. There, behind a short stack of boxes, he picked up the Weatherby .257.

———

For Caitlin, the process of picking out the cake took even more concentration and time.

"No, Bryan hates white frosting," she reminded her mother. "Do you have that same cake, only with a chocolate fudge inside?" she asked the clerk.

Caitlin and her mother rolled their cart out to their car and stuffed the back of the Prius with a cake, balloons, hats, and an assortment of other supplies.

———

With the rifle in his hand, Bryan stepped and ducked his way back to the attic's entrance. The heat and humidity were stifling. Sweat dripped in beads off his nose. He pulled up a strip of fiberglass against a wall near the hatch door. Tucked against intersecting 2x4s was a square cardboard box marked REMINGTON. It was heavy and clinked like it was full of coins when Bryan lifted it. He flipped back the flap, pulled out a single brass cartridge, and sat down to examine it. It looked to him like a small, gold rocket ship—round and squat at the bottom, tapering to an aerodynamic cone at the top. He thought about putting it back. He closed his eyes. Sweat dripped in beads from his nose.

———

Caitlin and her mother turned off the freeway exit that led to their house. They stopped at a traffic light. And then another. It was rush hour.

———

Bryan grabbed the rifle and stood. He lifted the bolt, which made a loud metallic *click* in the dim quiet of the attic. He yanked the bolt back, slid the cartridge into the chamber, jammed the bolt forward, flipped it down, and clicked off the gun's safety. Then it was silent. Sweat dripped in beads from the tip of Bryan's nose. He was breathing hard from the heat and felt like he couldn't get a full breath amid the swelter.

———

On their way home, Caitlin shouted to her mother in delight, pointing toward the eastern sky at the double rainbow. Her mom pulled to the side of the road so they could both admire it. Caitlin clapped and said it must be a sign of good luck.

———

Bryan placed the barrel firmly under his chin. He was breathing fast and loud. He then lifted his chin, pushed the barrel away, and paused. Sweat dripped in beads from his nose. He took a deep breath, held it, and placed the barrel back beneath his chin. His finger inched toward the trigger.

The explosion ripped through the attic and filled the empty house with a muffled boom.

The Weatherby .257 shoots one of the highest-velocity bullets available. And the bullet performed as designed when Bryan touched the trigger. It entered the soft tissue in his lower mandible at 2,300 miles per hour. The lead tip of the bullet immediately began to flatten and mushroom. It tore through his tongue and then exploded into the palate bone in the roof of his mouth, sending shards piercing through his brain. The bullet ripped a wound cavity through his gray matter of at least three inches in diameter. A supersonic cloud of burning gas and smoke followed directly behind the bullet. Because the shot was at point-blank range, the superheated cloud had nowhere to go but inside the cranium. It billowed outward in a flash, inflicting catastrophic damage to nearly every structure in the brain. The bullet finally exploded through the top of the cranium, pulling tissue, bone fragments, and blood with it in the vacuum of its wake and leaving behind a wound covering at least a quarter of the skull.

Bryan slumped backward a few inches, his back propped against the wall. He was still standing, still gripping the gun. His body twitched and convulsed, his blue eyes frozen wide.

And then it was quiet.

Blood gushed from his gaping wound, down his arm, and in a rivulet to the drywall ceiling below. The blood pooled and spread and ran along the base of the 2x4s. It trickled over the edge of the attic entrance, splattered onto the stepladder, and soaked deep and red into the beige carpet that covered the closet floor.

—◦—

Caitlin and her mom pulled into the garage. Caitlin grabbed a bag of party supplies and skipped into the house. She immediately went to the dining room table and began planning the seating chart for the party guests.

Her mom followed with one hand carrying a cake and balloons. She hollered upstairs in a singsong voice, "Bryy-aan, come help." She went back to the garage, closed the car doors, grabbed the two remaining bags, and returned to the living room, this time hollering a louder "Bryyy-aaan."

She went to the kitchen and began setting out food for the guests who would begin arriving in about twenty minutes.

"Caitlin, honey? Run upstairs and get your brother."

Caitlin scampered up and then scampered back down after about a minute.

"He's not there, Mom," Caitlin said matter-of-factly, returning to her party decorations.

"Hmm," her mom said. She had to run upstairs anyway to bring down some of Caitlin's presents she'd wrapped and hidden earlier in the week in her closet.

Bryan's mom walked by his room and saw the door open. She walked to his desk and saw a stack of unopened books.

She stepped into her room and immediately noticed the stepladder in the closet. She approached slowly and let out a shriek when she recognized blood on the ladder and the carpet.

She ran to the ladder, pleading, "Bryan! Bryan! Bryan!" as she frantically climbed the rungs, her hands already wet and sticky and red. She grabbed a 2x4 that ran next to the open hatch and struggled to pull herself up. She clambered to her knees, looked to her right, and peered through the dim light.

"Bryan! Bryan! Oh, my poor boy! Bryan! What have you done?" She screamed until she couldn't breathe.

He was still slumped against the wall, upright, and holding the gun.

She checked for a pulse. He was bloody and blue and there was none.

She lowered herself out of the attic, banged her knee hard coming down the ladder, and turned to run. Caitlin stood at the door, terrified by her mother's screams.

"Caitlin, Caitlin," her mother breathlessly squeaked. "Something's happened to Bryan. Go to your room now and close the door. Don't come out."

Caitlin ran down the hall to her room. Her mother ran down the stairs and to the neighbor's house.

"Mike! Mike!" she screamed, banging on the front door and ringing the bell.

He answered and followed Bryan's mom back into the house and to the closet. Mike called 911 on his cell phone from the attic.

Bryan's father was a captain at the firehouse. He was on duty that night and saw the call come across the screen with his home address. "Male teen. Deceased. Apparent self-inflicted gunshot wound to head. Body in attic."

Bryan's father immediately knew. He stood to leave. He exhaled and couldn't inhale. His knees buckled. His coworkers had seen the same call. They immediately knew, too. They helped him into the red fire department Jeep, buckled him in, and accelerated out of the station, lights flashing, sirens blaring.

—❧—

My knees wobbled, too, when my wife called me on my cell phone with the news. It was a terror and a horror that all gunshot victims come to know. It is something so sudden, so final. It is wanting to reach into the stream of time and take just one moment back.

—❧—

In the days that followed, the neighbors took turns taking care of anything the family needed. We made calls. Took care of pets. Cleaned the house. Brought meals.

Three days after, it was our turn to bring them dinner. I had made enchiladas and was waiting for my wife to come home from work so we could take the meal over together.

My wife called.

"Honey, I have a crisis here at the office. I'm going to be late. You're going to have to bring the dinner over yourself."

"No," I replied. "I can't do that."

"But you have to. They're counting on us. Why not?"

"I'm sorry, but I just can't go without you."

"That's ridiculous. You have to. I can't get away for another hour."

"Well, then, dinner can wait for an hour."

"Seriously?" my wife asked. "You really can't go? Why?"

"I'm not strong enough," I said. "I'm not strong enough to walk into that house by myself. I'm sorry, I can't do it. I won't. I'll wait."

And it was true. I was strong enough to do plenty of things. I'd seen a lot over the years and harbored fewer and fewer fears. But this? No, I wasn't nearly that strong. Few people are.

<hr />

My wife rang the doorbell. I stood holding the casserole dish. My hands were clammy. I tried to take deep, steady breaths.

The door slowly opened. Caitlin waved us in. Bryan's dad shuffled slowly across the living room. He talked in hushed tones. I set the enchiladas on an empty space on the granite countertop in the kitchen. There were already enough meals there to last a month.

Bryan's dad glanced over. "Yeah, none of us has been too hungry."

"Caitlin," he whispered. "Run upstairs and see if your mother is able to come down."

I couldn't look Bryan's dad or anyone in the eye. All I could do was stare at my feet and try to breathe steady just to keep from sobbing inconsolably.

Bryan's mom padded slowly down.

She didn't say a word. She and my wife hugged and both began wailing.

I lowered my head and closed my eyes.

I took a deep breath, looked up, and before me hung a large painting. It was a bright and cheerful portrait, filled with pastel blues and pinks and yellows. It was painted from a picture Bryan's mother had taken of Bryan and Caitlin about seven years earlier while they were playing on the beach at the edge of the ocean.

I began sobbing and couldn't stop.

CHAPTER FIFTY-SIX

I was hiking with my grandfather alongside Big Elk Creek in southeastern Idaho, fishing pole in hand, nearly a year after I'd shot my foot.

The creek side was lush with late-summer green, and breezes whispered through the pine-covered slopes. Cold water welled up from deep, roiling pools, and the air chilled as it passed over.

A waist-high sign appeared on the trail. It said simply WELCOME TO WYOMING.

"I think this is the first time I've ever been in Wyoming," I mused. "How about you, Grandpa?"

"Oh, I've been lots," he said.

"Really? When?"

"A long time ago. I sheared a lot of sheep in Wyoming. Shot some antelope, too."

"How come you don't hunt anymore?" I asked.

"Oh, just lost interest. I think in this country we've shot just about all the animals that ever needed shooting, and then some."

"But you hunted a lot when you were a kid."

"Oh, sure. In Montana we hunted all the time."

"Did you ever hunt bear?"

"No. I've seen plenty, but never hunted them."

"How about buffalo? Have you ever shot a buffalo?"

"No. They were all gone by the time I came around. But I collected buffalo skulls when I was a kid. There were places along the Yellowstone River where there were still piles of buffalo bones. My dad shot some buffalo, and my grandfather shot an awful lot. In fact, my dad used to go hunting with Two Moons. Do you know who Two Moons was?"

"No."

"He was chief of the Cheyenne. He was at Little Bighorn with Sitting Bull."

"Wow, really?" I asked, retaining a sliver of skepticism. This was from a grandfather who delighted in telling me Bigfoot stories.

"Did your dad know Sitting Bull?"

"He might have, but my grandfather certainly did."

"Wow. So what did they hunt—your dad and Two Moons?"

"Deer and elk, I suppose," he said. "He used to come to our ranch with his wives and put up his tepee. He and my grandfather were friends. They used to talk."

"Your grandfather could speak Indian."

"Oh, sure. My grandfather could speak some. My dad knew some words, too."

"Can you speak Indian?"

"Sure."

"Say something."

"Nee-haw pa wah may."

"What does that mean?"

"Shut up. You'll scare the fish."

We came to a large bend in the creek. A smooth, black rock formation jutted into the water. We walked onto it and set down our fishing poles. The big ledge backed up a clear, deep pool. The far side of the creek rushed by, crashing with whitecaps over submerged boulders. By contrast, the pool was mesmerizing and serene. The water pushed its way upward, creating small, roiling circles that spread calmly along the surface.

My grandfather knelt next to the water. I knelt, too. Sweat glistened off his face and forehead.

He gazed at the water and the trees along the bank. Then he turned to me.

"How's your foot, Chief Holy Toe?"

I chuckled. "Oh, it's fine. I'm going to be on the basketball team this fall."

"That's great." Then he added, "I should've never given you that gun."

Embarrassed, I stared into the pool. I could see white sand and smooth rocks wavering and shimmering deep at the bottom.

My grandfather reached into the water with his cupped hands. I did the same. The cold was bracing and almost painful to the touch.

We splashed our faces, ran dripping fingers through our hair, and rubbed the wet cold on our necks.

To our right, the waters of Big Elk Creek rushed ceaselessly by.

A Note from the Author

Let's get one thing clear: *Thunder in the Mountains* is not an antigun book.

I would never presume it to be so. Not in America. Not in 2014.

Plus, that is not for me to decide. Or presume. That job—complete with heavy lifting—is for the reader.

I am reminded of the rambling prologue of sorts that Kurt Vonnegut Jr. tacked on to the opening of *Slaughterhouse-Five*, his novel that is ostensibly about the World War II firebombing of Dresden, Germany, but ends up being mostly about life, death, time, the nature of man, and flying saucers from the planet Tralfamadore. I think. Vonnegut leaves to his readers much heavy lifting. As he should.

Here's what he says. Listen:

Over the years, people I've met have often asked me what I'm working on, and I've usually replied that the main thing was a book about Dresden.

I said that to Harrison Starr, the movie maker, one time, and he raised his eyebrows and inquired, "Is it an anti-war book?"

"Yes," I said. "I guess."

"You know what I say to people when I hear they're writing anti-war books?"

"No. What do you say, Harrison Starr?"

"I say, 'Why don't you write an anti-glacier book instead?'"

What he meant, of course, was that there would always be wars, that they were as easy to stop as glaciers. I believe that, too.

And even if wars didn't keep coming like glaciers, there would still be plain old death.

The part about the glaciers, in retrospect, is a bit of a hoot. But in 1969 very few people saw the coming of global warming. How could Vonnegut know? Still, we get the point. And the gravitas of Harrison Starr is neither lost nor diminished by our now carbon-sullied atmosphere.

More than 1,200 American and British bombers were dispatched to Dresden in February of 1945. The Allied pilots and crews were expert in flattening and incinerating the once grand and historic city on the banks of the Elbe. Up to 25,000 people, nearly all civilians, were killed. So it goes.

More than 32,000 people, nearly all civilians, are killed by guns each year in the United States. So it goes.

But enough about war, death, and sadness. Let's get back to *Thunder in the Mountains*.

It is a book of literary nonfiction. Two names have been changed out of courtesy and care, but everything contained within actually occurred. And everything that occurred, happened as depicted. More or less.

Few people want to read antiseptic studies and statistics of gun violence. We have reams of those, and, by all accounts, readership is quite low. I've perused many. Be thankful you've been spared.

While there are no aliens or flying saucers in *Thunder in the Mountains*, there is some time travel, I suspect. The historical sections of the book are as factual as I could make them without sucking the life out of the prose. That's where the "literary" part of literary nonfiction comes in. I don't know what one gunslinger said to the other, verbatim. I don't know if the hanged man's shirt was blue or red. I can't remember the exact dialogue I had with my brother when I was thirteen. I don't know exactly what was going through a classmate's mind as he stood alone in a field with a gun. No one does. But I can imagine. And in most cases I have a pretty good idea what was said or how someone might have reacted or what might've happened next. In most cases.

But as a practitioner of literary nonfiction, it's my job to fill in the blanks. To do my best to keep the story moving. To keep the reader engaged; enraptured, even. To interpret the past. To use all the tools available to a writer—imagery, foreshadowing, symbolism, plot, denouement. All those things that can provide clarity in art but usually elude us in real life—in the here and now. To paint a picture—with strokes both broad and fine—all the while keeping as true as possible to the essence of the story at hand.

It's quite a trick—an artful balancing act—no matter if one is writing fiction or nonfiction.

While fact-checking this book, I was struck by how little anyone from my past was willing to talk to me about their brush with gun violence. Understandably, it is a difficult and painful thing to approach. Even after four decades, in many cases. How do you begin?

"Hi, this is Craig Collins. Not sure if you recall, but we were great friends in the eighth grade. Remember when your brother got shot and killed? Good times, huh?"

Of course, I was more tactful than that, but no matter what was said or how delicately it was phrased, the message between the lines seemed just as coarse. Guns are a touchy subject in America. And the pain of gun violence within a family never subsides. The years never come close to wearing down the sharp edges of grief.

For that reason, the cloak of silence about guns is exceedingly thick. And I don't doubt that I've made some people as mad as hornets for even attempting to pull back that cloak and let the light shine in. But it can't be helped. It's an issue whose time has long since come.

Thomas Wolfe and John Steinbeck poked at beehives in their home-towns of Asheville, North Carolina, and Salinas, California, with their thinly veiled works of fiction, *Look Homeward, Angel* and *East of Eden*. There were swarms of angry villagers buzzing in the wakes of those tomes, hurling invectives and launching diatribes. But all these years later, the anger has faded, the villagers have passed—as have the authors. So it goes. What remains are two iconic novels—treasures, really—enduring monuments to truth and beauty.

It's all any writer, if they're honest, can aspire to.

Craig K. Collins
San Diego, California

Acknowledgments

To my mother, Ellen, who encouraged my talents as a writer from the time she gushed over a poem I'd written in the fourth grade. It was about a mountain. Go figure.

To my father, Ben, who, more than once, carried me on his back and showed me the correct path.

To my stepmother, Iva, without whose solid grounding I might've wandered into the wilderness of my teen years and perhaps not come out the other side fully intact.

To my brother Kirk and sister Camille, who have both, more than once, slapped me back into reality.

To my stepbrother Monte—sorry for ratting you out about the owl.

With much love to my wife, Janice, who has put up with me through thick and much thin, and who told me when we first met that she'd dreamed of marrying a writer. Sorry it took so long.

To my talented son Christopher, who has been my world, and whose story I watch unfold with great love, fascination, and hope.

To my agent, Alice Martell, who recognized something of beauty and import in my first manuscript, and who still fights the good fight on my behalf.

To my editor, Erin Turner, a fellow Westerner, who immediately perceived the truth in my writing that many in New York initially failed to see.

To Jennifer Ellis, who, after reading a writing sample of mine some time ago, told me I had the talent to become a renowned author. I laughed. But she didn't relent until I finally produced a manuscript, which she put in front of my now-agent, sending me on my way.

To Kelly Studer, my executive coach, who, after I'd expressed outrage at the Newtown tragedy, suggested I do something—anything—like write a three-page opinion piece. So I did. Then I wrote three pages more—and three more and three more and three more. This book is the faraway destination reached only by taking that first step.

To Robin: Sorry for dragging you into this. Fare thee well.

To Dan, Kelly, and Caitlin: Thank you for your courage and for the honor of allowing me to share Bryan's story. Your sadness is mine. And Janice's. And Christopher's. May we all find peace.

BIBLIOGRAPHY

Di Maio, Vincent J. M. *Gunshot Wounds: Practical Aspects of Firearms, Ballistics, and Forensic Techniques.* Boca Raton, FL: CRC Press, 1998.

Hickson, Howard. "Last Horsedrawn Stage Robbery," *Northeastern Nevada Historical Society Quarterly* (Winter 1981).

Mathias, Donald E., and Valerie S. Berry. *A Place Called Jarbidge.* Glendora, CA: Self-published, 1997.

McGrath, Roger D. "The Badmen of Bodie," "Vigilantism," "The Heritage of the Trans-Sierra Frontier." In *Gunfighters, Highwaymen & Vigilantes: Violence on the Frontier*, 199–260. Berkeley and Los Angeles: University of California Press, 1984.

Toll, David. "Butch Cassidy and the Great Winnemucca Bank Robbery," *The Historical Nevada Magazine: Outstanding Historical Features from the Pages of Nevada Magazine*, edited by Richard Moreno, 28–39. Carson City: Nevada, 1998. Originally published in *Nevada Magazine* (May/June 1983).

Whitney, Ellen M. The Illinois State Historical Library. *The Black Hawk War, 1831–1832.* Springfield, 1970.

ABOUT THE AUTHOR

Craig K. Collins was born in Pocatello, Idaho, in 1960 and was raised in small towns throughout the Great Basin—Carson City, Nevada; Winnemucca, Nevada; and Bishop, California. He attended college in San Diego, where he has lived since, and holds a BA in English and an MBA from San Diego State University. After a stint as a journalist, he served as a senior executive for Fortune 500 companies. Later, he founded a series of venture-backed technology start-ups. He has won a number of professional awards for writing, marketing, innovation, and entrepreneurship. *Thunder in the Mountains* is his first book. His second—*Midair*—is due out in 2015.